DO CHRISTIANS, MUSLIMS, AND JEWS WORSHIP THE SAME GOD?

Books in the Counterpoints Series

Church Life

Evaluating the Church Growth Movement
Exploring the Worship Spectrum
Remarriage after Divorce in Today's Church
Understanding Four Views on Baptism
Understanding Four Views on the Lord's Supper
Who Runs the Church?

Bible and Theology

Are Miraculous Gifts for Today?
Five Views on Apologetics
Five Views on Biblical Inerrancy
Five Views on Law and Gospel
Five Views on Sanctification
Five Views on the Church and Politics
Five Views on the Extent of the Atonement
Four Views on Christian Spirituality
Four Views on Christianity and Philosophy
Four Views on Creation, Evolution, and Intelligent Design
Four Views on Divine Providence
Four Views on Eternal Security
Four Views on Hell
Four Views on Moving Beyond the Bible to Theology
Four Views on Salvation in a Pluralistic World
Four Views on the Apostle Paul
Four Views on the Book of Revelation
Four Views on the Church's Mission
Four Views on the Historical Adam
Four Views on the Role of Works at the Final Judgment
Four Views on the Spectrum of Evangelicalism
Genesis: History, Fiction, or Neither?
How Jewish Is Christianity?
Show Them No Mercy
Three Views on Creation and Evolution
Three Views on Eastern Orthodoxy and Evangelicalism
Three Views on the Millennium and Beyond
Three Views on the New Testament Use of the Old Testament
Three Views on the Rapture
Two Views on Homosexuality, the Bible, and the Church
Two Views on the Doctrine of the Trinity
Two Views on Women in Ministry

DO CHRISTIANS, MUSLIMS, AND JEWS WORSHIP THE SAME GOD? FOUR VIEWS

Wm. Andrew Schwartz
John B. Cobb Jr.
Francis J. Beckwith
Gerald R. McDermott
Jerry Walls
Joseph L. Cumming
David W. Shenk

Ronnie P. Campbell and Christopher Gnanakan, General Editors
Stanley Gundry, Series Editor

COUNTERPOINTS
► BIBLE & THEOLOGY ◄

ZONDERVAN
ACADEMIC

ZONDERVAN ACADEMIC

Do Christians, Muslims, and Jews Worship the Same God? Four Views
Copyright © 2019 by Ronnie P. Campbell, Christopher Gnanakan, Wm. Andrew Schwartz,
John B. Cobb Jr., Francis J. Beckwith, Gerald R. McDermott, Jerry L. Walls

ISBN 978-0-310-53803-5 (softcover)

ISBN 978-0-310-53804-2 (ebook)

Requests for information should be addressed to:
Zondervan, *3900 Sparks Dr. SE, Grand Rapids, Michigan 49546*

Cover design: Tammy Johnson
Cover image: © denisgo / Shutterstock

Printed in the United States of America

19 20 21 22 23 24 25 26 27 28 29 /LSC/ 15 14 13 12 11 10 9 8 7 6 5 4 3 2 1

CONTENTS

CONTRIBUTORS

John B. Cobb Jr. (PhD, University of Chicago) is an American theologian, philosopher, and environmentalist. One of the preeminent theologians in the world and the global leader of process theology, he is the author of more than fifty books. He is a cofounder of the Center for Process Studies and professor emeritus at Claremont School of Theology and Claremont Graduate University.

Wm. Andrew Schwartz (PhD, Claremont Graduate University) is executive director of the Center for Process Studies, cofounder and executive vice president of EcoCiv, and assistant professor of process and comparative theology at Claremont School of Theology. His recent work has been focused on comparative religious philosophies and the role of big ideas in the transition toward ecological civilization.

Francis J. Beckwith (PhD, Fordham University) is professor of philosophy and church-state studies and associate director of the graduate program in philosophy at Baylor University, where he also serves as a resident scholar in Baylor's Institute for Studies of Religion. He has published widely in the areas of political philosophy, jurisprudence, applied ethics, philosophy of religion, and theology.

Gerald R. McDermott (PhD, University of Iowa) is Anglican Chair of Divinity at Beeson Divinity School. McDermott has been the author, coauthor, or editor of more than twenty books. An Anglican priest, he is teaching pastor at Christ the King Anglican Church and is married to Jean. Together they have three sons and twelve grandchildren.

Jerry L. Walls (PhD, University of Notre Dame) is scholar in residence and professor of philosophy at Houston Baptist University. He is the author or editor of over twenty books and has published widely in philosophy of religion, ethics, philosophical theology, and apologetics.

Joseph L. Cumming (MA, MPhil, Yale University) is pastor of the International Church at Yale. He worked fifteen years in the Islamic Republic of Mauritania and now lectures regularly at Islamic and Christian institutions in the Middle East and elsewhere. At Yale he organized the first Common Word conference.

David W. Shenk (PhD, New York University) is a global consultant for Eastern Mennonite Missions, where he serves on a team dedicated to Christian-Muslim relationships, Peacemakers Confessing Christ. He has written twenty books.

Ronnie P. Campbell Jr. (PhD, Liberty University) is associate professor of theology at Liberty University. He has published in the areas of theology, comparative theology and philosophy, Christianity and film, and apologetics.

Christopher Gnanakan (PhD, Leeds University, UK; DMin, South Asia Institute of Advanced Christian Studies, India) is professor of theology and world religions at Liberty University and director of Leadership Development for *Christar*, a missionary agency for the least reached peoples.

DO CHRISTIANS, JEWS, AND MUSLIMS WORSHIP THE SAME GOD?

RONNIE P. CAMPBELL JR. AND CHRISTOPHER GNANAKAN

The main question of this book is not a new one, and we are not the first to ask it. But this question came to prominence among evangelicals in 2015 when tenured Wheaton professor Larycia Hawkins was placed on paid administrative leave for comments made on social media, which, in turn, led to a fury storm of articles written about this topic on the worldwide web.[1]

On Facebook, Hawkins posted a picture of herself donning a hijab and made the following statements: "I stand in religious solidarity with

1. Francis J. Beckwith, "Do Muslims and Christians Worship the Same God?," *The Catholic Thing*, December 17, 2015, https://www.thecatholicthing.org/2015/12/17/do-muslims -and-christians-worship-the-same-god/; Beckwith, "Why Muslims and Christians Worship the Same God," January 7, 2016, https://www.thecatholicthing.org/2016/01/07/why-muslims-and -christians-worship-the-same-god/; William Lane Craig, "#459 Do Muslims and Christians Worship the Same God?," *Reasonable Faith*, January 31, 2016, https://www.reasonablefaith.org/ writings/question-answer/do-muslims-and-christians-worship-the-same-god; Peter Leithart, "Muslims, Christians, and the Gods." December 23, 2015. https://www.patheos.com/blogs/ leithart/2015/12/muslims-and-christians/; Gerald R. McDermott, "More on Whether Muslims and Christians Worship the Same God," *Patheos*, December 20, 2015, https://www.patheos .com/blogs/northamptonseminar/2015/12/20/more-on-whether-muslims-and-christians -worship-the-same-god/; Lydia McGrew, "The 'Same God' Debate is Too Important to Leave to Philosophers," *The Gospel Coalition*, January 15, 2016, https://www.thegospelcoalition.org/ article/the-same-god-debate-is-too-important-to-leave-to-philosophers/; R. Albert Mohler Jr., "Do Christians and Muslims Worship the Same God?," AlbertMohler.com, December 18, 2015, https://albertmohler.com/2015/12/18/do-christians-and-muslims-worship-the -same-god; Jerry Walls, "Wheaton, Allah, and the Trinity: Do Muslims Really Worship the Same God as C. S. Lewis?," Seedbed, January 13, 2016, https://www.seedbed.com/jerry-walls -wheaton-allah-the-trinity-do-muslims-really-worship-the-same-god-as-c-s-lewis/.

Muslims because they, like me, a Christian, are people of the book," and that, "as Pope Francis stated last week, we worship the same God."[2] Administrative leave came not from wearing a hijab, but from what the school believed to be "significant questions regarding the theological implications"[3] of the reasoning for her actions. As an Evangelical institution, Wheaton believed that the core issue was one of doctrine surrounding this question of whether Christians and Muslims worship the same God, especially since orthodox Christianity has held that God is a triunity of persons, and statements like the one made by Hawkins were not aligned with the school's doctrinal and theological commitments.

Why This Question Matters

The purpose of this book is not to answer whether Hawkins's statements were appropriate or whether Wheaton College's actions were just but to wrestle with the question of whether Christians, Jews, and Muslims worship the same God. In some ways, this question is both ambiguous and problematic, as will be demonstrated throughout the remainder of this book. After all, several additional subquestions arise from this one question. For example, what do we mean when we speak of worship? What does it look like for a Christian or a Jew or a Muslim to worship God? Do we mean here an outward expression or religious act? Do we mean an inner disposition toward God? Do we mean submission to God through daily living, actions, attitudes, and so on? Does worship require that we hold to correct beliefs about God?

Yet as complicated as the worship question may be, we are plagued with an even greater question: Who is the object of one's worship? Yahweh? Allah? Jesus? On the one hand, both Jews and Muslims hold to a unitarian view of God, which means that God is only one person. Christians, on the other hand, believe God to be a triunity of persons—Father, Son, and Holy Spirit. The Trinity question raises interesting questions for Christian worship. The New Testament Christians offered worship to Jesus,[4] especially through the act of prayer. As Richard Bauckham explains:

---

2. Bob Smeitana, "Wheaton College Suspends Hijab-Wearing Professor After 'Same God' Comment," *Christianity Today*, December 15, 2015, https://www.christianitytoday.com/news/2015/december/wheaton-college-hijab-professor-same-god-larycia-hawkins.html.

3. Smeitana, "Wheaton College Suspends."

4. For extended discussion, see Arthur W. Wainwright, *The Trinity in the New Testament* (Eugene, OR: Wipf and Stock, 2001), 93–104; Larry W. Hurtado, *Lord Jesus Christ: Devotion*

Acclamations and prayers addressed to Jesus go back to the earliest times. The Aramaic cry *Maranatha* ("Our Lord, come!": 1 Cor. 16:22; *Did. 10:6*; cf. Rev. 22:20), whose preservation in Aramaic in Greek-speaking churches indicates its very early origin, implies not only the expectation of the Parousia, but present religious relationship with the one who is to come, whether or not it was associated with a Eucharistic presence from the beginning. The New Testament evidence for personal prayer to Jesus as a regular feature of early Christianity has sometimes been underestimated. Paul (2 Cor. 12:8; 1 Thess. 3:11–13; 2 Thess. 2:16–17; 3:5, 16; cf. Rom 16:20b; 1 Cor. 16:23; Gal. 6:18; Phil. 4:23; 1 Thess. 5:28; 2 Thess. 3:18; Phlm. 25) and Acts (1:24; 7:59–60; 13:2) take it for granted (cf. also 1 Tim. 1:12; 2 Tim. 1:16–18; 4:22). The dominant practice was undoubtedly prayer to God, but since Jesus was understood as the active mediator of grace from God (as in the epistolary formula, "Grace to you and peace from God our Father and the Lord Jesus Christ": Rom 1:7 and elsewhere) and as the Lord for whose service Christians lived, prayer addressed to him was natural. John 14:14 (where the correct reading is probably "if you ask me") makes prayer to Jesus a principle of regular petition.[5]

But if God is one, as Christians and other monotheists believe, then how could these earliest Christians worship Jesus? Would it not count as idolatry or blasphemy, implying there are multiple gods? Central to the heart of the Christian faith is the belief that there is only one God, who has existed eternally as Father, Son, and Spirit. In Jesus, one of the divine persons (the Son) became incarnate, adding to himself a human nature, in order that we might receive salvation. Through his death, he reconciled us to God (Col. 1:22), and through his resurrection, he demonstrated God's defeat over death (1 Cor. 15:54–57), offering humanity eternal life and renewed relationship with God. In other words, God through the person of the Son became like us (John 1:1, 14)

to Jesus in Earliest Christianity (Grand Rapids: Eerdmans, 2003), 134–53; Richard Bauckham, Jesus and the God of Israel: God Crucified and Other Studies in the New Testament's Christology of Divine Identity (Grand Rapids: Eerdmans, 2008), 127–81.

5. Bauckham, Jesus and the God of Israel, 128–29.

yet without sin (Heb. 4:14; 1 Peter 2:21–22; 1 John 3:5), so that we can be forgiven of our sins and brought into right relationship with God. We point all of this out to show that there is a significant connection between our finer theological beliefs and worship. Perhaps, however, the above is a false dichotomy, and something more is going on.

What Do We Mean by "the Same"?

Much of how we answer the question of whether the three world monotheistic religions worship the same God hinges on what we mean by "the same." We want to know how much overlap is needed in one's beliefs in order to claim that two (or more) conceptions of God are one and the same God of worship. After all, Calvinists and Arminians, Catholics and Protestants, Openness and Classical theists all have different conceptions of God, yet most would not suggest that these Christians are worshiping a different God. Rather, they would argue that we have the same God in reference but different understandings of what this God is like. Here, philosophers will often differentiate between "sense" and "reference." Genoveva Marti explains the difference as follows:

> worship; doctrine
>
> The "reference" of an expression is the entity the expression designates or applies to. The "sense" of an expression is the way in which the expression presents the reference. For example, the ancients used "the morning star" and "the evening star" to designate what turned out to be the same heavenly body, the planet Venus. These two expessions have the same reference, but they clearly differ in that each presents that reference in a different "sense."[6]

When we speak, we might be referring to the same object (reference), for example, the planet Venus, but we might have different understandings of what the object is like (sense), for example, the morning or evening star. But is this what's happening with Christians, Jews, and Muslims when they claim to worship the same God?

Monotheists agree that ontologically there can be only one God. Moreover, they agree that God has certain properties, such as omnip-

6. Genoveva Marti, "Sense and Reference," in *New Routledge Encyclopedia of Philosophy*, ed. Edward Craig, vol. 8 (London: Taylor and Francis, 1998), 684–688, https://www.rep.routledge.com/articles/thematic/sense-and-reference/v-1.

otence, omniscience, and eternality. They also agree that God is the creator of all things. But is monotheism enough to claim that we have the same God in reference? Does the God of Judaism share all the same attributes as the God of Islam? Do they have the same character? Does the God of Christianity have properties (e.g., the property of being triune or the property of the Son's being incarnated) that the Muslim God does not? Some will resort to history and suggest that Jews, Christians, and Muslims all share a common ancestry and worship the God of Abraham? But, again, do each of the monotheistic views have the same conception of God, despite the common ancestry? Is the Father of Jesus the God of Muhammad? Do the Tanakh (Old Testament) and the Qur'an reveal God in the same way? If there are significant differences in properties or in character, can two conceptions refer to the same God? This distinction between reference and sense plays a significant part in the debate on whether Christians, Jews, and Muslims worship the same God, as we will see later in this book.

The Conbributors and Their Views

Having explored some preliminary questions, shall we now consider each of the views represented in this volume. In each response, the authors have been asked to explore subquestions that are implied in their answers to our main question, namely:

- Jews, Christians, and Muslims all hold to monotheism, but is monotheism enough to claim that adherents of each religion worship "the same" God?
- Does the doctrine of the Trinity matter in this debate? If so, to what extent?
- Much of the current debate hinges on what one means by "the same." What do we mean by "the same," and how do we make sense of the differences underlying each religion's understanding of God?
- What is included in worship? Is worship necessary for salvation? Furthermore, what place does the worship (or reverence) of Jesus Christ have for understanding the sameness of the God of Christianity, Judaism, and Islam and to what extent does this matter?

- Does affirming sameness lead to inclusivism or pluralism with respect to salvation, or does denying sameness imply exclusivism?

All Worship the Same God: Religious Pluralist View

In the first essay, Wm. Andrew Schwartz and John B. Cobb Jr. take the religious pluralist stance. Schwartz and Cobb demarcate between two kinds of pluralism—identist and deep pluralism. Identist pluralism, as found in the work of John Hick, suggests that though they might have different perspectives, adherents of various world religions orient themselves toward the same object of worship, whether that object is called "God," "Brahman," "the Real," or something else. Deep pluralism, on the other hand, suggests that there may be, indeed, different objects of worship or of religious concern, and even different salvations. Moving forward, Schwartz and Cobb then marshall a variety of arguments in favor of the thesis that Christians, Jews, and Muslims worship the same God. First, they provide a historical argument, which centers on the fact that Abraham is the father of each of the monotheistic traditions. The second argument emphasizes divine character, suggesting that each monothesitic religion takes it that there is only one God, that God is knowledgeable and relational, that God is loving and merciful, that God is creator, and that God is mysterious. Their third and final argument is ontological and suggests that if only one God exists, then Muslims, Christians, and Jews worship the same God since there is no other God to worship. They conclude their paper by considering the possibility of deep pluralism. According to process theology, there is not just one ultimate, but three ultimates (God, World, and Creativity) that make up ultimate reality. They suggest that perhaps the question is not so much whether Christians, Jews, and Muslims worship the same God, but whether Jews, Muslims, and Christians worship the same ultimate reality.

All Worship the Same God: Referring to the Same God View

Francis Beckwith, like Schwartz and Cobb, takes the affirmative view that Christians, Jews, and Muslims worship the same God. Yet there are some notable difference between Beckwith's view and the religious pluralist view of Schwartz and Cobb. Beckwith argues that although Christians, Jews, and Muslims have different understandings—sometimes deep and contrary theological differences—of what God is like, they nevertheless refer to the same God. Ontologically, there can be only one God who is absolute, uncaused, and perfect. God is not just one being among many within the universe; rather, God is the creator, sustainer, and absolute source of all things that exist. While creation has participatory existence, God alone is fully self-existent. On this understading of God, Christians, Jews, and Muslims all agree. They differ on the finer points of what their individual faith traditions and scriptures reveal about such things as the divine nature, humanity, morality, and salvation. But what about doctrines of the Trinity and incarnation? Beckwith recognizes that there are profound differences between Jews, Christians, and Muslims on the Trinity and the deity of Jesus. But he does not think we can even consider these issues until we first get the doctrine of God right. It is only because Christians, Jews, and Muslims get the divine nature right that their views on such teachings as the Trinity and incarnation can be viewed as contrary to one another.

Jews and Christians Worship the Same God: Shared Revelation View

Gerald McDermott takes the third view, which suggests that Christians and Jews worship the same God, but Muslims do not. Central to his argument is that Christians and Muslims disagree on a number of key issues about the nature and character of God. For example, it is often said that Muslims and Christians agree on the greatest two commandments—to love God and to love others. However, as McDermott stresses, neither of these commands are found within the Qur'an. Rather, the central focus of the Qur'an is on God's justice and not of God as a father or God as love. Furthermore, McDermott suggests there are some significant differences between the Christian and Muslim views on God. Both are monotheists, who hold to God as the eternal creator of the world, and both hold to some common attributes (e.g., omniscience or omnipotence) in God. Despite these similarities, the differences are far too significant, especially in relation to how Christians and Muslims understand the doctrines of the Trinity and deity of the Son of God. But what of Christians and Jews? McDermott points out that the authors of the New Testament never suggest the earliest Christians, who were worshiping Jesus, were now worshiping a God different from that of biblical Judaism. McDermott recognizes that some Christians will have doubts about whether Jews and Christians worship the same God based on three key issues: incarnation, resurrection, and Trinity. In response, McDermott builds an argument showing that each of these core Christian ideas are firmly grounded in biblical Judaism and are in no way contradictory to Christian teaching.

None Worship the Same God: Different Conceptions View

Dissenting from the previous three views, Jerry Walls takes the fourth and final position, that none worship the same God. Certainly, Christians, Jews, and Muslims share common beliefs about God, but Walls questions whether such shared beliefs are enough to maintain that the same God is in view. Drawing from recent studies in the philosophy of language, particularly the notion of "reference shifts," he first argues that it is doubtful whether Muslims and Christians can even claim to refer to the same thing when they speak of God. But even if a reference shift has not occurred, it is still not clear that the conditions necessary for worship obtain. Walls then provides another argument grounded in New Testament revelation, which, if successful, would show that Christians, Jews, and Muslims have radically different conceptions of God. He distinguishes between the order of being and the order of knowing. According to the order of being, God has eternally been a triunity of persons. Yet with respect to the order of knowing, this is something that was not revealed until the incarnate Son rose from the dead—something Christians recognize as progressive revelation and is established by the New Testament. Jews and Muslims both reject these distinctive elements of God's revelation to us, namely, the incarnation and resurrection of Jesus and the triunity of God. The thrust of Walls's argument suggests that for those Muslims and Jews who have been properly informed of the incarnation and resurrection of the Son of God, and yet who reject this revelation given to us by God through the New Testament, are not worshiping the same God as properly informed Christians, since those who reject are denying something that is true about God.

Ministry Reflection Essays

In addition to the four main views, this book also provides the reader with two ministry reflection essays. Both contributors have significant ministry experience with adherents of the Islamic faith and share their own take on how we should approach ministering to Muslims. For the first ministry essay, Joseph Cumming emphasizes focusing on common ground in Christian-Muslim relationships. He answers the question of whether Muslims and Christians worship the same God, saying, "Yes and no. But mostly yes" (p. 210). Cumming recognizes that Christians and Muslims have deep theological differences and that these deep theological issues should not be ignored. Yet his top priorities in ministering to Muslims center on communicating (in word and deed) something about the loving Person of Christ and on religious liberty. David Shenk, on the other hand, takes up our second ministry essay with a focus on respectfully held differences in Christian-Muslim relations. Like Cumming, Shenk recognizes the similarities between Christians and Muslims but claims that these two religions ultimately have different centers. For Shenk, it is our key distinctions that often lead to fruitful ministry opportunities. In no way should placing emphasis on key differences keep us from a commitment to peacemaking in the way of Christ.

Implications for Christian Ministry and Evangelicalism

Readers will find this book's insightful contributions rewarding, as have we. I (Chris Gnanakan) would like to posit a few challenging implications for "evangelicals" wrestling with the question at hand, irrespective of the view we gravitate toward. I raise these concerns having grown up in pluralistic India, serving among Muslims for over twenty years, taking trips to the Holy Land, and engaging in regular dialogue with Jewish-Islamic leaders in the Washington, DC, area.[7] It is intriguing that no other religion has a clear, compelling mandate for mission like our three Abrahamic faiths (Buddhism comes close). On one hand, we must be concerned for Judaism—the smallest and shrinking of the major world's religions. For Jews, Hexham notes, "Christianity is a systematic distortion of Jewish religion that creates something almost totally unrecognizable."[8] Should Christians beat them, join them or make them "jealous for Jesus"? (Rom. 11:14) On the other hand, trends predict

---

7. Chris Gnanakan, "Any Which Way but Win? Christian Mission in a Religiously Pluralistic Society," ASM Paper, Bali, Indonesia, June 2018; Gnanakan, "To God Be the Glory," in *Lord of All: Embracing Unity and Eternity through Jesus Christ in Northern Virginia and Beyond*, ed. Casey Veatch (Washington, DC: Believe Books, 2015).

8. Irving Hexham, *Understanding World Religions: An Interdisciplinary Approach* (Grand Rapids: Zondervan, 2011), 251.

Islam—the fastest growing militant faith, will in two decades be the largest. Islamophobia stems out of "terror text" and so-called jihadists at work. Christians must ask, and answer: "Are Muslims friends to win or foes to fight?!" William Temple aptly warned, "If your concept of God is wrong, the more religion you get the more dangerous you become to yourself and to others!" As religious pluralisms and postmodernity surmount, there is an apologetical and missiological need for evangelicals to come to objective terms with "who" they truly worship and "how" seriously they must take Christ's Great Commission. For any practical ministry and effective mission in multi-faith communities, our theology and methodology matter.

A useful approach is to start with the essentials or nonnegotiables of "evangelical" faith, which often align with the volatile issues central to this book—the Trinity, Christology, and missiology. Often, defining the problems lies in defining the problematic terms related to God's name and our act of worship. We may start with common good and move to common grace, but we must use common sense. Christian worship occurs in spirit and in truth (John 4:24). Our subjective experiences must be logically geared to objective obedience to God's revealed Word as absolute truth. This integrates and engages the human mind, will, and body in ascribing worth and offering sacrifice to God, who is worship's transforming object. So theoretical concepts must relate to contextual and cultural realities, even at grassroot levels, especially among unreached peoples. Let us consider some missional consequences under three headings: revelation, redemption, and regeneration.

Revelation: What the Father Has Said in His Word

Christians must admit the strict monotheism that Jews and Muslims subscribe to and clarify their reasonable worship of the Bible's one true God in three persons. The primary and critical need is to establish which book—the Hebrew scripture, the Christian Bible, or the Qur'an—is the inspired, inerrant, and therefore authoritative "Word of God." Beyond mystery or paradox, "evangelicals" anchor the basis and criteria for their faith in divine self-disclosure: (1) God has spoken, and (2) it is written. Before the fifth century, the church councils and creeds identified YHWH's name as "the God and 'Father' of our 'Lord' Jesus," as pronounced in the benediction (2 Cor. 13:14). It is characterized principally by sacrificial love seen precisely in him sending Jesus, the Jewish Messiah. The church's canon of scripture understood the risen Jesus to be the full and final revelation of YHWH's person and redeeming purposes. Thomas confessed him as "God," and Jesus did not object (John 20:21). Christians thereafter consider the Lord Jesus "one with the Father" to be worshiped and obeyed. Any different view is deemed unorthodox or heretical since this endangers the Bible's authority, Christ's deity, and the church's apostolic mission.[9]

In the New Testament it is evident how Jesus's Jewish disciples boldly confess Jesus as Messiah, the Christ, the incarnate Son of God. They worship him as the risen Lord and proclaim a "global gospel" that offers him as the only savior of both Jews and gentiles. As Ghassan Khalaf notes, "The point at issue is not whether Christians believe in the Jewishness of Jesus, because that is a fact. The more important issue is for Jews to believe in the 'Christian' Jesus."[10] By the sixth century, the prophet Muhammad and the Qur'an affirmed that Jews and Christians were "the people of the Book." We now have a problem: if we were created specifically to worship God who reveals himself "in Christ," then Christian mission gains impetus because people need God's love to worship Christ.[11] God's nature of reciprocal love within the Trinity is best embodied in the Father's grace that sent Jesus to put away sins by sacrificing himself.

Redemption: What the Son of God Has Done on the Cross

One of the earliest mentions of Word worship is in direct relation to Abraham's obedience in sacrificing his son (Gen. 22:1–5). The Jewish *Seder* is a reminder of the Paschal lamb that still represents "the four stages of redemption, from the Exodus to the future coming of messiah."[12] Jews, Christians, and Muslims use the term *messiah* with different meanings and expectations. However, at the heart of all "Christian"

---

9. Cf. W. St. Clair Tisdall, *Christian Reply to Muslim Objections* (London: SPCK, 1904; Colorado Springs: Al-Nour, 2005).

10. Ghassan Khalaf, "Jesus and Judaism," *Arabic Christian Theology*, ed. Andrea Zaki Stephanous (Grand Rapids: Zondervan, 2019), 210.

11. John Gilchrist, "The Love of God," *Sharing the Gospel with Muslims* (Cape Town: Life Challenge, 2003), 137.

12. Christopher Partridge, "Worship and Festivals," in *Introduction to World Religions* (Minneapolis: Fortress, 2013), 326.

worship is a sacrifice which is vividly portrayed in Jesus, the Son of God, offering his body and blood as the Lamb of God (John 1:29). It is gratefully commemorated in communion as the Eucharist. The litmus test for Christianity is Christological—faith in God's grace produces salvation in Jesus's person and atoning work. Christ's cross symbolizes faith in God's mercy, and true worshipers respond by offering themselves as "living sacrifices" as their logical act of worship that God accepts and is pleased with (Rom. 12:1–2). Besides belief in one God in three persons, Jews and Muslims find it illogical that there can be one person with two natures, human and divine, and blasphemous that he is being worshiped![13]

Ultimately, Christians receive the doctrine of Christ's incarnation as revealed truth, not something to be biologically simplified or philosophically rationalized. Jesus's death and resurrection are precisely how the God of Abraham declared Jesus's Lordship (Rom. 1:4). Christians believe this truth as a historical fact and an experiential reality that their day of worship was changed from the Jewish Sabbath to Sunday. Muslims intentionally prefer Friday. This raises ontological and functional questions about the redeeming love of the God who each Abrahamic faith approaches in worship. Moreover, this God's promise of eternal life "in Christ" is the Christian gospel. It is inclusive, universal in scope, and Jesus's followers are mandated to share it to make disciples of all people. Yet it is exclusive in that it claims to be the true God's only way of salvation for all!

Adopting a pluralistic, syncretic, or universalistic view of God's way of salvation raises serious questions: Does one's faith have a need for and any divine means or provision for redemption? Does the worshiper of the particular God have personal assurance of sharing their afterlife with him in heaven or paradise? If so, on what basis? Worship, although sincere, can be vain, false, or demonic (Matt. 15:9; John 4.19–26). Hence, the worthiness of the object of worship must be clearly and boldly affirmed with integrity. All three faiths agree that "worship" (literally worth-ship) is ascribed only to God since he alone is worthy.

---

13. "While Q 2.10 commands Muslims to be kind to the People of the Book, but its ruling is abrogated by later texts that command them to fight (Q 5.29). To have *shirk* in Allah: to have a partner in his reign . . . the noun is *al-shirku* . . . to associate with Allah a partner in his Lordship." "People of Other Faiths," *The Quran Dilemma: Former Muslims Analyze Islam's Holiest Book*, vol. 1 (Seattle: WaterLife, 2011), 139.

For Christians, in the final analysis, people from every nation, tongue, and tribe will worship Jesus crying, "Worthy is the Lamb, who was slain, to receive power and . . . honor and glory and praise" (Rev. 5:12; cf. 4:11). With this future trajectory and eschatological hope, in what sense are all three faiths worshiping the same God?

Regeneration: What the Holy Spirit Does by Grace in the Believer

If accepting Jesus's deity is difficult for Jews and Muslims, affirming the Spirit's person and role in worship and for ministry is even more so. Authentic worship is an awesome encounter with God that exudes his glory. For Muslims this is prescribed in the Qur'an, and for Jews it is seen in the law of Moses written on stones. Paul contrasts this with the truth of God's Word in a new covenant written on human hearts by the Spirit of God. Moses experienced God's glory temporarily with his face veiled. True worshipers "in the Spirit" with unveiled faces behold God's glory "by the Spirit" and are transformed into the same image from glory to glory (2 Cor. 3:18). The Spirit points believers to Jesus and then transforms them to be conformed to his image—the purpose for which God created and redeems people (Rom. 8:28).[14] We tend to become like the gods we worship! In short, the goal of "Christian" worship is Christlikeness—the Spirit's fruit or love in believers (Gal. 5:22). Worship produces a religion that is governed and guided by the moral power of love, not the love for political power. This begs for the question: to what extent is this an evidential reality in Jewish, Muslim, or Christian worship and missions?

Further critical concerns emerge regarding the exercise of the Spirit's gifts for evangelistic ministry. Such endowments of the Spirit's manifestation are so underserved that their worshipful expressions, like salvation, are a "celebration of grace." It is obvious in the Bible and from church history how the Holy Spirit's incoming and empowering of Jesus and his followers is critical to both their worship and witness to the end of the earth.[15] So the goal of God's creation and redemption is the worship of Christ. Missions exists because there are places where

---

14. For a good exegetical study of God's missional Spirit, see Gordon Fee, *God's Empowering Presence* (Grand Rapids: Baker Academic, 2009).

15. Winfield Bevins, "Connecting Liturgy with Mission," in *Ever Ancient, Ever New* (Grand Rapids: Zondervan, 2019), 175–87.

the worship of Jesus as Lord does not! If all the three religions under consideration already worship the same God, is there a need for conversion? What would missions look like for the Jew, Muslim, or Christian? More could be discussed, yet within the fine contributions that follow, you will find enough substance to agree with and more issues to be challenged by.

ALL WORSHIP THE SAME GOD:
RELIGIOUS PLURALIST VIEW

WM. ANDREW SCHWARTZ AND JOHN B. COBB JR.

Religious pluralism can be broadly understood as standing between absolutism (only one perspective is true) and relativism (all perspectives are true). As such, pluralism asserts that more than one perspective, more than one path, can be true or efficacious. In what follows, we argue for a pluralistic view of the Abrahamic traditions of Judaism, Christianity, and Islam.

A vast array of theories of religious pluralism exists—a plurality of pluralisms. One version of pluralism, emphasizing an underlying unity, might say that Muslims, Jews, and Christians all worship the same God though experienced and expressed in different ways. This type of pluralism, often affiliated with John Hick, is what David Ray Griffin has referred to as "identist." As Griffin explains, "According to *identist* pluralism, all religions are oriented toward the same religious object (whether it be called 'God,' 'Brahman,' 'Nirvana,' 'Sunyata,' 'Ultimate Reality,' 'the Transcendent,' or 'the Real') and promote essentially the same end (the same type of 'salvation')." [1] Alternatively, the tradition of deep pluralism, often affiliated with process theology and the work of one of the authors of this chapter, John Cobb, says that "religions

---

1. David Ray Griffin, ed., *Deep Religious Pluralism* (Louisville: Westminster John Knox, 2005), 24.

promote different ends—different salvations—perhaps by virtue of being oriented toward different religious objects, perhaps thought of as different ultimates. Differential pluralism is, in other words, pluralistic soteriologically and perhaps also ontologically." [2] In this way, a *deep* pluralist might conclude that Christians, Muslims, and Jews do not worship the same "God," yet all can be oriented toward very real ultimates, with paths that are more or less equally efficacious. [3] This essay will present both the identist and deep pluralism perspectives.

One point of clarification up front: the ambiguity inherent in the question "Do Christians, Muslims, and Jews worship the same God?" requires that the best we can offer is a qualified yes, a yes from a certain perspective or in a certain sense. No doubt there are many ways in which it can be demonstrated that the three Abrahamic traditions do not worship the same God, just as it can be demonstrated that Christians don't all worship the same God, or that no two people worship the same God. [4] Therefore, much of what follows will be an attempt to clarify the conditions under which we believe the three Abrahamic traditions can rightly be said to be worshiping the same God. But before describing the conditions under which this qualified yes can be asserted, we wish to first unpack the core question of this book.

What Is Meant by "Christians," "Muslims," and "Jews"?

Do Christians, Muslims, and Jews worship the same God? The question itself begins with what could be considered a hasty generalization—namely, that there is some group called "Christians," or some group called "Muslims," or some group called "Jews" that can be easily identified and evaluated. This is far from the case.

Take Christianity: What is Christianity, and who are Christians? Is Christianity defined by a set of beliefs? If so, which beliefs? Perhaps we can make some broad assertions, such as belief in God, belief in the divinity of Christ, and so on. But the more detailed we get (e.g., what is meant by belief, what is meant by God, what is meant by belief in God, and so forth), the more difficult it becomes to parse out "Christian"

---

2. Griffin, *Deep Religious Pluralism*, 24.

3. Want to know how this is possible? Keep reading. The deep pluralism perspective will be presented in greater detail later in this chapter.

4. We will explain this in the next section.

from "non-Christian" beliefs. Undoubtedly, this is the very problem the church has been struggling with for nearly two thousand years. The pursuit of <u>orthodoxy</u> in contrast to heresy has been, among other things, an attempt to answer the question "What is Christianity, and who are Christians?" But who decides which beliefs are orthodox? The proliferation of Christian sects/denominations since the time of Martin Luther, as well as the distinctive branches of Christianity prior to Luther, is evidence of this struggle to identify Christian orthodoxy. Perhaps we could point to the Nicene or Apostles' Creeds as representative of orthodox Christian belief. But even then interpretations of creedal affirmations vary greatly. Using doctrine to identify "Christians" is problematic.

Does identifying Christians through practice rather than belief avoid this difficulty? Unfortunately not. The pursuit of <u>orthopraxy</u> is met with the same challenges as that of orthodoxy. Which practices should be identified with "true" Christianity, and who decides on them? We could point to something like the ritual of the Eucharist, but there remain great variations in method—one cup versus individual cups, bread versus wafers, dipping versus successive consumption, and so on. Not to mention the variations on beliefs related to core practices, such as transubstantiation, consubstantiation, and varying beliefs about the presence of Jesus's body and blood in the eucharistic bread and wine.

Since orthodoxy and orthopraxy fail to offer clear paths toward identifying "the Christians," could we rely on history—historical affiliation and succession? In a sense, this is what the Catholic Church has attempted to do with apostolic succession, by which the authority of bishops comes from tracing the lineage of teaching back to the original apostles of Jesus. But historical succession doesn't guarantee any degree of consistency in belief or practice. Furthermore, we have no reason to assume that the early church is a pure expression of "true" Christianity. In reading the Gospels, we witness story after story in which the apostles clearly didn't understand Jesus's core teachings.[5]

So what is Christianity, and who are Christians? In short, there is no single Christianity. In so far as we use the label *Christianity* to refer to a tradition, it must be understood as dynamic and diverse. Consider

---

5. See Luke 18:34, "The disciples did not understand any of this. Its meaning was hidden from them, and they did not know what he was talking about." Unless noted otherwise, scripture quotations in Schwartz and Cobb's essay and responses come from the NIV.

the development of Christian thought—from Origen and Irenaeus to Augustine, Thomas Aquinas, Martin Luther, John Calvin, and John Wesley to contemporary voices like Marjorie Suchocki, Thomas Jay Oord, and Catherine Keller. Each of these thinkers has been influential for specific groups of Christians, yet significant differences can be seen across their thought. Not only does the Christian tradition change, but the various manifestations are interconnected. Protestant Christians protested Catholic Christianity. The Five Articles of Remonstrance were developed to contrast the Five Points of Calvinism. The evolution of Christianity is not uniform or singular. There are many Christianities.[6] Even if we were to examine a single thinker such as Martin Luther, we would need to be careful to recognize the dynamic development of his thought.[7] Theology is not static. Theology is not uniform. Neither are the world's wisdom traditions.

Because of the diverse expressions of each tradition, there are times when the differences within Christianity are greater than the differences between Christian, Jewish, and Muslim thinkers. For example, the Christian panentheism of Charles Hartshorne, a twentieth-century Christian thinker, is more similar to the Islamic panentheism of Ibn Arabi, a twelfth- to thirteenth-century Muslim thinker, than to the classical theism of Christian thinkers like Augustine.

Christianity is not alone in its diversity. There are also many Judaisms and many Islams. With the absence of singular unchanging subjects—Christian, Jew, and Muslim—to be compared, all conclusions regarding whether the three worship the same God should be made conditionally. We might even say it depends on which Christians, Jews, and Muslims we are talking about at any particular moment.

The Fallacy of the Perfect Dictionary and Problem of Sameness

In addition to recognizing the complexity around Jewish, Muslim, and Christian identity, we should take note of the ambiguity surrounding the words *worship*, *same*, and *God*. We should not be surprised, for all words have an element of ambiguity. We must be careful to avoid the fallacy

---

6. In a sense, to affirm that diverse ways of being Christian are acceptable is to be a pluralist—to allow that more than one perspective or path can be efficacious.

7. See Berndt Hamm, *The Early Luther: Stages in a Reformation Reorientation* (Minneapolis: Fortress, 2017).

of the perfect dictionary. As one of us has written elsewhere, "A perfect dictionary would be one in which some set of words was unambiguously defined and all the others were defined in terms of them. We would then have the possibility of communicating univocally, that is, without the possibility of diverse understanding of what we mean."[8] However, we believe this is impossible. It is important to remember that as we pursue more and more exact meanings for terms, we will never reach a final point where some set of words can be universally and unambiguously understood. There is no perfect definition of *worship*, *same*, or *God*, such that the terms could be understood unambiguously. The limits of language always require that communication involve some intuitive and imaginative leap.

Even if we get to a place where we are satisfied with an explanation of what is meant by the question "Do Christians, Muslims, and Jews worship the same God?" we are still met with the epistemic gap between ourselves and the subjects in question, particular Christians, Muslims, and Jews. In other words, how do we know what someone else believes? How do we know whom they worship? At best, through dialogue, we can come to make judgments about what the other has in mind; we do this all the time in daily life. Yet we must also recognize that these judgments are not always accurate. Language is symbolic. The words and concepts we use are always pointing beyond themselves.

To add to the difficult challenge at hand, addressing the question as to whether Muslims, Jews, and Christians worship the same God is a task that requires translation. Not simply linguistic translations (i.e., Hebrew, Greek, Arabic, etc.), but a translation of conceptual frameworks that vary across historical-cultural contexts. This is a major challenge of all comparative theological and philosophical work. It is more clearly a challenge in East-West comparisons like Christianity and Buddhism, for which assuming that nirvana is simply the Buddhist version of Christian heaven results in an imperialistic misappropriation of concepts. Yet there is also a risk of conceptual chauvinism when comparing and contrasting the Abrahamic traditions. We should be slow to assume that the YHWH of Judaism, Allah of Islam, and God of Christianity are different ways of referring to one and the same divine ultimate.

Finally, much of the current debate regarding whether or not the three

---

8. John B. Cobb Jr. *Whitehead Word Book: A Glossary with Alphabetical Index to Technical Terms* (Claremont, CA: P&F Press, 2008), 14.

Abrahamic traditions worship the same God hinges on what one means by the "same." There is a sense in which Andrew Schwartz today is the same person as Andrew Schwartz twenty-five years ago. He has the same parents, the same siblings, the same origins. Yet there is a sense in which he is not the same person he was back then (there are pictures to prove it!). If the police were to put out an APB on thirty-three-year-old Andrew Schwartz but used the description of eight-year-old Andrew, they would have a difficult time tracking him down. Moreover, the cells in our bodies regenerate over and over to the point that the physical makeup that constituted Andrew's eight-year-old body is not the *same* stuff that constitutes his body today. This conundrum is well documented in philosophical discourse on identity, with examples like the Ship of Theseus.

Imagine a ship that leaves from Los Angeles, arriving in Shanghai a month later. During the voyage the ship requires extensive repairs, such that by the time it arrives in Shanghai none of the parts that constitute the ship are the original parts that constituted the ship upon its departure from LA. There is a sense in which the ship that left Los Angeles is not the "same" ship that arrived in Shanghai—different deck, different sails, and so on. Yet there is another sense in which it is the same ship, albeit transformed. So, in one sense "same" can imply no difference, and in another sense it can incorporate difference. What then does it mean for Christians, Jews, and Muslims to worship the *same* God?

While we wish to acknowledge the ambiguity of language, the complexity of Christian, Muslim, and Jewish identities, and the difficulty of the notion of sameness, we won't let this prevent us from attempting to say something positive about the main question of whether the three worship the same God. Sure enough, there are many ways in which it can be said that Christians, Jews, and Muslims do *not* worship the same God. Some examples are given above, and other examples will be discussed at length by other authors in this book. Our goal, however, is to identify how we can positively assert that all three groups *do* worship the same God.

The God of Abraham: A Historical Argument

Do Jews, Christians, and Muslims worship the same God? From a historical perspective, absolutely! Muslims worship the God of Abraham, Christians worship the God of Abraham, and Jews worship the God of Abraham.

Perhaps you recall the Bible school song that declares that "Father Abraham had many sons, many sons had Father Abraham. I am one of them and so are you, so let's just praise the Lord." While not likely intended as a pluralistic affirmation of Jewish and Muslim expressions of faith being compatible with Christianity, there is something significant about the realization that all three traditions claim a similar origin.

Consider the above example of the ship that travels from LA to Shanghai. Imagine we knew nothing about the origins of the ship that arrives on the Shanghai shore, and that we know nothing about the destination of the ship at the LA harbor. Imagine a photo is taken of the ship before leaving LA and upon arriving at Shanghai, and that a detailed description of the ship's makeup is provided before departure in LA and after arrival in Shanghai. If someone were asked, based on the disparate descriptions and photographic evidence, whether the LA ship and the Shanghai ship are the *same* ship, one would be justified in concluding that they are not. Yet when we know something about the origins of the Shanghai ship and the journey of the LA ship, we are inclined to overlook differences in appearance, material, location, and so forth and conclude that the two ships are one in the same. This is the power of history.

The same logic can be applied to the Abrahamic traditions. Despite any differences in description, nature, or expression, if we are able to trace the origins of the God of Christianity, Allah of Islam, and YHWH of Judaism to the same historical root—the God of Abraham—we can conclude that all three traditions worship the same God, despite any differences. So, do all three worship the God of Abraham? Consider the following argument:

1. The God of Abraham is the God of Judaism.
2. Jesus worshiped the God of Abraham.
3. Christians worship the God of Jesus.
4. Therefore, Christians worship the God of Judaism.

The first premise (that the God of Abraham is the God of Judaism) is not particularly controversial. After all, Jews themselves claim Abraham as a central figure and a source of their understanding of God. Abraham is referred to as the first patriarch, is credited with being the one who brought knowledge of the one true God (YHWH), and is the one through whom God made a covenant with Israel. The first book of the Torah records, "I am the Lord, the God of Abraham" (Gen. 28:13 NRSV). So premise 1 seems true—the God of Abraham is the God of Judaism.

Now let's turn to premise 2, that Jesus worshiped the God of Abraham. Take, for instance, that which Jesus declares as the greatest commandment.

> One of them, an expert in the law, tested him with this question: "Teacher, which is the greatest commandment in the Law?"
>
> Jesus replied: "'Love the Lord your God with all your heart and with all your soul and with all your mind.' This is the first and greatest commandment. And the second is like it: 'Love your neighbor as yourself.' All the Law and the Prophets hang on these two commandments." (Matt. 22:35–40)

Not only is Jesus referencing Jewish scripture (Tanakh) when he speaks of the Law (the Torah—five books of Moses) and the Prophets (Nevi'im), but he actually quotes two passages from the Torah, namely, Deuteronomy 6:5 ("Love the Lord your God with all your heart and with all your soul and with all your strength.") and Leviticus 19:18 ("Do not seek revenge or bear a grudge against anyone among your people, but love your neighbor as yourself. I am the Lord."). This shouldn't be a surprise, since the Jesus we find in the Christian Gospels was in fact Jewish. As such, when he urges us to "Love the Lord your God," he has in mind the one true God, his *Abba*, the God of Abraham, the God of Judaism. Hence, premise 2 seems true—Jesus worshiped the God of Abraham.

What then of premise 3? Is it true to say that Christians worship the God of Jesus? Surely this too is not particularly controversial. After all, what is a Christian if not a follower of Jesus? And what would it mean to be a follower of Jesus if not, at minimum, to worship the God that Jesus instructed us to worship? After more than two thousand years of development, there remains an important practice within Christian liturgy, the recitation of the Lord's Prayer. In his groundbreaking Sermon on the Mount, Jesus instructs the people how to pray, which begins with "Our Father in heaven" (see Matt. 6:9–13). This particular prayer continues to have significance across the sects of Christianity throughout the ages. Whether a Catholic mass or an evangelical tent revival, the Lord's Prayer seems to have a uniting quality for Christians around the world. It unites Christians around the globe because it affirms that all are praying to the same God (*our* Father in heaven). Likewise, it unites Christians with Jesus, in that they continue to pray to the same God to whom Jesus prayed—"Our Father in heaven." Hence, premise 3 seems true; Christians worship the God of Jesus. And, if premises 1, 2, and 3 are true, then the conclusion is sound: Christians worship the God of Judaism.

Thus, it is reasonable to say in a historical sense that Christians and Jews worship the same God. But what about Muslims? Within Islam, Abraham is—as in Judaism—recognized as a central patriarch that proclaimed the oneness of God. Revered as a prophet in Islam, Abraham is also considered the constructor of the Ka'bah—the most sacred site in Islam—which Muslims all around the world face when praying. The *hadj*, one of the five pillars of Islam, is a holy pilgrimage to Mecca, which is sometimes referred to as the City of Abraham. In fact, the Qur'an explicitly claims the God of Abraham stating, "Who but a fool would forsake the religion of Abraham?" (2:130). Moreover, as stated in the Qur'an, "We [Muslims] believe in God, and in what has been revealed to us, and what was revealed to Abraham, Ishmael, Isaac, Jacob, and the Tribes, and in what was given to Moses, Jesus, and the Prophets from their Lord" (3:84). So it seems that, according to Islamic scripture, Muslims worship the God of both Abraham and Jesus, implying that Jesus worshiped the God of Abraham, and essentially affirming that Muslims worship the same God as Jews and Christians.

As Michael Lodahl brilliantly points out, while Islam, Judaism, and Christianity each claim Abraham as their father, "the ways in which they construe Abraham's patronage and story are so divergent as to yield some very different Abrahams."[9] We agree with Lodahl. But remember the ship from LA to Shanghai. Imagine three different people giving an account of the ship by describing Los Angeles, the ship's point of origin. One person describes Venice Beach, another describes Disneyland, and another describes the San Gabriel Mountains. Are varied descriptions of the complex LA region reason to believe that the three people are

---

9. Michael Lodahl, *Claiming Abraham: Reading the Bible and the Qur'an Side by Side* (Grand Rapids: Brazos, 2010), 4.

talking about different cities and therefore different ships? We think not. Lodahl's concern regarding different Abrahams isn't so much a question as to multiple historical figures called Abraham, but diverse theological interpretations connected to that shared historical origin. Like trying to compile an image of a father based on descriptions from his three children, the fact that each offspring provides a unique description of their father doesn't entail that they aren't siblings. Similarly, the fact that Muslims, Christians, and Jews have varying accounts of Abraham doesn't entail that they don't share the same historical root. That all three worship the God of Abraham, is one way in which Christians, Muslims, and Jews can be said to be worshiping the same God.

A Loving Creator: A Divine Character Argument

Another way to answer the question of whether Christians, Muslims, and Jews worship the same God positively is by focusing on what is meant by "God." One way to do this is to identify characteristics, or attributes, of the Divine. Perhaps you've heard it said, "If it looks like a duck, walks like a duck, and quacks like a duck, then it's probably a duck." Similarly, we might say that if the God of Christianity is described with the same attributes as the God of Judaism and Islam, then it would stand to reason that they are in fact describing the same divine entity and therefore should be said to be worshiping the same God. So, are YHWH, God, and Allah described as having more or less similar characteristics? It seems so.

God is one. That all three Abrahamic traditions are monotheistic means each affirms that there is only one God. The scriptures of each tradition are quite clear on this. As expressed in the shared Christian and Jewish scriptures, "Hear O Israel: The Lord our God, the Lord is one" (Deut. 6:4). Additionally, "I am the Lord, and there is no other; apart from me there is no God" (Isa. 45:5). Likewise, Islamic scriptures are clear on the oneness of God: "God! There is no God but He, the living the Everlasting" (Qur'an 2:255). Additionally, "Do not call out to any other god beside God, for there is no god but Him" (Qur'an 28:88). As demonstrated throughout their scriptures, Islam, Judaism, and Christianity all describe God as "one"—the only one.

God is knowledgeable and relational. Another shared attribute of God is the most knowledgeable. As the Qur'an states, "Our Lord, You know well what we conceal and what we reveal: nothing at all is hidden from God, on earth or in heaven" (Qur'an 14:38). This is echoed by the Christian and Jewish psalm, which reads,

> O Lord, you have searched me and known me.
> You know when I sit down and when I rise up;
>   you discern my thoughts from far away.
> You search out my path and my lying down
>   and are acquainted with all my ways.
>   (Ps. 139:1–3 NRSV)

Furthermore, the kind of knowledge attributed to God by these traditions is relational. God doesn't just know "about" humanity; God *knows* humanity in an intimate way, such that we cannot keep secrets from God. As the Qur'an explains, God is closer to us "than a jugular vein" (50:16).

God is loving and merciful. Not only does God know our innermost beings, but all three traditions describe God as loving and merciful. Within Christianity, God's love is often lifted up as a central attribute—a sentiment supported by scriptures like 1 John 4:8, which simply states that "God is love." Similarly, Jewish scripture describes God in this way:

> The Lord is gracious and merciful,
>   slow to anger and abounding in steadfast love.
> The Lord is good to all,
>   and his compassion is over all that he has made.
>   (Ps. 145:8–9 NRSV)

The picture of a gracious and merciful God found in Judaism and Christianity is paralleled in Islam, with such statements as "If you tried to count God's blessings, you could never take them all in: He is truly most forgiving and most merciful" (Qur'an 16:18).

God is creator. Thus far, we have seen that all three traditions describe their God as the one true God who is loving and merciful, and who knows all creatures intimately. Additionally, God is described by all three as the creator of the heavens and the earth. The very beginning of the Christian Bible and the Jewish Torah affirm that "in the beginning

God created the heavens and the earth" (Gen. 1:1). Not surprisingly, Islam too affirms God as creator: "It is God who created the heavens and the earth and everything between them in six Days" (Qur'an 32:4). To be the creator of the heavens and the earth, of which humans are a part, is to identify God as the author of human existence. Just as when all three traditions claim a shared origin in Father Abraham, claiming to worship the creator of the heavens and the earth (a cosmic reality shared by Christians, Muslims, and Jews alike) implies that all three worship the same God, the creator of our world.

God is mysterious. While these Abrahamic traditions go to great lengths to describe the object of their worship, there is also the deep recognition that God is ultimately mysterious, hidden, and beyond our understanding. As Zophar asked Job,

> Can you find out the deep things of God?
>> Can you find out the limit of the Almighty?
> It is higher than heaven—what can you do?
>> Deeper than Sheol—what can you know?
> Its measure is longer than the earth
>> and broader than the sea. (Job 11:7–9 NRSV)

Isaiah said of God, "Truly, you are a God who hides himself" (Isa. 45:15 NRSV). The Qur'an echoes this in such statements as "No vision can grasp Him, but His grasp is over all vision; He is above all comprehension, yet is acquainted with all things" (Qur'an 6:103).

Now, one might object to the above Divine character argument, since describing God in the same terms doesn't necessarily mean the same God is being described. Imagine two people, one describing a fir tree in Oregon, another describing a fir tree in Germany. Both descriptions might be similar since the fir trees might be similar. But that doesn't mean only one fir tree is being described, just one referent for two descriptions. However, when we combine the shared origin argument with the Divine description argument, we find that parallel descriptions of God across the traditions greatly strengthen the likelihood that the God described and revered in Islam, Christianity, and Judaism is one in the same—the one and only loving and merciful Creator who knows our innermost beings.

There Is Only One God: An Ontological Argument

Christians, Muslims, and Jews are all very clear on the declaration that "there is only one God." If we begin with this declaration, the question as to whether all three worship the same God is strange indeed. After all, what would it mean for them to worship different Gods if there is only one God? From an ontological perspective, if there is, in fact, only one God available to worship, then it is reasonable to conclude that Muslims, Christians, and Jews worship the same God—that is, the only God.

Imagine a scenario in which there are only two people in the world, and they happen to be married. It would be strange if one day the wife asked her husband whether or not he had a "Sally on the side" (was having an affair with another woman) since there aren't any other women to have an affair with. Similarly, since Christians, Jews, and Muslims believe that there is only one God, to worship *a* God entails worshiping *the* God. Put another way, how could they be worshiping different Gods if there are no other Gods to worship?

If there is only one God, then, for Christians, Muslims, and Jews to worship *some* God is to worship the *same* God. By the logic of monotheism, one can either worship God or not worship God. To state from a Christian, Muslim, or Jewish perspective that the other Abrahamic faiths worship different Gods is to undermine monotheism by implying the existence of other Gods. Since the existence of multiple Gods as distinct objects of worship is incompatible with monotheism, all three Abrahamic traditions should not—from within their own theological commitment—allow the possibility that the others are worshiping different Gods. In this sense, Muslims, Christians, and Jews can rightly be said to be worshiping the same God.

Now, some may be inclined to distinguish between the "real" God and "false" gods. But what reason does a Christian or Muslim or Jew have for believing that the others worship a fake god? Consider the example of three sons. Each claims the same man as his father. Each describes the man the same way. Then imagine that one son turns to the others and says, "Your father is not real; only my father is real." That would be a strange response. Clearly all three sons have a father (I mean, they came from somewhere, right?). What would it mean to have a fake father? What is intended here is actually "Your father is not my father."

But if there is only one father (one creator) and everyone has a father, then everyone has the same father.

In the spirit of Robert DeNiro's character from *Taxi Driver*, we might imagine God looking at the world and, in response to the prayers of Muslims, Jews, and Christians, replying, "You talkin' to me? You talkin' to me? Well I'm the only one here. Who . . . do you think you're talking to?" From this perspective, Muslims, Jews, and Christians worship the same God because there are no other gods to worship. This ontological argument is strengthened by the Divine character argument, that all three religions describe God in similar ways, and the historical argument, that all three claim the same origins—the God of Abraham.

Many Paths, One Mountain: Identist Pluralism

As mentioned above, there are many different types of religious pluralism. One version is described by the phrase "many paths up one mountain." According to this form of pluralism, the mountain can be said to represent reality, while the mountaintop is the end (and presumed goal) of all those who climb to the summit. What makes this position pluralistic is that it doesn't matter if you climb the mountain from the east or the west, if your path is straight or winding, because eventually all paths lead to a single summit. This kind of pluralism is called *identist* because there is an identical goal, or single ultimate, to which the many religions are oriented.

From the identist perspective, Christians, Jews, and Muslims can be said to worship the same God because all are oriented to the singular ultimate reality or religious end. Not only so, but renowned pluralist John Hick explains how all religions can be oriented toward the same ultimate even though there are diverse practices and expressions. Essentially, he claims an ontological unity amid epistemic diversity. Ultimate reality (what Hick calls "the Real," and others might call God) is known and experienced in many diverse ways by many different people in many different contexts throughout history. Therefore, many diverse expressions could be said to capture the diverse ways of knowing God; but this doesn't entail that there are many Gods. Just like the idea that there are many paths up one mountain, an identist pluralist might say that there is "one God but many religions."

Hick's identist approach is further explained through his use of a

Kantian distinction between the *noumena* (reality as it is in itself) and the *phenomena* (reality as perceived). Like the mountain, for Hick, there is only one—only one ultimate reality. But knowledge of that reality is always mediated through our experiences in a particular context by particular people—many paths. Therefore, according to Hick, we should be careful to delineate between reality and our perception of reality, between God and our perception of God. The important question to consider here is whether differences in the way God is perceived entails different Gods. Hick thinks not.

To explain this, Hick uses the Indic parable of the blind men and the elephant. Imagine six blind men are touching different parts of an elephant. Each describes the elephant differently (for example, like a rope when holding the tail, like a fan when holding the ear, like a wall when touching the side). Often this analogy gets used to make a point about epistemology—the limitations of our coming to know an entity as akin to blindness, which explains why there are different religious accounts. But there is also an ontological insight here. Yes, there are many descriptions of the elephant (reality), but there is only one elephant. It doesn't matter how many descriptions there are, there is still only one elephant. So, from the perspective of identist pluralism, even though Christians, Jews, and Muslims have distinct religious traditions with distinct beliefs and practices, all worship the same God because there is ultimately only one God to worship—one mountain. As you can see, identist pluralism goes hand in hand with the ontological argument above.

Many Paths, Many Mountains: Deep Pluralism

Alternatively, the ontological situation may be more complicated than the simple identist understanding portrayed above. Instead of "many paths up one mountain," what if there are many mountains—multiple unique ultimates and distinct religious ends? Like the analogy of the blind men and the elephant, it is incontrovertible that the many religions of the world express themselves through distinct beliefs and practices. But why should we presume that there is only one elephant? Why presume that ultimate reality is singular? This is where "differential" (or "deep") pluralism comes in. According to process philosophy, ultimate reality is best thought of as a complex unity of three distinct but inseparable ultimates. As David Ray Griffin explains:

One of these [ultimates], corresponding with what Whitehead calls "creativity," has been called "Emptiness" ("*Śūnyatā*") or "Dharmakaya" by Buddhists, "Nirguna Brahman" by Advaita Vedāntists, "the Godhead" by Meister Eckhart, and "Being Itself" by Heidegger and Tillich (among others). It is the *formless* ultimate reality. The other ultimate, corresponding with what Whitehead calls "God," is not Being Itself but the *Supreme* Being. It is in-formed and the source of forms (such as truth, beauty, and justice). It has been called "Amida Buddha," "Sambhogakaya," "Saguna Brahman," "Ishvara," "Yahweh," "Christ," and "Allah" . . . [the third ultimate is] the cosmos, the universe, "the totality of [finite] things . . . illustrated by forms of Taoism and many primal religions, including Native American religions, that regards the cosmos as sacred.[10]

These three ultimates (God, World, and Creativity) can also correspond to three types of religion described by Jack Hutchinson: theistic, cosmic, and acosmic, respectively. In this way, deep pluralism acknowledges that the many religions of the world don't have to be oriented to the same elephant (the same ultimate) in order to be oriented toward something truly ultimate in the nature of things.

So, to slightly adapt the core question of this book, instead of asking whether Jews, Christians, and Muslims worship the *same God*, we could ask whether all three worship *ultimate reality*. But what is the relationship between God and ultimate reality? Should the two be treated as synonymous? We think not. Like Paul Tillich, who urged Christians to worship the God beyond the Bible, we believe it is helpful to distinguish between a *supreme personal being* (i.e., God), and the *source of all being* (i.e., Being Itself, the Ground of Being, or what Alfred North Whitehead calls "Creativity").

Consider a painting. The canvas, the paint, and the artists are all distinct but necessary elements. The canvas is the space which makes the intent of the artists possible, which is expressed in the particular images constituted by the paint. Likewise, we might say that God (the cosmic artists) creates the world of particularities (paint). But this is only

---

10. Griffin, *Deep Religious Pluralism*, 47, 49.

possible because there is a canvas—the Ground of Being, Being Itself, or Creativity.

Tillich rightly saw that the Bible does not introduce the concept of Being Itself, which suggests that the God of Abraham is not Being Itself. Therefore, when answering the question of whether the Abrahamic traditions all worship the same God, it may be helpful to determine whether Christians worship the God of the Bible or whether the object of Christian devotion was redirected to Being Itself. This distinction, between Supreme Being and Being Itself, can also be understood as the difference between worshiping a personal deity on the one hand and engaging in a mystical quest for unity with a formless ultimate reality on the other.

Within Christianity, Thomas Aquinas affirmed that Supreme Being and Being Itself are one and the same. This has been mainstream Catholic teaching since then. The general pattern has been to regard the characteristics of the Supreme Being as valuable symbols for Being Itself so that they retain the dominant role in worship and personal piety and an important place in theology where the language is used with the caveat that applying language descriptive of creatures to God can never be literal. This introduces deep tensions into traditional theology, especially philosophical theology. Meister Eckhart tried to liberate theology from these views. Some have called Being Itself Godhead and the Supreme Being God and then usually blurred the distinctions. Paul Tillich makes some use of traditional symbols to make it easier for Christians to identify Being Itself with God. But in the twentieth century, identifying Being Itself and the Supreme Being became more and more difficult, with Heidegger playing an important role. Much of the response has been to emphasize that all language, especially language about God, is symbolic, so that any question about what it refers to beyond language is excluded. If our language is not referential, then the issue is simply a pragmatic choice of images. There are as many gods as images. The Reformer's call for *sola scriptura* reduced, but did not eliminate, the effects of Thomas's discovery of Being Itself in Protestant theology.

Thomas did not want to do what Tillich does (i.e., invite Christians to change the object of their devotion), since he thought he was providing a more profound understanding of the Supreme Being that Christians worshiped. It could be argued, however, that Eckhart understood Thomas better than Thomas understood himself, which became clear in the twentieth century. Nevertheless, the Thomistic synthesis of Being Itself and Supreme Being remains the official Catholic doctrine.

The distinction between the personal God and Being Itself in a way introduces the notion of a plurality of ultimates in the context of monotheism, which can help account for mystical expressions in all three traditions. While Jews and Muslims have been less drawn to Being Itself, Muslim thinkers like Muhammad Iqbal and Jewish thinkers like Rabbi Michael Lerner provide examples to the contrary. For most of those who focus on Being Itself, a personal or I-Thou God is often considered unreal or inferior (non-ultimate). This is not unlike the Nirguna Brahman and Saguna Brahman distinction in Advaita Vedanta. However, Alfred North Whitehead allows us to say that both the God of Abraham and Being Itself (renamed Creativity) are ultimately real.

This adds to the complexity in answering the question of whether Muslims, Christians, and Jews worship the same God. In one sense, no two Christians worship the same God. But in our view, most Christians intend to worship the God of Abraham even though they understand God in very different ways. However, since Thomas Aquinas, the Christian worship of this God has been challenged by the realization that Being Itself has an equal or superior claim upon us. In general, until recently and with some dramatic exceptions such as Eckhart, the result has been to confuse and modify the God of Abraham for sophisticated Christians. Most Christians ignored this in their worship. Indeed, worship is not the human act for which Being Itself calls, which leads to mysticism rather than worship. Our view is that because of the role of the Bible in the church, the great majority of Christians worship the same God as Jews and Muslims (the Supreme Being). In fact, we consider this normative. Changing Gods is a very recent option. Our hope, and a widespread reality already, is that Christians through their worship of the God of Abraham will be freed to also engage in practices oriented to "creativity" and also to "the world." We take this to be the contribution of process theology to the present discourse.

The Benefits of Saying Yes

While we have not argued beyond all doubt that Muslims, Jews, and Christians worship the same God, the above arguments make it plausible to conclude affirmatively. More importantly, we believe there are significant benefits to affirming that all three worship the same God; such that if all things are equal, it would be in one's best interest to agree with us. These benefits include the following.

A more peaceful world. It is not essential to peace that we all agree. In fact, it is probably best that we don't. Yes, difference is often the source of conflict. But difference is also the source of beauty. Imagine a garden with only a single flower or a symphony with only one note. The beauty of the garden and the attraction of the symphony is found in diversity, not sameness. Likewise, we believe that diversity should not be subsumed for the sake of sameness, and that sameness is not essential for peace. That said, religious exclusivism—or more accurately, arrogant absolutism—has contributed to a great deal of the world's violence. It is for that reason that Sandra Lubarsky writes, "Religious pluralism is a tool for perfecting the world, helping to eliminate religious arrogance which has resulted in so much human suffering."[11] The recognition that Christians, Muslims, and Jews worship the same God can help unite the Abrahamic traditions and lead to greater peace among these major religions.

Generosity and humility. The principle of generosity is central to all three faiths. Yet too often Christians, Jews, and Muslims, make harsh judgments about the intentions of the others. What would it look like for Christians to assume the best of Muslims, and not the worst? How is assuming the best of religious others connected to affirming that all three worship the same God? As Sandra Lubarsky notes, renowned Jewish thinker David Hartman celebrates religious pluralism as spiritually redemptive, indicating that such a view "preserves the understanding that God is greater than any single faith community; it frees humans from the mistaken belief that any revelation is universal; and it reasserts the sacredness of all human life, regardless of different truth claims."[12] Affirming that the three Abrahamic traditions are oriented toward the same object of worship can help avoid undue arrogance and attitudes of superiority. After all, if Muslims, Jews, and Christians are all responding to and attempting to know the same deity, there are

11. Sandra Lubarsky, "Deep Religious Pluralism and Contemporary Jewish Thought," in Griffin, *Deep Religious Pluralism*, 118.
12. Lubarsky, "Deep Religious Pluralism and Contemporary Jewish Thought," 122.

probably insights from Judaism and Islam that can enhance a Christian's understanding of God.

Mutual transformation. As Christians, Muslims, and Jews interact with one another in a spirit of generosity and mutual respect, there is an increased chance of mutual transformation. To be changed, to be transformed, to become the best version of yourself, to become more like God and the prophets—these are among the goals of all three Abrahamic faiths. Might a Christian be transformed by reading the Qur'an? Might a Jew be transformed by going to a Christian worship service? We think so. In fact, we believe such mutual transformation, especially through interreligious dialogue, can and should occur regardless of whether or not the individuals in question believe they are worshiping the same God. However, if we begin with the view that Muslims, Jews, and Christians worship the same God, then all three traditions become another source of revelation, another means by which one can know God more deeply.

Importance of dialogue. Given this stance of generosity and mutual respect, proselytization is replaced with dialogue. Interfaith dialogue does not ask that we abandon our convictions. On the contrary, it is the convictions of all involved that make the dialogue valuable. Moreover, we believe the entire enterprise of attempting to answer the question of this book should hinge on the practice of interreligious dialogue. How do we know if we are talking about the same God or different Gods if we don't begin with dialogue? While the above arguments have attempted to answer the question through alternative means, the path of dialogue is by far the most promising in coming to a clear answer.

Take, for instance, theism and atheism. Conceptually and linguistically, these two are complete opposites, literally theism and not-theism. As such, it is commonly assumed that theism and atheism are incompatible. But there is a massive hole, an unasked and unanswered question at the heart of the incompatibility between theism and atheism. Namely, is the God that atheism rejects the same God the theist accepts? Much like the question of this book, one could ask, are theists and atheists talking about the same God? Of course, how can we know this without dialogue?[13] Through dialogue, we may come to discover that the God

---

13. While not technically part of traditional interfaith dialogue, we believe that comparative textual analysis (i.e., Christian writings and atheist writings) can shed some light on

that Richard Dawkins rejects (the old man in the sky who unilaterally determines all things, and is hence responsible for all evil and suffering in the world) is not the same God that Thomas Jay Oord accepts (a God whose nature is an uncontrolling love that does not unilaterally determine anything, but is always working cooperatively with creation to bring about the best possible outcome). Perhaps, if Oord and Dawkins were to engage in a dialogue, Dawkins would discover that the God he adamantly rejects is not the same God that Oord describes, such that Oord's theism remains compatible with Dawkins's atheism.

Likewise, to effectively answer the question of whether Christians, Jews, and Muslims worship the same God, we should begin with dialogue. Perhaps most significantly, the dialogue itself is transformative. While a Christian may enter the dialogue with the goal of figuring out whether a Muslim worships the same God, through the dialogue—through the process of sharing and listening, of getting to know our interlocutor—all parties involved are forever changed. This is simultaneously the risk and reward of dialogue. The person who enters the dialogue is, in a sense, not the same person who exits the dialogue. When we are transformed by our encounter with those of other faiths, the kinds of questions we have when the dialogue begins may not be the same questions we value when the dialogue ends. We may come to the realization that all three Abrahamic traditions worship the same God, but we may also transcend that question and discover new questions of significance.

As we humbly approach the great mysteries of God, as we engage one another with a spirit of generosity and hospitality, as we embark on the journey of a mutually transforming dialogue, we set the stage for a more peaceful world. The ambiguity inherent in the question of whether Christians, Muslims, and Jews worship the same God provides an opportunity. This is an opportunity for choosing generosity over judgment, unity over division, and peace over conflict.

---

answering this question without requiring two living people to engage in a real-time dialogue. That said, many of the challenges of comparative inquiry can be reduced through direct dialogue with a knowledgeable interlocutor.

RESPONSE TO WM. ANDREW SCHWARTZ AND JOHN B. COBB JR.

FRANCIS J. BECKWITH

Professors Schwartz and Cobb offer a strong case for why one should believe that Christians, Jews, and Muslims worship the same God. Because much of their case is consistent with my contribution to this volume, this response focuses on the few points they make with which I disagree.

Christian Orthodoxy and the Problem of Religious Identity

Schwartz and Cobb draw our attention to the problem of religious identity: What does it mean to say that someone is a Christian, Muslim, or Jew? They raise this question because they want the reader to understand that if the meanings of "Christian," "Muslim," and "Jew" are contested within those faiths, then figuring out whether Christians, Muslims, and Jews worship the same God is not a simple task. After all, not every member of a particular faith conceives of God, salvation, and religious practice in exactly the same way. For this reason, a classical Christian theist, like St. Thomas Aquinas (1225–74), holds to a view of God more in common with that held by the Jewish philosopher Moses Maimonides (1135–1204) than the one embraced by the Christian philosopher and open theist Richard Swinburne (1934–).[1]

Focusing on Christianity, Schwartz and Cobb point out that there have been disputes about what counts as orthodoxy and what counts as heresy since the beginning of the faith. Although they admit that some of the catholic creeds may be viewed as authoritative statements

---

1. Richard Swinburne, *The Christian God* (New York: Oxford University Press, 1994).

of doctrine, individual Christians interpret those differently. And even when it comes to practices that may seem to be held in common between Christians—such as, baptism, the celebration of the Eucharist—one finds throughout the Christian world a variety of views about the meaning, purpose, and nature of these practices.

As a Catholic, I must confess that this is not at all surprising, since the Catholic Church teaches that there is a deposit of faith, having developed over time, that has been passed on and received by the apostles' successors throughout the church's two-thousand-year history.[2] Summarized in the *Catechism of the Catholic Church*,[3] the very existence of this tradition implies that some who depart from the faith on certain matters embrace heretical views. In fact, many of the citations found in the *Catechism* are from the church's ecumenical and regional councils, which were convened to settle these very disputes. Schwartz and Cobb reject this Catholic account, arguing that apostolic "succession doesn't guarantee any degree of consistency in belief or practice" (12). But that's not quite what the Catholic Church teaches. It is not apostolic succession per se that guarantees orthodoxy, but it is the power of the Holy Spirit working through the church's magisterium—with all its human flaws and foibles—while it encounters new and differing challenges to its mission on earth as it moves through history.[4]

On the other hand, as I noted in my chapter, to be a Catholic, or any Christian for that matter, one does not have to be a theologian or even fully understand or grasp the complex subtleties with which the Church wrestled when it addressed these doctrinal controversies. To be a member of Christ's body requires assent to the faith, not comprehension of

---

2. "The apostles entrusted the 'Sacred deposit' of the faith (the *depositum fidei*), contained in Sacred Scripture and Tradition, to the whole of the Church. 'By adhering to [this heritage] the entire holy people, united to its pastors, remains always faithful to the teaching of the apostles, to the brotherhood, to the breaking of bread and the prayers. So, in maintaining, practicing and professing the faith that has been handed on, there should be a remarkable harmony between the bishops and the faithful.'" *Catechism of the Catholic Church: Revised in Accordance With the Official Latin Text Promulgated by Pope John Paul II*, 2nd ed. (Washington, DC: United States Conference of Catholic Bishops, 2000), 84, citations omitted.

3. See *Catechism of the Catholic Church*, 84.

4. "This living transmission, accomplished in the Holy Spirit, is called Tradition, since it is distinct from Sacred Scripture, though closely connected to it. Through Tradition, 'the Church, in her doctrine, life and worship, perpetuates and transmits to every generation all that she herself is, all that she believes.' . . . Thanks to the assistance of the Holy Spirit, the understanding of both the realities and the words of the heritage of faith is able to grow in the life of the Church." *Catechism of the Catholic Church*, 78, 94, citations omitted.

it.[5] In other words, you do not have to understand what "consubstantial with the Father" means, as St. Athanasius understood it, in order to believe it. For this reason, I think that Schwartz and Cobb, by emphasizing how individual believers may embrace contrary understandings of particular doctrines and practices, overintellectualize how people come to and maintain their Christian faith. (This, by the way, is something that we philosophers are prone to do. We often forget that the grandmas who work in the parish soup kitchen are not at all worried about falling into heresy, and neither is their pastor.)

Having said that, it is not clear how the problem of religious identity as it pertains to the three faiths discussed in this book—Christianity, Judaism, and Islam—is relevant to the question at hand, "Do Christians, Muslims, and Jews worship the same God?" Disagreements about what counts as heresy or orthodoxy are typically engaged within the confines of particular traditions and thus presuppose a common understanding of what constitutes a divine nature. Take, for example, an illustration I employed in my chapter: the dispute between Arius and St. Athanasius over whether the Son of God was made or begotten—whether he is merely a creature or the second person of the Trinity—assumes there is only one God who is *the absolute, uncaused, perfect, rational, unchanging, self-subsistent, eternal creator and sustainer of all that which receives its being from another.* The dispute concerned the nature of the Son of *that God*, not what constitutes a divine nature. Of course, if we come across a self-described Christian, Jew, or Muslim who denies that God is metaphysically ultimate and has underived existence, as, for example, Latter-day Saint doctrine teaches,[6] we will have found someone who has abandoned the logic of classical monotheism and for whom the "same God" question, as traditionally understood, could not in principle arise. On the other hand, as I noted in my chapter, those theists who depart from classical theism on certain points—such as Swinburne, William Lane Craig, and Alvin Plantinga—are nevertheless referring to the same God, since they are working within the same tradition and providing an account of the same reality, *the absolute underived unconditioned source*

---

5. A baptized infant technically does not assent, but her parents and godparents do by proxy on her behalf. But when the child is mature enough, she does assent as she receives the sacrament of confirmation.

6. See K. Codell Carter, "Godhood," in *The Encyclopedia of Mormonism*, ed. Daniel H. Ludlow (New York: Macmillan, 1992), 553–55.

of all contingent existence, just as Isaac Newton (1643–1727) and Albert Einstein (1879–1955) were writing about the same physical universe.

Identism and the Case for the Same God

The core of Schwartz and Cobb's chapter is their three-pronged case for the same God thesis. They offer (1) an historical argument, (2) a divine character argument, and (3) an ontological argument. The first argument appeals to the fact that each of the traditions traces its origin to the historical Abraham. The second points to the fact that each of the faiths holds to the same view of the divine nature: God is one, knowledgeable and relational, loving and merciful, and creator. The third maintains that God's oneness, according to each faith, means that there can in principle be only one God. According to Schwartz and Cobb, when we combine the conclusions of these three arguments, we have a powerful case for believing that Christians, Muslims, and Jews worship the same God.

Although I find their case compelling, I would like to suggest some small tweaks. When trying to account for the differences between the three faiths that all worship the same God, Schwartz and Cobb employ a version of the Ship of Theseus story. I am not sure that works, since the purpose of the story is to show the difficulty of affirming metaphysical identity of an artifactual thing over time whose parts are eventually all replaced. But to say that the God of Christianity, Islam, and Judaism is the same God, despite each faith's differing understandings of that God, requires an explanation that preserves God's substantial unity and unchanging nature while providing an account of the interfaith disagreements about that God. The Ship of Theseus story does not do that since it implies that the differing perceptions of God's nature and actions are the result of changes in God (as in the ship), not in our beliefs. For this reason, as I argue in my chapter, I think it is better to employ Aquinas's distinction between the preambles of faith and the articles of faith,[7] that the differences between the three religions are the result of what each tradition believes God has specially revealed through Sacred Scripture and/or authoritative figures.

---

7. St. Thomas Aquinas, *Summa Theologica* I. q. 2, a. 2, ad. 1, trans. Fathers of the English Dominican Province (1920), online edition, http://www.newadvent.org/summa/1002.htm #article2.

Also, I do not think that the same God thesis requires that one embrace an identist understanding of religious difference, as Schwartz and Cobb argue. They write that the three faiths are oriented toward the same ultimate reality but that the differences between them are culturally and historically conditioned expressions of what each perceives about that ultimate reality. This, it seems to me, violates Schwartz and Cobb's own warning that when comparing other religious traditions to one's own, one should not risk engaging in the "imperialistic misappropriation of concepts" or "conceptual chauvinism" (p. 27). Because the identist view, as they admit, "is further explained" by "a Kantian distinction between the *noumena* (reality as it is in itself) and the *phenomena* (reality as perceived)," (p. 37) it risks not taking seriously what each tradition teaches about its own beliefs and the truth of them. When, for example, a Muslim claims that it is his belief that there is no God but Allah and Muhammed is Allah's prophet, we should not appeal to the authority of the *Critique of Pure Reason* and suggest to this follower of Islam that he does not truly understand his own beliefs, that they are merely his perceptions of what God has revealed and thus not truly about what is real. We should, as a matter of charity, take the Muslim at his word, even if we think he is mistaken and that our own tradition or Kantian commitment is the correct one.

This is another place where the Thomistic distinction between the preambles of faith and the articles of faith can be helpful. Because human beings are oriented toward their ultimate good—the vision of God in the afterlife[8]—it is not at all surprising that the Christian may find much truth in religious traditions that she may otherwise believe are mistaken in some very important ways. This is why, as I note in my chapter, St. Paul's preaching on the Areopagus in Athens (Acts 17:22–28), in which he provides to his pagan audience a common reference to the divine nature, is a nice illustration of how a Christian and a non-Christian may both correctly identify the one true God and at the same time think that the other is wrong about how (if it all) God has been

---

8. Aquinas writes: "To know that God exists in a general and confused way is implanted in us by nature, inasmuch as God is man's beatitude. For man naturally desires happiness, and what is naturally desired by man must be naturally known to him. This, however, is not to know absolutely that God exists; just as to know that someone is approaching is not the same as to know that Peter is approaching, even though it is Peter who is approaching." Aquinas, *Summa Theologica*, I. q. 2, a. 1, ad. 1.

revealed in history. This approach does not fall prey to the conceptual chauvinism that Schwartz and Cobb rightly warn us to avoid.

Deep Pluralism and the Non-Ultimate God

Schwartz and Cobb introduce ideas associated with process theology in order to show that religious diversity may be the consequence of differing traditions associating God with one of three ultimates. On this account, the personal God of the Bible and the Qur'an is one ultimate (a supreme being) while Being Itself (the source of all being) and the cosmos (the totality of finite things) are two different ultimates. But this is not a real option for Christians, Jews, and Muslims who see God as their sacred writings and theological traditions see him: *the absolute underived unconditioned source of all contingent existence.*[9] For those believers, there can only be one ultimate since to place any being (or even Being Itself) outside of the providence and creative power of God is to reject the logic of classical monotheism.

The Benefits of Saying Yes

Although I agree with Schwartz and Cobb about the benefits of saying that Christians, Muslims, and Jews worship the same God—that it will lead to a more peaceful world, greater generosity and humility, and mutual transformation—I do not think this requires that believers in those traditions abandon exclusivism. In fact, to suggest otherwise, as Schwartz and Cobb do, leads to a new type of exclusivism: those who think their faith's revelation is the truest or most correct are excluded from the association of religions that properly understand their beliefs as nonexclusive. As we have seen in several very public incidents,[10] dissent-

---

9. See, e.g., *Catechism of the Catholic Church*, 279–324.

10. See, e.g., Associated Press, "Mike Pence Defends His Wife's Job Teaching at a School That Can Bar Gays," *Time*, January 18, 2019, http://time.com/5506565/karen-pence-school-homosexuality/; Ed Condon, "Judicial Nominee Faces Senate Scrutiny over Knights of Columbus Membership," *Catholic News Agency*, December 21, 2018, https://www.catholicnewsagency.com/news/senators-quiz-nominee-about-membership-of-extreme-knights-of-columbus-78683; Emma Green, "Bernie Sanders's Religious Test for Christians in Public Office," *The Atlantic*, June 8, 2017, https://www.theatlantic.com/politics/archive/2017/06/bernie-sanders-chris-van-hollen-russell-vought/529614/; Ian Millhiser, "The Overlooked Line That Let Us Know How Justice Kennedy Really Feels about Homophobes," *Think Progress*, December 6, 2017, https://thinkprogress.org/kennedy-homophobes-good-people-13111f1bf40e/; *Christian Legal Society v. Martinez*, 561 U.S. 661 (2010), in which the Supreme Court holds that the University of California Hastings College of Law may withhold funds from a Christian student group on the grounds that it violates an

ers from orthodox nonexclusivism pay the price of being mocked and shunned simply because they have the temerity to believe that their own religious traditions are true and to publicize it. If we are really serious about respecting differing religious traditions in a pluralistic society— the sort that arises from a rock-ribbed liberalism, not a hegemonic one—we cannot, as a condition of dialogue, impose nonexclusivism on those who cannot in good conscience acquiesce to it.

"all comers" policy that requires that all student groups, including religious ones, not discriminate based on religion or sexual orientation in membership or leadership.

RESPONSE TO JOHN B. COBB JR. AND WM. ANDREW SCHWARTZ

GERALD R. MCDERMOTT

John Cobb and Andrew Schwartz are insightful. They rightly complain of "conceptual chauvinism" when religious people presume that other religious traditions assume the same referents behind words that appear to be similar. Christians, for example, (wrongly) think Buddhist *nirvana* must be another word for heaven. I applaud their warning to be slow to assume that the YHWH of Judaism, the God of Christianity, and Allah of Islam are different ways of referring to the same divine ultimate. And they are on target when they affirm that Christians worship the God of Judaism.

But their thesis is broader, that Christians and Jews worship the same God whom Muslims worship. In support of this thesis, they first argue that there are many disagreements over what Christianity is. Therefore, if one finds one kind of Christianity that disagrees with the God of Islam, one can find another kind of Christianity that agrees with what Muslims mean by Allah. The problem with this approach is that, contrary to what Cobb and Schwartz claim, there *is* one discernible Christian tradition that is called orthodoxy. Others call it the Great Tradition. Different people can disagree with this part or that part, but there is an enormous consensus through history from East to West on its basic shape. C. S. Lewis called it "Mere Christianity" and wrote a book by that title to describe it—what most Christians in most times and places have agreed on. And this conception of God and worship is at odds with what Muslims mean by God and worship.

Cobb and Schwartz say that the Gods of these three religions are "described with the same attributes." I disagree. As I write in my essay, while Christians point to the Bible's declaration that God is love, Muslims deny this. Allah is so transcendent, they say, that such a statement using the word "love" makes God too much like a human being. As readers will know from my essay in this volume, the Muslim writer Murad Wilfried Hofmann has written that "a love of God for His creation . . . must be ruled out as incompatible with the very nature of God s sublime and totally self-sufficient."[1] The Qur'an is ambiguous on whether Allah has love for anyone, but even if he does, his love is only for his Muslim followers. Allah does not love all human beings. As Muslim scholar Daud Rahbar puts it, "Unqualified Divine Love for mankind is an idea completely alien to the Qur'an."[2]

Cobb and Schwartz try to prove that Allah is "loving and merciful" by citing the Qur'anic verse where Allah is said to be "most forgiving and merciful." But a being can be merciful without being loving. A president, for example, can forgive slights against him for any number of reasons, and that forgiveness can be said to be merciful. But merely forgiving a wrong against him does not make that president loving. Neither does mercy make Allah loving, especially when Muslims themselves say that Allah is not loving.

For Muslims, love is not at the heart of Allah's character. Instead, for them, the heart of Allah's character is his being sovereign Lord of the cosmos. The Qur'an teaches that the principal human response is fear, for human beings are his servants or slaves. This is the assessment of both Muslim scholars and Christian specialists in Islam, such as Sir Norman Anderson, longtime professor of Islamic law at the University of London.[3]

So consider the contrast: Christians say that the most essential description of the Christian God's character is love, while Muslims say that Allah has little or nothing to do with love. Even for the minority of Muslims who say Allah has love, that love is only for Muslims and not for all human beings. Therefore we cannot say that Muslims and Christians describe God with the same attributes. An honest assessment

---

1. Murad Wilfried Hofmann, "Differences between the Muslim and Christian Concepts of Divine Love," Bismika Allahuma, September 22, 2008, www.bismikaallahuma.org/archives/2008/differences-between-the-muslim-and-christian-concepts-of-divine-love/.

2. Daud Rahbar, *God of Justice: A Study in the Ethical Doctrine of the Qur'an* (Leiden: Brill, 1960), 172.

3. See my essay for this.

must consider the possibility that if the Muslim God and the Christian God are so fundamentally different in what Christians consider to be most essential, then the Muslim and Christian objects of worship might be two different entities. Cobb and Schwartz's analogy to three sons with the same father does not work because they say that each son "describes the man [their father] the same way." Since the descriptions are very different, there must be two different fathers.

Does this undermine monotheism by implying that there are other gods, as Cobb and Schwartz claim? Not at all. Consider Paul's statement that when Corinthian Christians participated in worship of other deities besides the God of Israel and his Son Jesus, they were participating in worship offered "to demons and not to God" (1 Cor. 9:20). He also said, "There may be so-called 'gods' and many 'lords'—yet for us there is one God, the Father, from whom are all things and for whom we exist, and one Lord, Jesus Christ, through whom are all things and through whom we exist" (1 Cor. 8:5–6 ESV). In other words, other supernatural powers ("gods" and "lords") masquerade as God and Lord, and pagans worship them. Paul sometimes calls them "principalities and powers" (Eph. 6:12) and other times, such as here (1 Cor. 10:20), he calls them "demons." For him, they are real spiritual entities that animate other religions. But they are neither the Creator of the world nor its Redeemer. The Creator is the Father God of Israel and the Redeemer is his Son the messiah Jesus. They alone are God and Lord. With the Spirit, they created and redeemed the world, and as the church later taught, they are three divine persons in one divine being.

While Paul's referents in Corinth were pagans, I do not mean to suggest that Muslims are pagans who refuse monotheism. Unlike most pagans, Muslims clearly assert that there is only one God ruling the cosmos. My point is that in discussing the paganism at Corinth Paul suggested that other religions might be animated by supernatural powers that are not the true Creator and Redeemer of the world. In other words, he attributed competing religions to other spiritual powers that rivalled the true God for the titles God and Lord. Yet at the same time Paul was a monotheist—as Christian theologians have recognized for thousands of years. Therefore, recognizing that other religions may be animated by spiritual powers does not undermine monotheism. If it does, then the apostle Paul was undermining monotheism.

Cobb and Schwartz also suggest that because Thomas Aquinas affirmed that Supreme Being and Being Itself are one and the same, and because Thomas thought he was providing a more profound understanding of the Supreme Being by pointing to Being Itself, "Being Itself has an equal or superior claim upon us" (p. 40). And since "worship is not the human act for which Being Itself calls" (p. 40), mysticism rather than worship is the better Christian response to the Ultimate. In mysticism, there are no determinate words or concepts that might contradict one another, but only Being Itself. In that way of viewing things, it is much easier to say that Christians and Muslims worship the same object because it is indeterminate Being Itself.

But there are problems with this approach. Thomas Aquinas did not regard his description of the triune God as Being Itself as superior to his description of the personal God in Trinity. Being Itself was simply his philosophical way of rendering the God of the scriptures. In fact, for Thomas it was far superior to relate in faith and love to the triune God than to think about God as Being. Only the former was saving.[4] Secondly, for Thomas, God demands worship, not simply meditation as in mystical reflection on Being Itself.[5] So it cannot be said with accuracy that the premier Christian philosophical theologian recommended meditation on Being rather than worship of the Triune God. Therefore that way—the mystical way focused on indeterminate Being Itself—to equate the God of Muslims and the God of Christians cannot be said to be a legitimate way for the mainstream of Christian orthodoxy, which Thomas represents. And for Christian orthodoxy it is most certainly not a "superior" way.

Finally, Cobb and Schwartz recommend pluralism for pragmatic reasons. They claim it leads to less violence and more peace, makes us more humble and generous, and does a better job of inducing mutual transformation. My response is also pragmatic: the results on the ground don't prove any of these things. First of all, the Middle East is riven by

---

4. Thomas said humans can know by reason that God is Being Itself, but that knowledge is insufficient for salvation: "It was necessary for the salvation of man that certain truths which exceed human reason should be made known to him by divine revelation." *Summa Theologiae*, trans. Fathers of the English Dominican Province (Westminster MD: Christian Classics, 1981), Ia.1.1.

5. "God ought to be worshiped not only by internal but also by external actions" and especially in the Christian liturgy to the triune God (ST 2a.2ae. 81.7).

violent conflict between Shi'ites and Sunnis; both worship the God of Islam. The real conflicts are about dominance, led by Persians (Iran) or Arabs (Saudi Arabia and other Sunni states such as Egypt and the Gulf states). More than a half-million Syrians have died in a conflict between the Assad regime and rebels trying to overthrow it. While Russia, the United States, and Iran support differing factions, almost all the fighters in the field believe that Allah is the God of the cosmos. Agreement on the identity of God has not reduced violence or contributed to peace.

There have indeed been plenty of religious wars in history. But far more people were killed by godless totalitarian empires in the twentieth century (Nazism, Soviet communism, Maoist communism, Pol Pot's Khmer Rouge) than by all the religious wars of history put together. If we want more peace and less violence, history suggests that we should fear not the religious but the nonreligious, especially when the latter promise that their use of coercive state power will bring peace and equality. Hitler, Lenin, Stalin, Mao, and Pol Pot preached (eventual) peace and equality but demonized religion and brought death and destruction to hundreds of millions. In *The Myth of Religious Violence*, William Cavanaugh argues that even the early modern religious wars were not battles over rival gods but secular contests for political power that used religion as a pretext.[6] Hence, it was not theological conflict but plain old lust for power and wealth that drove the "religious wars" commonly used to prove that theological difference is the greatest cause of violence.

Does pluralism make us more humble? Perhaps we would regard religious others as more like us if we thought their worship was the same as ours at some level. But this pluralism also thinks that Muslims and Jews and Christians are wrong insofar as they think their Gods are different. Yet most Christians, Jews, and Muslims think precisely that, and more so Muslims and Christians than Jews and Christians. Most Christians think that Muslims have a different religion and God, while most Christians and Jews recognize their closer historical relation to one another. Pluralists think that most believers in these three religions are wrong and that they—the pluralists—are right about the true object of their worship. Believers on the ground think the other religions worship

---

6. William T. Cavanaugh, *The Myth of Religious Violence: Secular Ideology and the Roots of Modern Conflict* (New York: Oxford university Press, 2009).

a different God, but pluralists think they are wrong. That attitude might not result in the kind of humility that "thinks others as better than yourself" (Phil. 2:3).

Does pluralism lead to more generosity? That remains to be seen. There is no Church of Pluralism today, though the Unitarian Universalists might claim to be that. They have never been able to attract more than a statistically insignificant number, so we have no large-scale way of knowing if pluralism leads to generosity. But we do know that the antipluralist Judeo-Christian tradition has been chiefly responsible for the greatest systems of humanitarian action in the world.[7] More schools, hospitals, and charitable institutions have been founded by Christians and Jews than by any other religious groups in the world. And almost all of them have been religious exclusivists who have believed that Muslims had a different book and a God quite different from theirs.

In sum, it is not at all clear that affirming that we all worship the same God will necessarily lead to less violence or more humility and benevolence.

---

7. See, e.g., Peter Brown, *Through the Eye of a Needle: Wealth, the Fall of Rome, and the Making of Christianity in the West 350–550 AD* (Princeton, NJ: Princeton University Press, 2014); Gregg Gardner, *The Origins of Organized Charity in Rabbinic Judaism* (Cambridge: Cambridge University Press, 2015); Demetrios Constantelos, *Byzantine Philanthropy and Social Welfare* (New Brunswick, NJ: Rutgers University Press, 1968).

RESPONSE TO WM. ANDREW
SCHWARTZ AND JOHN B. COBB JR.

JERRY L. WALLS

I appreciate Andrew and John's forthright defense of the religious pluralist view even as I thoroughly disagree with it. As a preliminary matter, I am much more confident than they are that we can satisfactorily define the terms "Christians," "Muslims," and "Jews." The plausibility of their case hinges on their strategy of contending that all the terms in the question at the heart of this debate are fraught with ambiguity and open-ended uncertainty. They believe there is no identifiable thing called Christianity but only various and diverse Christianities. Indeed, they apparently believe there are as many Christianities as there are Christians and as many Islams as there are Muslims since "no two people worship the same God" (p. 24).

But these claims are greatly exaggerated. While there are to be sure many distinct Christian traditions and numerous theological variations, there is also a reasonably clear and identifiable set of core beliefs and practices that make up the "mere Christianity" that is affirmed by the overwhelming majority of Christians, whether Orthodox, Roman Catholic, or Protestant. It is far more plausible to think that millions of these believers do in fact worship the same God, as they would surely insist, than to think not even two of them do.

Turning now to more substantive issues, let us consider their historical argument, which depends on the following conditional statement: "Despite any differences in description, nature or expression, if we are able to trace the origins of the God of Christianity, Allah of Islam, and YHWH of Judaism to the same historical root—the God of Abraham—we can conclude that all three traditions worship the same

God, despite any differences" (p. 29). Conditional statements like this are false if the antecedent is true but the consequent is false. And I think that is the case with this statement. The antecedent is indeed true, for we can trace the origins of all three religions to the same historical root—the God of Abraham. However, I would argue that the consequent is false. It does not follow from the truth of the antecedent all these religions worship the same God, despite whatever differences they now have between them.

Let us look at the argument they present (p. 29), which begins with the uncontroversial premise that "the God of Abraham is the God of Judaism." When we come to the second premise, "Jesus worshiped the God of Abraham," things are not so simple. Indeed, this premise cannot be affirmed by orthodox Christians except in a highly qualified sense. Does the Son of God worship the Father? Or to put it even more starkly, does the second person of the Trinity worship the first person of the Trinity? What these questions point up is that we can only affirm the second premise in the sense that the incarnate Son of God, as a human being, worshiped the Father just as other human beings properly do.

But let us move on to the third premise, "Christians worship the God of Jesus," where these issues come squarely into focus. What is the referent of "the God of Jesus," whom Christians worship? The correct answer, I would contend, is the Trinity, the Father, Son, and Holy Spirit, who was fully revealed only in the life, death, and resurrection of Jesus and in the coming of the Holy Spirit at Pentecost. The Trinitarian God is the only God that exists and is the referent of all true statements about God, his activity, and his nature. So the referent of "the God of Abraham" is the same as the referent of "the Trinity," namely, the God who eternally exists in three persons: Father, Son, and Holy Spirit. The sense of "the God of Abraham," of course, is not the same as the sense of "the Trinity," but the referent is the same.

What this points up is that Andrew and John's argument founders on the jagged rocks of equivocation. This is quite apparent in the conclusion of the argument, which claims that "Christians worship the God of Judaism." This is true for Messianic Judaism, but it is not true of non-Messianic Judaism. Again, the revelation of Jesus changes everything. Before the coming of Christ and the development of the doctrine of the Trinity, Judaism was non-Trinitarian only in the sense that the

Trinity had yet to be fully revealed. After the coming of Christ, it is non-Trinitarian in the sense that it explicitly rejects the resurrection of Jesus, the incarnation, and the Trinity. So "the God of Judaism" in premise one is not identical with "the God of Judaism" in the conclusion. Christians will take the referent of "the God of Judaism" in premise one to be the Trinity, but it is hard to see how the referent of "the God of Judaism" in the conclusion can be the Trinity since Judaism now expressly rejects that doctrine.

To see how the revelation of Jesus changes everything, consider his conversation with the Jews in John 8, where they claim to be children of Abraham. Jesus denies their claim because he says they are not doing what Abraham did. Indeed, Jesus even claims that in some sense, "Abraham rejoiced that he would see my day; he saw it and was glad" (John 8:56). So those who are truly worshiping the God of Abraham will accept Jesus and embrace his teaching. As Jesus put it, "If God were your Father, you would love me, for I came from God and am now here" (John 8:42). When the Jews took offense at his claim that Abraham rejoiced to see his day, and questioned how that could be true since Jesus was not even fifty years old, Jesus replied to them, "Before Abraham was, I am" (John 8:58). In so doing he claimed the divine name for himself, reiterating his claim to be the Son of God. Now that Jesus has come to us, there can be no relationship to God that denies the claims of Christ or bypasses him.

Next, let us look briefly at their divine character argument. This one has little force for the simple reason that it ignores what is most interesting and distinctive about the Christian account of God. In listing various generic attributes of God, the authors note that God is one, that he is creator, that he is loving and merciful, that he is mysterious, and so on. But they ignore altogether the Judeo-Christian belief that God is a savior. To highlight this attribute is to bring into focus the specific ways God has acted to save us and to demonstrate his love for us, most notably in sending his Son to die for our sins and to be raised from the dead to save us from death and destruction.

Indeed, other attributes in their list take on a whole new meaning in light of God's action in Christ to save us from our sin. Consider the attribute of mystery. When the Word became flesh and dwelt among us, he revealed the Father in intimate terms that nothing else can even begin to emulate: "We declare to you what was from the beginning, what we have heard, what we have seen with our eyes, what we have looked at and touched with our hands, concerning the word of life—this life was revealed, and we have seen and testify to it, and declare to you the eternal life that was with the Father and was revealed to us" (1 John 1:1–2).

To be sure, the doctrines of incarnation and Trinity produce mysteries of their own. But these are not mysteries of a distant God who remains aloof from the human condition. "For we do not have a high priest who is unable to sympathize with our weaknesses, but we have one who in every respect has been tested as we are, yet without sin. Let us therefore approach the throne of grace with boldness, so that we may receive mercy and find grace to help in time of need" (Heb. 4:15–16).

This brings us to Andrew and John's ontological argument, which, like their historical argument, hinges on a conditional statement: "From an ontological perspective, if there is, in fact, only one God available to worship, then it is reasonable to conclude that Muslims, Christians, and Jews worship the same God—that is, the only God" (p. 35). As with their historical argument, I judge this conditional statement to be false because the antecedent is true, but the consequent is false.

Andrew and John, however, think it is true and pose the following question: "But what reason does a Christian or Muslim or Jew have for believing that the others worship a fake god?" (p. 35). Well, I have explained the reasons Christians have for believing this in my essay, but let me reiterate the point that God's revelation defines the terms of genuine worship, and his definitive act of revelation is the life, death, and resurrection of Jesus. Anyone who is properly informed of this revelation and refuses to believe it and to respond with appropriate expressions of gratitude and praise is not worshiping the one and only God as he has revealed himself to us and instructed us to honor him.

This is not to say that those who fail to properly worship God cannot know anything about him or acknowledge any important truths about him. Indeed, they may truly recognize that there is only one God, that he has created the world, and so on. And yet despite all of this, some of their beliefs about him may be so deeply misguided in other ways that their worship is accordingly misguided and misdirected.

Andrew and John reject this conclusion, and attempt to support their case by telling us a story of three sons arguing over whose father is actually real. Here is a story that I think better captures the dynamics of this dispute.

There was an exquisitely beautiful house in the woods. It had obviously been built centuries ago, but its exact origin was controversial. The identity of the builder was in dispute, and some said no one really knew. A few even denied the house had a builder. Two men were discussing the matter, and they happened to agree that a man named Mr. Devine was indeed the builder, and they were both admirers of him and his work. As they continued their conversation, one of them commented that Devine and his family had moved here from Edinburgh in 1777 and had built the house the following year. The other replied: "Family? What family? Mr. Devine was a lifelong bachelor, and he took special pride in working alone and doing his architectural projects with no input from anyone else." "Well," the first man replied, "while Mr. Devine indeed designed the house, his wife and son played vital roles alongside him not only in designing it but also in crafting and constructing it. Moreover, he passed on to his son his extraordinary talent, and his son achieved equal fame with that of his father, and Mr. Devine delighted in him and his success to an extraordinary degree. The loving cooperation between them is legendary, and you cannot really appreciate Mr. Devine and his passion for his craftsmanship if you do not understand that. Indeed, there was a remarkable resemblance between the two, and while there is no portrait of Mr. Devine, there is one of his son, and those who knew him said that if you have seen the son, you have seen the father. Consequently, one cannot truly pay homage to Mr. Devine without similarly honoring his son." The second man listened politely, and then replied: "Yes, I have heard all that and more, but I completely reject it. I repeat, Mr. Devine was a lifelong bachelor, and he certainly had no son. The credit for building this house goes to him and him alone."

It is apparent, I take it, that there is little, if any, substantial agreement between these men, despite their nominal agreement that Mr. Devine built the house, and their shared admiration for his work. The disagreements between informed Christians and Muslims about the creator of our world and what he requires of us by way of worship are even more profound.

Finally, near the end of their essay, Andrew and John warn against an "arrogant absolutism" and urge that "affirming that the three Abrahamic traditions are oriented toward the same object of worship can help avoid undue arrogance and attitudes of superiority" (p. 41). It is no less a truth claim—and an exclusive one at that—to hold that all the Abrahamic traditions are "oriented toward the same object of worship" than it is to hold that they are not. Both of these mutually exclusive claims cannot be true. The question of which is true needs to be settled by forthright discussion and careful argument, not by a presumptuous claim to hold the moral high ground.

REJOINDER

WM. ANDREW SCHWARTZ AND JOHN B. COBB JR.

The central inquiry of this book is whether Christians, Muslims, and Jews worship the same God. Why ask this question? Because of the similarities *and* differences among the three traditions. If there were no differences, or only differences, then the "same God" question would never arise. In our initial chapter, we attempted to shed light on just how complicated this inquiry truly is. Sameness amid difference is not a simple matter. It involves bridging the gap between reality and perception, between identity and difference, between continuity and change, not to mention the ambiguity of language and the gaps between other minds. How much more complicated when the subject in question is noncorporeal and as mysterious as all agree!

We have argued that the dynamic and changing nature of faith, knowledge, and even God and the world all make it unlikely that any two people hold *identical* beliefs about God. This has not been contested by any of the contributors. All seem willing to accept that two or more people can be worshiping the same God even while disagreeing about what that God is like. By acknowledging great diversity across the Christian traditions while concluding that Christians worship the same God, our fellow contributors have provided a framework that can be extended to all Abrahamic traditions.

Gerald McDermott argues that "there *is* one discernible Christian tradition that is called orthodoxy. . . . Different people can disagree with this part or that part, but there is an enormous consensus through history from East to West on its basic shape . . . what most Christians in most times and places have agreed on" (p. 51). But consider McDermott's qualifications: "enormous" consensus, "basic" shape, "most" times and places. Such qualifications acknowledge that "orthodoxy" is a generalization abstracted from particular Christians and particular beliefs in a way that evaluates some differences as irrelevant. We agree that such generalizations and ambiguity are a practical part of living together. What is problematic is using these generalizations as exclusionary criteria. Lacking a nonarbitrary criterion to evaluate between meaningful and irrelevant differences (between "same God" and "different Gods" conclusions), we favor inclusion over exclusion.

All New Testament writers understood *God* to mean the Creator of Heaven and Earth. Even when they had somewhat different ideas, they all spoke of the same actor. Jews and Muslims also intend to be speaking of the Creator of Heaven and Earth. Their intention and our intention, therefore, are the same. We may differ about just how God was acting in Jesus. But there is not one Creator of Heaven and Earth who was incarnate in Jesus and another who was not.

If we say that Jews worship a different God, that means that Jesus and Paul worshiped a different God than Christians do. Surely that cannot be. Jesus asked that we become his disciples. Surely that means that we worship the God he, as a Jew, worshiped. If we must choose between Jesus and Nicaea, we will choose Jesus. We are more concerned to be faithful disciples of Jesus than to be "orthodox" in terms of very human councils and their often-confusing decisions. Fortunately, there is no indication that Nicaea thought that it was teaching a God other than the God of Jesus and Paul and the other Jews of their day.

Muhammad, too, certainly thought that he was speaking of the Jewish and Christian God. He never claimed to be introducing a different God. Christians may disagree with the Qur'an's teaching about the Creator of Heaven and Earth, but there are not two such creators of whom Christians worship one and Muslims another. To state our position once more, we make a major distinction between having the same entity in view and agreeing about what it is like.

We introduced ideas associated with process theology to explain how differences can be complementary rather than contradictory. Francis Beckwith argues that our plurality of ultimates proposal is incompatible with classical monotheism. To clarify, when we speak of different ultimates we aren't proposing some form of polytheism. The plurality of ultimates are not competing ultimates because they do not exist on the same level. The supreme being is ultimate in a different way than the ground of being. Like giving different answers to different questions, God (personal supreme being) and Godhead (formless ground of being) can both exist as ultimates without conflict.

We do agree with all three authors who note that pluralists can be just as arrogant as exclusivists. For this volume, we were tasked with representing one of four views and have attempted to do so constructively. However, our underlying approach is to recognize the complexity of this inquiry and caution against hasty conclusions in favor of dialogue with specific Muslims, Jews, and Christians. Our approach is not one of an absolutist pluralism (i.e., "pluralism is the only truth"). Given the entangled character of religious identity, the ambiguities at play in life and language, as well as the ultimately ineffable nature of God, we urge humility—being open to the possibility that one's own faith perspective is not exclusively valid. Is such humility equivalent to arrogance? We think not.

Likewise, we agree wholeheartedly with Beckwith, who argues that "if we are really serious about respecting differing religious traditions in a pluralistic society . . . we cannot, as a condition of dialogue, impose nonexclusivism on those who cannot in good conscience acquiesce to it" (p. 50). We agree that this is a real danger. Many of our friends emphasize inclusivity but tend not to include those who do not do so. We hope it is clear that we do not make this mistake, since we are currently in dialogue with people who are not pluralists.

In contrast to some forms of religious pluralism, we appreciate those who hold fast by their distinctive convictions and commitments. Our special interest in dialogue both with critics of pluralism and many of its practitioners is that embracing Christian uniqueness does not require exclusivism. "We do not need to relativize our beliefs. . . . We can affirm our insights as universally valid! What we cannot do, without lapsing back into unjustified arrogance, is to deny that the insights of other traditions are also universally valid."[1] Pluralism of this variety does not have to be a "new type of exclusivism," as Beckwith suggests, but can be truly inclusive, where "yes—and" replaces "yes—no," thereby empowering us to embrace our own insights as universally valid without denying the universal validity of others.

---

1. John B. Cobb, Jr., *Transforming Christianity & The World: A Way Beyond Absolutism and Relativism*, Ed. Paul Knitter (Orbis Books: 1999), 137.

CHAPTER TWO

ALL WORSHIP THE SAME GOD:
REFERRING TO THE SAME GOD VIEW

FRANCIS J. BECKWITH

> Jesus said to her, "Woman, believe me, the hour is coming when you will worship the Father neither on this mountain nor in Jerusalem. You worship what you do not know; we worship what we know, for salvation is from the Jews. But the hour is coming, and is now here, when the true worshipers will worship the Father in spirit and truth, for the Father seeks such as these to worship him."
>
> John 4:21–23[1]

As a kid I collected comic books. My favorite character was Superman. According to his origin story, he was born on the planet Krypton and was given the name Kal-El. Soon after his birth, he was rocketed as an infant to Earth by his parents right before Krypton was destroyed as a result of its unstable core. Kal-El was discovered in a field in Kansas by a childless couple, Jonathan and Martha Kent, who eventually adopted Kal-El and gave him the name Clark, Martha's maiden name. As the young boy grew older, the Kents discovered that their adopted child was no mere mortal. He had superpowers, among which were the abilities to fly, bend steel with his bare hands, employ x-ray and heat vision, and

---

1. Unless otherwise indicated, all scripture quotes in Francis Beckwith's chapter and responses come from the NRSV.

run faster than a speeding bullet. Realizing the responsibility of someone possessing such powers, the Kents trained Clark to be a virtuous person. When he had grown up, Clark decided to use his awesome powers for the advancement of good and the defeat of evil. But so as not to draw attention to his family, as well as to have the semblance of a normal life, Clark took on the alter ego Superman. Clark eventually found work as a reporter in the city of Metropolis at the *Daily Planet*, where he became friends with a colleague named Lois Lane, who had been assigned to cover the new phenomenon known as Superman. But as far as Lois was concerned, Superman and Clark Kent were two different men. To make matters even stranger, she would soon begin dating Superman, while having no idea that her colleague at the *Daily Planet* was the same man she was dating.

During high school, Clark's girlfriend was a young woman named Lana Lang. After college, Lana took up residence in Metropolis, where she began to date Clark once again. Whenever they dined together, Lana would ask Clark about how it was to work with Lois and whether he had seen or spoken to Superman. Not wanting either to lie or to reveal his secret identity, Clark gave vague and ambiguous answers, though they seemed to satisfy Lana's curiosity. So, as far as Lana was concerned, her boyfriend, Clark, was a human being born in Kansas, and Clark worked with a woman, Lois, whose boyfriend was Superman, a nonhuman son of the planet Krypton.

We and the Kents know that the terms *Superman* and *Clark Kent* refer to the same being, for we and the Kents know that they have the same *reference*, Kal-El. But for Lois and Lana, *Superman* and *Clark Kent* have different *senses*, and they believe that those senses are true descriptions of who we and the Kents know as Kal-El. Yet these senses are inconsistent, and some are even false: Clark is human, and Superman is not; Superman has superpowers, while Clark is a mere mortal; Clark was born on Earth, but Superman was born on Krypton; Clark is employed as a reporter, while Superman has no employment unless you count his membership in the Justice League.

We make this distinction between sense and reference all the time. Suppose you have a friend, Tom, who, while watching YouTube, comes across films of boxing matches involving Cassius Clay (1942–2016). He tells you, "Boy, that guy Clay was some boxer. I wonder what happened to him." You gently explain to Tom that Cassius Clay was the birth name of Muhammad Ali (1942–2016), who changed his name after he converted to Islam. But in Tom's mind, prior to your correcting him, he believed that there were things true of Clay that were not true of Ali, even though in reality they were the same person. Imagine another friend, Frankie. She gets up every morning at 6:00 a.m., walks outside, and for a few moments stares at the morning star. And every evening, right before she retires to bed, she takes some time to stroll in the back-yard and stare at the evening star. She comes to believe that there are two stars in the sky, the morning star and the evening star, and over time she catalogs their differences and begins to speculate where they may reside in the vastness of space. But it turns out that the morning star and the evening star are not even really stars! They are just one thing, the planet Venus. Although Frankie has different *senses* about what she thinks are two objects in the sky, the fact of the matter is that each has the same reference.

In this chapter, I will argue that just as Lois and Lana are referring to the same man even when they attribute different characteristics to Superman and Clark Kent, Christians, Muslims, and Jews are referring to the same God even though each group believes different, and some-times contrary, things about that God. To accomplish this task, I will first provide a reference to that one God and explain why the believers in these three faiths all worship that one God. For unlike the Cassius Clay/ Muhammad Ali and morning star/evening star illustrations, where the references are well known, God is not a thing in the universe to which we can point or for which we can use a Google image search. For most religious believers—Christians, Muslims, and Jews included—God is the absolute source of all existence, meaning that creation has partic-ipatory existence whereas God does not. That is, all creation receives existence while God alone gives it. Therefore, God cannot be *a thing* in the universe, but the being on which all things in the universe depend.

After establishing the reference to God, I will provide an account of the three Abrahamic faiths that shows that their members worship the same God despite their profound theological differences. And finally, I will respond to four objections to the view I am defending in this chapter.

Before I move on, I should note that I am writing for my fellow Christians. I am not trying to convince my Jewish and Muslim friends that they worship the same God that Christians worship, though I believe they do. All I am trying to do here is to convince my fellow Christians that we worship the same God that Jews and Muslims worship. Nevertheless, I do think that my case in this chapter should be able to convince observant Muslims and Jews that they worship the same God as Christians do, even though the devotees of each tradition do not always use the term *God* in the same sense.

Philosophy Class with Adam, Baaqir, and Candida

Meet Adam, Baaqir, and Candida. All three are freshmen philosophy majors at Fordham University, each one arriving in the Bronx from different religious and geographical backgrounds: Adam, who grew up in Brooklyn, is Jewish; Baaqir, a native of Queens, is Muslim; and Candida, a resident of Manhattan, is Christian. After taking Professor Skeptic's course, Philosophy and Religion, each abandons not only his or her childhood faith but belief in God as well. Another faculty member in the department, Professor Faith, hears about what happened to Adam, Baaqir, and Candida. She is not convinced that Professor Skeptic had exposed them to the best arguments for God's existence. For this reason, she offers to lead each of them in a directed study course on works of three of the greatest theologians from the religious traditions that Adam, Baaqir, and Candida had once embraced: the Muslim Avicenna (980–1037), [2] the Jewish Moses Maimonides (1135–1204),[3] and the Christian Saint Thomas Aquinas (1225–74).[4] Because each student meets with Professor Faith separately, none is privy to the conversations that take place in the others' directed studies.

After fifteen weeks of poring over a variety of works from each thinker, Adam, Baaqir, and Candida decide to meet in an Italian diner off of Arthur Avenue to compare notes and discuss what they have learned. Adam, the former Jew, speaks first: "I was surprised to discover that I was convinced by Aquinas's argument."

Baaqir pipes up, "Really? I found myself unable to offer a plausible rebuttal to Maimonides's case."

---

2. See, e.g., Avicenna, *The Metaphysics of the Healing*, trans. Michael E. Marmura (Provo, UT: Brigham Young University Press, 2005).

3. See, e.g., Moses Maimonides, *Guide for the Perplexed*, trans. Michael Friedländer, 2nd ed. (London: Routledge Kegan Paul, 1904).

4. See, e.g., St. Thomas Aquinas, *On Being and Essence*, trans. Armand Maurer, 2nd ed. (Toronto: Pontifical Institute of Mediaeval Studies, 1968).

Interjecting, Candida exclaims, "This is really going to blow your mind. But I thought that Avicenna's reasoning was so persuasive that I now consider myself a theist, a believer in God."

Excited about what they have ascertained, they visit Professor Faith to tell her the news. She says, "You now all believe in God. But who or what is he?"

Candida says, "The self-existent absolute source of everything."

Baaqir adds, "Uncaused, perfect, rational, and unchanging," until Adam interrupts with, "Self-subsistent, eternal creator and sustainer of all that which receives its being from another." At that point, they realize that they all more or less believe the same things about God: he is *the absolute, uncaused, perfect, rational, unchanging, self-subsistent, eternal creator and sustainer of all that which receives its being from another.*

"That is indeed a mouthful," Professor Faith observes. So she asks, "Is there a more efficient way to define God?"

They look at each other and then simultaneously answer, "He who is metaphysically ultimate and has underived existence."

Professor Faith further probes, "Does that mean that anything that might not have existed—like me, you, the planet Mars, Professor Skeptic, or my dog Tosh—exists only because it 'receives its being from another'?"

Adam, Baaqir, and Candida answer in unison, "Yes."

"So," Professor Faith reasons, "does it not follow from this that there can in principle be only one God?"

Candida promptly replies, "Yes. If there could be more than one God, then God would be only one of a kind even if there only happened to be one God. Imagine, for example, that a nuclear disaster wiped out the entire human race except for Professor Skeptic. Although there literally would now be only one human being, there is nothing about human nature that requires that only one human exists. After all, prior to the nuclear disaster, there were billions of other human beings."

Baaqir picks up from there: "That can't be the case with God, since in order for there to be a 'second God,' he would have to differ in some way from the 'first God.' But two Gods can only differ from each other if the one has what the other lacks."

Pausing for a moment, Baaqir is interrupted by Adam, who goes on to say, "If God is he who is metaphysically ultimate and has underived existence, doesn't that mean that he lacks no perfection? But to say that God-2 lacks what God-1 has and vice versa implies not only that neither one is perfect but that neither one is metaphysically ultimate, and thus neither one is God. If God were like that, it's not clear how he would not be just a more elaborate version of Zeus or Poseidon or even the Flying Spaghetti Monster. But in that case, he wouldn't really be 'God,' since he would only be one of a kind, like the last remaining dodo bird was one of a kind. So, it seems right to say that if God is what we think he is—he who has metaphysical ultimacy and underived existence—then in principle there can only be one God. What's more, by lacking nothing and having underived existence, God would be the fullness of being. But you can no more have a second fullness of being than you can have a second number one or a five-sided square."

Professor Faith replies, "And in that case, God cannot be one of a kind. He must be Being Itself, which means that he is the absolute source of all the kinds of things that do exist."

If what Professor Faith is saying is correct, then it must be *God's nature to exist*. What does that mean? Think, for example, of anything one may encounter in the world, such as frogs, trees, human beings, and automobiles. None of these things exists by nature. All require another thing or things to bring them into being and keep them in existence. But God cannot be like that, since it would mean that he is creaturely, and thus he would not be self-existent. As Aquinas points out, a being that receives its existence from another, like a frog, a tree, a human being, or an automobile, is "a being by participation," which means that a participating being cannot be the ultimate source of its own existence. If it were not God's nature to exist, or to use Aquinas's language, if God were not essentially his own existence, he would just be another being who has existence by participation, like you, me, Muhammad Ali, or any of the Greek gods (if any of them were to exist). But in that case, "[God] will not therefore be the first being—which is absurd. Therefore God is His own existence."[5]

So, Adam, Baaqir, and Candida, after leaving the faith traditions in which they were reared, became atheists for a short time while studying with Professor Skeptic. That soon changed as a result of the work they

---

5. St. Thomas Aquinas, *Summa Theologica*, I, q. 3, a. 4, trans. Fathers of the English Dominican Province (1920), online edition, www.newadvent.org/summa/1003.htm#article4.

did with Professor Faith, who introduced each of them to the writings of Avicenna, Maimonides, and Aquinas. Adam, Baaqir, and Candida came to believe in the existence of what they concluded must be the one true God: *the absolute, uncaused, perfect, rational, unchanging, self-subsistent, eternal creator and sustainer of all that which receives its being from another.*

Can anyone deny that Adam, the former Jew; Baaqir, the former Muslim; and Candida, the former Christian, all believe in the same God? Of course these former atheists are now just mere theists, since none of them has returned to the religion in which he or she was raised. It is not even clear whether it is accurate to say they now have *faith* in God, since, at least from a Christian perspective, true faith cannot be summoned by human effort, including the intellectual appropriation of arguments: "For by grace you have been saved through faith, and this is not your own doing; it is the gift of God" (Eph. 2:8). Even Aquinas distinguished between the preambles of faith—those things we can know through natural reason or just happen to correctly believe, such as "the existence of God and other like truths about God"[6]—and the articles of faith—those things we can know only as a result of God specially revealing them to us. Nevertheless, at this point it seems obvious that Adam, Baaqir, and Candida not only believe in the same God, but when they talk about God with Professor Faith, they are referring to the same God and using the term *God* in the same sense.

From Reason to Faith and Disagreement

Adam, Baaqir, and Candida eventually graduate from Fordham. Over the subsequent years, they find themselves spiritually dissatisfied with belief in mere theism, since it seems to them to be more like a philosophical theory than an avenue to religious devotion. (Have you ever heard of someone martyred for the principle of sufficient reason?) As they get on with their lives, Adam, Baaqir, and Candida begin to reflect more deeply on several profound existential questions: What is the point of life, if there is even a point to it? Is there an afterlife, and if there is, what is it like? Is there a heaven, a hell, or a purgatory? And if there is, are there correct or incorrect ways by which one gets in or out? Is there a right way to live one's life, such as the Ten Commandments, the

---

6. Aquinas, *Summa Theologica* I. q. 2, a. 2, ad. 1, http://www.newadvent.org/summa/1002 .htm#article2.

lessons of Jesus of Nazareth, or the instructions of Muhammad? Are there proper or improper ways to pray to God, assuming that God wants one to pray to him? Has God specially revealed things about himself and the world, including human beings, that are not accessible by way of our natural reason?

Adam, Baaqir, and Candida realize that the best way to try to answer these and similar questions is to critically reexamine the religious traditions they embraced in their youth. So each of them makes a commitment to read not only the Jewish Bible, the New Testament, and the Qur'an, but also scores of theologians, philosophers, mystics, converts, and apologists found in the Christian, Muslim, and Jewish traditions. Adam, Baaqir, and Candida also pledge to attend a variety of liturgical and prayer services practiced by different groups within each tradition.

After about eighteen months of sustained and prayerful investigation, Adam, Baaqir, and Candida each decide to enter one of these faiths. Adam, the former Jew, becomes a Christian. Baaqir, the former Muslim, becomes a Jew. Candida, the former Christian, becomes a Muslim. And yet each of them *still believes* that God is *the absolute, uncaused, perfect, rational, unchanging, self-subsistent, eternal creator and sustainer of all that receives its being from another.* For this reason, none of them thinks of his or her conversion as a "change in Gods," for they continue to believe that in principle there can only be one God. They each think of their own religious transition as a result of learning more about the God they had not fully known before they converted. This is because all of the converts now believe that God has specially revealed in the scriptures and traditions of their respective faiths additional things about the divine nature, creation, humanity, morality, salvation, and the like that were unavailable to them when they were mere theists. Consequently, when Adam partakes in the Divine Liturgy, when Baaqir goes to shul, and when Candida says her five daily prayers (*salat*), they all are worshiping the same God.

Nevertheless, there are important differences between their faiths. Adam as a Christian now believes that God is triune and that Jesus of Nazareth is God's Son as well as the second person of the Trinity. He also affirms the divine inspiration and authority of the New Testament. The Jewish Baaqir now believes that only the Jewish Bible is God's word, denying that the Qur'an and the New Testament are divinely inspired.

Just as he did as a Muslim, Baaqir denies that God has begotten a son. It is, of course, a belief he shares with the Muslim Candida, who now accepts the authority of the Qur'an, which states: "[God] begetteth not nor was begotten" and "It befitteth not (the Majesty of) Allah that He should take unto Himself a son." [7] On the other hand, Candida agrees with Adam that Jesus was the Messiah, which is a belief that Baaqir denies. However, Candida and Baaqir maintain that Adam is wrong in believing that God is triune, while Adam and Baaqir think that Candida is mistaken in claiming that Muhammad was a true prophet. Nevertheless, they all agree that God made a covenant with Abraham and that he called Moses to lead the children of Israel out of Egypt.

These are far from minor disagreements, for the very integrity of each faith tradition depends on them. A Muslim who denies that Muhammad was God's prophet is hardly a Muslim, and a Christian who agrees with mainstream Judaism about the person of Jesus is probably not really a Christian. Although some Jewish converts to Christianity identify themselves as "messianic Jews," such a designation is not recognized by the state of Israel and is universally rejected by Judaism's foremost rabbis. [8] Yet all these profound differences between Christianity, Islam, and Judaism are not enough to defeat the view I am defending in this chapter, that Christians, Muslims, and Jews worship the same God. The reason is remarkably simple. Each faith tradition holds the same basic understanding of what constitutes a divine nature: God is *the absolute, uncaused, perfect, rational, unchanging, self-subsistent, eternal creator and sustainer of all that which receives its being from another.* So, when Christians, Muslims, and Jews speak of God, they have the same reference. [9]

Now consider the illustrations we covered at the beginning of this chapter. Although we know that the names Clark Kent and Superman refer to the same being, Lana Lang does not know this. She mistakenly believes that her boyfriend Clark is one person—a human being who works at the *Daily Planet* and whose parents are from the state of Kansas—while Superman is another person—a superhero whose parents

---

7. Qur'an 112:3; 19:35, as quoted in *The Meaning of the Glorious Koran: An Explanatory Translation by Mohammed Marmaduke Pickthall* (New York: New American Library, 1988), 454, 223.

8. See David Novak, "When Jews Are Christians," *First Things* 17 (November 1991): 42–46.

9. See, e.g., Deut. 6:4; the Nicene Creed; and *Qur'an* 59:22–24.

were from the planet Krypton. Before you corrected him, Tom attributed differing properties to Cassius Clay and Muhammad Ali, since he believed that they were two different people. And what about poor Frankie? She thought she was seeing two different stars—one in the morning and the other in the evening—when in fact they were really one and the same thing. And it wasn't even really a star! These illustrations show us that people can have different senses about the same thing while believing they are referring to two different things, even though they are really referring to the same thing. Similarly, although there is no doubt that Christians, Muslims, and Jews hold contrary beliefs about God, which entail that the other faith traditions are mistaken on very important matters, these conflicts are at the level of sense, not reference, even if it turns out that one of the senses is correct. Given what we have covered so far in this chapter, it is difficult to see how this cannot be true.

First, in the story of Adam's, Baaqir's, and Candida's shift from atheism to theism, we saw that there can in principle be only one God. Second, when we read of their conversions to Christianity, Judaism, and Islam, respectively, we saw that the disagreements between these traditions arise from what each group considers to be divinely revealed truths inaccessible by natural reason. Remember, when Adam, Baaqir, and Candida shifted from atheism to theism and then converted to their newfound faiths, they gave up nothing about the divine nature that they had held when they were mere theists. To be sure, upon conversion, they embraced what they came to believe were truths specially revealed by God. But as a consequence, they did not come to believe less about God; rather, they came to believe more about him. Thus, the differences between the Christian, Muslim, and Jewish views of God are not differences of reference, but differences of sense. As you may recall from reading the early chapters of Genesis, our first parents were not tempted to fall because their reference to God was mistaken but because they accepted what they thought was a revealed truth about the one true God, a revelation that turned out not to be so: "'You will not die; for God knows that when you eat of [the fruit of the tree in the middle of the garden] your eyes will be opened, and you will be like God, knowing good and evil'" (Gen. 3:4–5).

Perhaps one more illustration will help. Although they were philosophy majors in college, Adam, Baaqir, and Candida decided to pursue careers in archaeology, each becoming a professor of archaeology at Baylor University. (They loved philosophy, but they wisely examined the job market before embarking on five years of graduate work in the discipline.) Adam, Baaqir, and Candida often go on digs together. On a dig with their friend Aristotle, who holds an endowed chair in archaeology at another institution, they come across a small unexplored mountain, which they name "Zion." They notice that residing at the foot of Zion are three villages of three indigenous peoples: the Robinsons, the Kirks, and the Cartwrights. Before beginning their exploration of the mountain, they talk to the leader from each group: John Robinson, Jim Kirk, and Ben Cartwright. Adam, Baaqir, Candida, and Aristotle ask each leader two questions: What do you call the mountain? What is inside its caves? John answers, "Its name is Jupiter 2, and inside the caves are nothing but ancient pottery." Jim answers, "Its name is Enterprise, and inside the caves are nothing but bears and lions." Ben answers, "Its name is Ponderosa, and inside the caves are nothing but bars of silver." Each says that his people came to believe these things because of what is written in their village's historical records, which have been handed down by the village leadership over several generations. After discussing the answers among themselves, Adam, Baaqir, Candida, and Aristotle explain to each other which account of the mountain he or she thinks is correct. Adam says he believes John. Baaqir says he believes Jim. Candida says she believes Ben. But Aristotle is not persuaded by any of them. He has his doubts about the reliability of each village's official history.

All four archaeologists now hold contrary views about, and have different names for, Zion. But they are nevertheless talking about the same mountain. When the archaeologists first came upon the mountain, that event was analogous to how Adam, Baaqir, and Candida had come to believe in God through their natural reason while they were undergraduate philosophy students. They realized, as a consequence of studying Avicenna, Maimonides, and Aquinas, that an absolute underived source of all contingent reality must necessarily exist, even though they also realized that they could know only a few things about this being by means of their natural reason. After arriving at the foot of Zion with their friend Aristotle, and getting to know the indigenous peoples that live there, the archaeologists became privy to contrary claims about Zion that each of the village's leaders believed were based on reliable historical records. This is analogous to the deliverances of special revelation that Adam, Baaqir, and Candida had come to believe when they converted to Christianity, Judaism, and Islam, respectively. Although each thought he or she had now learned more about the absolute underived source of contingent existence than what he or she knew previously, each was fully aware that it could not be the case that none of them was mistaken, even though they agreed that their additional views about God were referring to the same absolute underived source of contingent existence.

Of course, their friend Aristotle is skeptical about the veracity of the historical records, though he does not doubt that he and his friends are talking about the same mountain, just as the preconversion Adam, Baaqir, and Candida were skeptical about the religious traditions in which they were raised, even though they did not doubt that the God in which they had come to believe by way of natural reason referred to the same God affirmed by those faiths.

So, if we assume that one of the three sets of historical records is correct, either Adam, Baaqir, or Candida knows more about the mountain than he or she knew before questioning the leader of each village. But none of them knows less, and none of them believes they are not referring to the same mountain, even though each of them embraces contrary senses about Zion (or Jupiter 2 or Enterprise or Ponderosa). In the same way, when it comes to their current religious beliefs, Adam, Baaqir, and Candida do not believe less than what they believed as mere theists, and for this reason, none of them believes they are not referring to the same God, even though each now embraces contrary senses of that God.

Scripture and History

Apart from the philosophical illustrations I have used thus far in this chapter, there are also good scriptural and historical reasons to believe that Christians, Muslims, and Jews worship the same God, irrespective of their profound theological disagreements. Consider first that well-known scene in the book of Exodus. Moses finds himself in the presence of God at the burning bush on Mount Horeb. In an event affirmed by all three religious traditions,[10] this exchange between Moses and God transpires:

---

10. For the Qur'an's account of Moses at the burning bush, see Qur'an 20.

But Moses said to God, "If I come to the Israelites and say to them, 'The God of your ancestors has sent me to you,' and they ask me, 'What is his name?' what shall I say to them?" God said to Moses, "I am who I am." He said further, "Thus you shall say to the Israelites, 'I am has sent me to you.'" (Ex. 3:13–14)

Christians have traditionally read this passage as God affirming to Moses a deep metaphysical truth about the divine nature: God, as "I am who I am," is announcing that he is *Being Itself*, he who has underived unconditioned existence, and thus is the self-existent source for all that which is not self-existent.[11] When, for example, Aquinas provided this very interpretation of Exodus 3:14 in his *Summa Contra Gentiles*, he was simply passing on to his pupils what he had inherited from many of his predecessors in the church, including Saint Jerome (347–420) and Saint Augustine (354–430):[12] "But God is the first being, with nothing prior to Him. His essence is, therefore, His being. This sublime truth Moses was taught by our Lord. When Moses asked our Lord: 'If the children of Israel say to me: what is His name? What shall I say to them?' The Lord replied: 'I am who I am. . . . You shall say to the children of Israel: He who is has sent me to you' (Exod. 3:13, 14). By this our Lord showed that his own proper name is He who is."[13]

Unsurprisingly, Christians, who believe that Jesus is the second person of the triune Godhead, have read certain passages in the New Testament as Christ referring to himself as "I am," the very same one who revealed himself in the burning bush to Moses.[14] Take, for example, John 8:58: "Jesus said to them, 'Very truly, I tell you, before Abraham

---

11. See Matthew Levering, *Scripture and Metaphysics: Aquinas and the Renewal of Trinitarian Theology* (Oxford: Blackwell, 2004), chap. 2; and Jaroslav Pelikan, *The Christian Tradition: A History of the Development of Doctrine*, vol. 1, *The Emergence of the Catholic Tradition (100–600)* (Chicago: University of Chicago Press, 1971), 53–54.

12. See St. Jerome, "Letter 15" (ca. 376), in *Letters of St. Jerome*, trans. W. H. Fremantle, G. Lewis and W. G. Martley, in *Nicene and Post-Nicene Fathers, Second Series* (hereafter *NPNF²*), vol. 6, eds. Philip Schaff and Henry Wace (Buffalo, NY: Christian Literature Publishing Co., 1893), rev. and ed. for New Advent by Kevin Knight, http://www.newadvent.org/fathers/3001015.htm; St. Augustine, *On the Trinity* (400–428) 5.2, trans. Arthur West Haddan, in *NPNF²* 6, http://www.newadvent.org/fathers/130105.htm.

13. See, e.g., St. Thomas Aquinas, "That in God Being and Essence Are the Same," in *Summa Contra Gentiles* 1.22.10, trans. Anton C. Pegis, Dominican House of Studies Priory, https://dhspriory.org/thomas/ContraGentiles1.htm#22.

14. See Levering, *Scripture and Metaphysics*, 40–41, 63–64.

was, *I am*'" (emphasis added). His critical listeners undoubtedly took Christ to be claiming that he was God: "So they picked up stones to throw at him, but Jesus hid himself and went out of the temple" (v. 59). But when God revealed to Moses that he was the great "I am," the self-existent one, he conveyed nothing about his triune nature to the Hebrew patriarch. He did not say, "Oh, Moses, by the way, I am three as well. Try explaining *that* to the children of Israel!" According to the Christian understanding of progressive revelation, it was only later, under the new covenant, that God revealed he is Father, Son, and Holy Spirit, and even then the full implications of what that means for the universal church were not settled until well into the fourth century at the Council of Constantinople in 381.[15]

This is why it seems counterintuitive for one to claim that Moses (not to mention, Abraham, Isaac, or Jacob) did not worship the same God as Aquinas (not to mention, Saint Augustine, Martin Luther, or Billy Graham) simply because Moses's understanding of God did not include the Son and the Holy Spirit. Although Moses's sense of God differed from that of Aquinas, they nevertheless had the same reference: *the absolute, uncaused, perfect, rational, unchanging, self-subsistent, eternal creator and sustainer of all that which receives its being from another.* Or, for the sake of brevity: *the absolute underived unconditioned source of all contingent existence.*

This seems to be the God whom the apostle Paul had in mind when he addressed his pagan inquirers in a sermon he delivered on the Areopagus in Athens:

> Athenians, I see how extremely religious you are in every way. For as I went through the city and looked carefully at the objects of your worship, I found among them an altar with the inscription, "To an unknown god." What therefore you worship as unknown, this I proclaim to you. The God who made the world and everything in it, he who is Lord of heaven and earth, does not live in shrines made by human hands, nor is he served by human hands, as though he needed anything, since he himself gives to all mortals life and breath and all things. From one

---

15. The Nicene Creed. See generally Lewis Ayers, *Nicaea and Its Legacy: An Approach to Fourth-Century Trinitarian Theology* (New York: Oxford University Press, 2004).

ancestor he made all nations to inhabit the whole earth, and he allotted the times of their existence and the boundaries of the places where they would live, so that they would search for God and perhaps grope for him and find him—though indeed he is not far from each one of us. For "In him we live and move and have our being"; as even some of your own poets have said,

"For we too are his offspring." (Acts 17:22–28)

At this point, Saint Paul was just warming up, for he had yet to deliver the gospel to his Athenian listeners. But when he did, it was clear that he was moving from a philosophical account of the divine nature to what he believed God had specially revealed in human history: "[God] has fixed a day on which he will have the world judged in righteousness by a man [Jesus Christ] whom he has appointed, and of this he has given assurance to all by raising him from the dead" (Acts 17:31).

Those familiar with Acts 17 know that prior to his sojourning to Athens, Paul was in Thessalonica with Silas, where they visited a synagogue in which Paul identified Jesus of Nazareth as the promised Jewish Messiah. This is why he had to argue from the scriptures that the Messiah was supposed to suffer, die, and rise from the dead (vv. 1–3). Some who listened converted to Christianity, though not all. Saint Paul surely believed that the Jews with whom he was arguing believed in the same God he did, that the question at issue was not what constituted a divine nature, but rather, whether Jesus of Nazareth was the Messiah promised in the Jewish Bible by the God of Abraham, Isaac, Jacob, and Moses.

It follows from Paul's disputations that he believed both Christians and Jews refer to the same God, even though they have different senses of that God. After all, the Jews who rejected Paul's message and walked away were not denying the existence of the God Moses encountered in the burning bush; they were rejecting the apostle's claim that God had revealed himself in a unique and profound way in the person of Jesus of Nazareth. On the other hand, when engaging his Athenian critics later in Acts 17, Paul began by establishing the right reference to God: "In him we live and move and have our being" (v. 28).

Saint Paul did not have to do this in the synagogue in Thessalonica, since the reference to God was obvious given the speaker, the audience, and the subject matter. It is furthermore clear from the text that if the Athenians had all accepted Paul's reference to God while never embracing the gospel, they would have believed in the same God as Christians believe, even though they would have lacked faith in Christ. In both cases—with the Jews and with the pagans—Paul never suggested that his listeners "change Gods" in order to become followers of Christ, since in each case the reference to the correct God had already been established prior to the apostle's presentation of the gospel.

As I noted earlier, the full implications of the meaning of the Trinity for the universal church were not settled until well into the fourth century. The catalyst for this settlement was the Arian Controversy. At the time, Christians disagreed over how best to understand the New Testament's depiction of Jesus as the Son of God and his relationship to the Father. Some bishops embraced the position defended by Arius of Alexandria (AD 256–336), who taught that Jesus, although the Son of God, had not always existed. As Arius put it, "There was a time when the Son was not,"[16] and he maintained that the Son of God was made by the Father before he became incarnate in Jesus of Nazareth.[17] The leader on the other side of this dispute was Saint Athanasius of Alexandria (AD 296–373). He taught that because Christ is the Word mentioned in John 1:1, and because the text says that the Word is God, then it follows that Christ, who is the Son of God, is God, and thus uncreated.[18] The dispute between Arius and Athanasius was thus over the nature of the Son of God. Was he, as Arius claimed, made and not begotten, of a different substance than the Father, or was Christ, as Athanasius maintained, "begotten, not made, con-substantial with the Father?"[19] As providence would have it, Athanasius's view was the one that triumphed, embraced by the First Council of Nicaea (AD 325), the same conciliar body that confirmed Arianism as a christological heresy.

Does the council's judgment mean, though, that Arius and Athanasius were not referring to the same God when they sparred over the

---

16. Quoted in Socrates of Constantinople, *Church History* (ca. 439) 1.5, trans. A.C. Zenos, in *NPNF²* 2, http://www.newadvent.org/fathers/26011.htm.

17. J. N. D. Kelly, *Early Christian Doctrines*, 5th ed. (San Francisco: HarperCollins, 1978), 226–31.

18. Athanasius, *De Synodis* (359–361), trans. John Henry Newman and Archibald Robertson, in *NPNF²* 4, www.newadvent.org/fathers/2817.htm.

19. The Nicene Creed.

nature of God's Son? Actually, quite the opposite, if you think about it. If two theologians disagree about whether the Son of *that God*—the God of Abraham, Isaac, Jacob, and Moses—is a creature, they cannot *not* be referring to the same God, in the same way that Paul could not have *not* been referring to the same God when he was addressing his Jewish and pagan audiences, once he established the correct reference to the one true God. After we get our heads around that, we realize very quickly that Arius's non-Trinitarian view of God's nature seems indistinguishable from the non-Trinitarian views embraced by Avicenna (a Muslim) and Maimonides (a Jew). But if Arius, Avicenna, and Maimonides believed in the same God, and Athanasius and Arius believed in the same God, would it not follow that Avicenna, Maimonides, and Athanasius also believed in the same God? It is difficult to imagine how this could not be so.

Some Objections

I first wrote on the "same God" topic in December 2015 in an online magazine called *The Catholic Thing*,[20] in which I had been a regular columnist for several years. I published two essays addressing the case of Larycia Hawkins, an associate professor of political science at Wheaton College, an evangelical school. On December 15, 2015, the college put her on administrative leave for this Facebook post: "I stand in *religious solidarity* with Muslims because they, like me, a Christian, are people of the book. And as Pope Francis stated last week, we worship the same God."[21] Wheaton held that Professor Hawkins's public statement raised serious questions as to whether it "faithfully represent[s] the College's evangelical Statement of Faith."[22] Based on the kind of reasoning I present in this chapter, I argued that the school's grounds for suspending Professor Hawkins were not convincing. Unsurprisingly, some writers

20. Francis J. Beckwith, "Do Muslims and Christians Worship the Same God?," *The Catholic Thing* December 17, 2015, www.thecatholicthing.org/2015/12/17/do-muslims-and -christians-worship-the-same-god/; and Francis J. Beckwith, "Why Muslims and Christians Worship the Same God," *The Catholic Thing*, January 7, 2016, www.thecatholicthing. org/2016/01/07/why-muslims-and-christians-worship-the-same-god/.

21. See Ruth Graham, "The Professor Wore a Hijab in Solidarity—Then Lost Her Job," *New York Times Magazine*, October 13, 2016.

22. Wheaton College Statement Regarding Dr. Larycia Hawkins, Wheaton College, December 11, 2015, https://web.archive.org/web/20151216161646/https://www.wheaton .edu/Media-Center/Media-Relations/Statements/Wheaton-College-Statement-Regarding -Dr-Hawkins.

disagreed. What follows are my responses to a few of their objections. Because of space constraints, my answers will be brief.

Why Prioritize God as Creator over God as Triune?

Lydia McGrew writes, "Islam says more than that God doesn't happen to be triune or that God didn't in fact come down as man. Islam insists God cannot be triune or incarnate. It denies Jesus could be the Son of God, much less God himself. Why is the fact that Allah (as conceived in Islam) is the Creator more important to the question at hand than the fact that he cannot be triune or incarnate?"[23] McGrew is certainly correct in saying that there are distinct and profound differences between Christianity, Judaism, and Islam on matters such as the Trinity and the incarnation. But one cannot discuss those doctrines without first getting the divine nature right. Imagine, for example, a religious group that identifies as Christian and claims to believe in the Trinity, but they understand that doctrine to mean that there exist three incredibly powerful physical beings whose proper names are Father, Son, and Holy Spirit, and that the unity of the Trinity is the result of their common purpose and not of their being of one substance. Members of such a group, because they get the divine nature so spectacularly wrong, could not assent to the Nicene Creed, even though they may think like McGrew that the doctrines of the Trinity and the incarnation are of utmost importance. On the other hand, because Christianity, Judaism, and Islam get the divine nature right—*the absolute underived unconditioned source of all contingent existence*—their disagreements over the Trinity and the incarnation are appropriately viewed as contrary beliefs about the same God to which each faith refers.

Worshiping One God Does Not Entail Worshiping the Same God

Tomas Bogardus and Mallorie Urban write, "Perhaps fans of Democritus, fans of Plato, and fans of Aristotle agree that *only one* of those three can be the greatest philosopher. It hardly follows that these three groups of fans celebrate *the same* philosopher as the greatest. Similarly, the fact that Muslims, Christians, and Jews all believe in *only one* God doesn't

---

23. Lydia McGrew, "The 'Same God' Debate Is Too Important to Leave to Philosophers," *The Gospel Coalition*, January 16, 2016, www.thegospelcoalition.org/article/the-same-god-debate-is-too-important-to-leave-to-philosophers/.

prove that they all worship *the same* God." [24] But I am not arguing from the monotheism of each faith to the conclusion that they all worship the same one God. Rather, I am arguing that because there can only in principle be one God—*the absolute underived unconditioned source of all contingent existence*—and because the theologies of each of these faith traditions refer to that one God, it stands to reason that they all worship the same God, even though they disagree about aspects of that God as a result of what each believes is special revelation. (I should note that Bogardus and Urban do not attribute to me the argument they critique. Rather, they offer it as a "retooled" version of an argument that I do in fact make. But because they believe my argument assumes too much theological knowledge on the part of ordinary believers, they reject it. I address that criticism in my response to the fourth objection below.)

The Terms for God Do Not Have the Same Truth Value

William Lane Craig writes,

> A further wrinkle is that "worships *x*" is what philosophers call an intensional (as opposed to extensional) context, where the term "*x*" need not refer to anything at all (as in, *e.g.*, "Jason worships Zeus"). In an intensional context co-referring terms cannot be substituted without impacting the truth value of the sentence. For example, even though "Jupiter" may refer to the same god as "Zeus," still Jason, a Greek, does not worship Jupiter and may have never even heard of the Roman god. So one cannot say that Abdul, a Muslim, worships Yahweh, even if "Yahweh" and "Allah" are co-referring terms. [25]

Craig is absolutely correct and, ironically, seems to make my point, since all he is saying is that "Yahweh" and "Allah" have different senses for the Christian and the Muslim, respectively, even if the terms are referring to the same being. That is no different than saying that *Superman* and

---

24. Tomas Bogardus and Mallorie Urban, "How to Tell Whether Christians and Muslims Worship the Same God," *Faith and Philosophy* 34, no. 2 (2017): 178.

25. William Lane Craig, "#459 Do Muslims and Christians Worship the Same God?" *Reasonable Faith* (blog), January 31, 2016, www.reasonablefaith.org/writings/question-answer/do-muslims-and-christians-worship-the-same-god#_ednref1.

Clark Kent have different senses for Lois Lane and Lana Lang, respectively, even if the terms are referring to the same being.

Ordinary Believers Do Not Believe in the "God of the Philosophers"

Borgadus and Urban write, "One may reasonably wonder whether all members of these religions really are classical theists worshiping the God of the philosophers in the way Avicenna, Maimonides, and Aquinas did, or even a sufficient number to ground the claim that Christians and Muslims worship the same God. Have all or even most or even ten thousand of these folks heard of divine simplicity, for example, let alone understood it, let alone endorsed it? It's a heavy hike from the prayer hall to the lecture hall, and few make it." [26]

That is certainly true, but irrelevant. Being a religious believer within a particular faith tradition is not a matter of taking a theology test or fully grasping all the subtle distinctions that have preoccupied scholars, priests, and mystics for millennia. Rather, it's a matter of assenting to certain general beliefs about which others have done all the heavy lifting. When my sainted grandmother, Frances Guido (1913–2002), recited the Nicene Creed at mass every Sunday, I am pretty sure she had no idea about the philosophical pedigree of the phrase "begotten not made, consubstantial with the Father." But I would be hard pressed to say that she didn't believe it. For she had, what Aquinas called, *implicit faith*: "Therefore, as regards the primary points or articles of faith, man is bound to believe them, just as he is bound to have faith; but as to other points of faith, man is not bound to believe them explicitly, but only implicitly, or to be ready to believe them, in so far as he is prepared to believe whatever is contained in the Divine Scriptures. Then alone is he bound to believe such things explicitly, when it is clear to him that they are contained in the doctrine of faith."[27]

When we study a particular faith tradition, we appropriately look to what the institution teaches over generations, not to what a few devotees here and there claim they think the faith teaches. Even in cases where we find sophisticated believers of a particular faith departing from a classical understanding of the divine nature—as in the cases of

---

26. Bogardus and Urban, "How to Tell," 178.
27. Aquinas, *Summa Theologica* II-II, q. 2, a. 5, http://www.newadvent.org/summa/3002.htm.

Craig,[28] Alvin Plantinga,[29] and Richard Swinburne[30] within Christianity—these thinkers are virtually always working through problems and issues *within* the tradition, relying on its long-standing philosophical, theological, and scriptural resources. This is why it seems right to say that Craig, Plantinga, and Swinburne worship the same God as Augustine, Aquinas, Avicenna, and Maimonides, since they are trying to provide a coherent account of the same reality—*the absolute underived unconditioned source of all contingent existence*[31]—just as Ptolemy and Galileo were trying to provide a coherent account of the movement of the same sun.

Conclusion

It would be a mistake to interpret the case I seek to make in this chapter as a call to an interfaith ecumenism in which the deepest convictions of each religious tradition should be considered secondary or peripheral to its true essence. To distinguish between a belief in God that we can know apart from special revelation (or that we may simply hold in common) and beliefs that we cannot know without divine disclosure is actually to imply the opposite, as the emotional and dismissive responses of Paul's listeners in Acts 17 reveal. To quote the esteemed Catholic theologian David B. Burrell, "To understand an apparently philosophical conclusion, then, one does best to try to identify the religious strands of which it is woven. Monotheism . . . is not a confession but an abstraction. However convenient it may appear, one is ill-advised to assume it describes a common faith."[32] Or to put it another way: in recognizing that three distinct religious traditions refer to the same God one is not contending that they share the same faith.[33]

---

28. William Lane Craig and J. P. Moreland, *Philosophical Foundations of a Christian Worldview*, 2nd ed. (Downers Grove, IL: InterVarsity, 2017), 510–39.

29. Alvin Plantinga, *Does God Have a Nature?* (Milwaukee, WI: Marquette University Press, 1980).

30. Richard Swinburne, *The Christian God* (New York: Oxford University Press, 1994).

31. Take, for example, these comments from Craig: "So on the traditional conception, God is what the philosopher Brian Leftow calls 'the sole ultimate reality,' the pinnacle of being, so to speak. For all other beings have been created by Him and therefore depend on Him for their existence, whereas God depends upon nothing else for His existence and is the source of existence of everything else." William Lane Craig, *God over All: Divine Aseity and the Challenge of Platonism* (New York: Oxford University Press, 2017), 2. It should be noted that in this book's second chapter, Craig argues that "the traditional conception" is the biblical conception that was subsequently affirmed by the church fathers.

32. David B. Burrell, CSC, *Knowing the Unknowable God: Ibn-Sina, Maimonides, Aquinas* (Notre Dame, IN: University of Notre Dame Press, 1986), 111.

33. Special thanks to my colleague Alex Pruss, who gave me some valuable feedback on this topic during the Spring 2018 semester.

RESPONSE TO FRANCIS J. BECKWITH

WM. ANDREW SCHWARTZ AND JOHN B. COBB JR.

Table for Three

Imagine that Lois Lane and Lana Lang went on a double date. Lois brings her boyfriend Superman, and Lana brings her boyfriend Clark Kent. Should they get a table for four or a table for three? Francis J. Beckwith's opening example of Clark Kent and Superman is helpful in illustrating the gap between knowledge and reality, between sense and reference. As Beckwith remarks, "So, as far as Lana was concerned, her boyfriend, Clark, was a human being born in Kansas, and Clark worked with a woman, Lois, whose boyfriend was Superman, a nonhuman son of the planet Krypton." Yet no matter what Lana or Lois believe, regardless of their conflicting conceptions, whether called Clark or Kal-El, whether thought to be human or Kryptonian, they are dating the same guy—they need a table for three.

Beckwith argues that this situation is analogous to Muslim, Jewish, and Christian relations to God. Despite diverse claims, names, and beliefs about God, YHWH, and Allah, the three Abrahamic traditions all worship the same deity. Moreover, one could argue that just as Lois and Lana become aware of their shared love interest during the double date, Muslims, Jews, and Christians might become aware of their shared object of worship through interreligious dialogue, interfaith worship services, and other collective gatherings.

The Superman example also illustrates the limits of intentionality on matters of truth. It doesn't really matter if Lana and Lois intend to be dating the same person. Belief and intention seem to have little to no effect on the verity of the situation. Just as the oneness of Clark Kent/Superman supersedes Lana's and Lois's intentions, so too does the oneness of God/YHWH/Allah supersede the intentions of Muslims, Christians, and Jews.

Beckwith's Identist Pluralism

While there is much in Beckwith's argument that seems reasonable, we wish to point out the limits of his position. What Beckwith provides is quite similar to the "ontological argument" we discussed in the previous chapter. If there is only one God—like there is only one referent for the names Clark Kent and Superman—then Jews, Christians, and Muslims should be said to be worshiping the same God. Beckwith goes on to defend the necessary oneness of God, declaring, "It seems right to say that if God is what we think he is—he who has metaphysical ultimacy and underived existence—then in principle there can only be one God" (p. 71).

But if there is only one God, why are there so many different religions? How do we make sense of the diverse conceptions of God across (and within) these three Abrahamic traditions if everyone is experiencing and describing the same God? Here, Beckwith explains that "these conflicts are at the level of sense, not reference, even if it turns out that one of the senses is correct" (p. 75). This distinction between sense and reference is not unlike John Hick's neo-Kantian distinction between the *phenomenal* Real (the Divine as experienced/perceived) and the *noumenal* Real (the Divine in itself).

Like Hick, Beckwith asserts that ultimate reality (what Hick calls "the Real" and Beckwith calls "God") is singular. That is, at the level of reference, there is only one God. Beckwith's level of reference is akin to Hick's noumenal Real. This is the level of objective reality—the way things are independent of our experience or understanding of them. By contrast, differences between Muslim, Jewish, and Christian conceptions of God are differences at the level of sense (akin to Hick's phenomenal Real). This is the level of subjective reality—the way things are as we perceive and understand them. According to Beckwith, although Lois and Lana have different understandings (grounded in different experiences) of Clark/Kal-El, these differences are only conflicting at the level of sense—the level of phenomena (reality as perceived). Yet diversity at this level doesn't entail diversity at the level of reference—the level of noumena (reality as it is in itself). Therefore, Beckwith's sense-reference distinction, like Hick's noumena-phenomena distinction, is used to defend the oneness of God amid a plurality of accounts.

Given the similarities between Beckwith's and Hick's arguments, it should come as no surprise to discover that they share similar problems. Perhaps the greatest problem with Beckwith's position is privileging unity over diversity. Both Hick and Beckwith assume a fundamental unity at the level of reference underlying a plurality of experience of the level sense. Consider the example used by Hick (and described in our chapter) of the Blind Men and the Elephant. If we are all blind, with access to only a limited piece of the whole reality, what reasons do we have for believing that we're touching the same elephant? Hick's position is often criticized on the grounds that it requires some actor standing in a privileged epistemic position (like being the only sighted person in a group of blind people), capable of identifying the unity of reference amidst the diversity of sense. This is not unlike Beckwith's Superman example, whereby the reader of the comic book stands outside the story in a privileged epistemic position to that of Lana and Lois. It is because of this unique position that the reader can see the truth of Superman's dual-identity, beyond Lois and Lana's limited understanding.

Please don't misunderstand, we aren't criticizing Beckwith for making positive claims about the nature of God (e.g., as fundamentally one). After all, such is the task of theology! Our concern is that Beckwith appears to presuppose a fundamental unity of reference but without a comprehensive metaphysical framework to back it up.[1] And without a comprehensive metaphysical system, Beckwith's position relies on some privileged access to the level of reference. Whether reading a comic book or a cosmic book, Beckwith's perspective depends on some privileged access to the level of reference; without it, he has no reason to assume a fundamental unity underlying the diversity of experience. Thus, it seems equally plausible that God, Allah, and YHWH are three distinct realities (referents) rather than a single reality experienced and described in different ways.

Is Oneness a Necessary Feature of Divinity?

In addition to his sense/reference identist pluralism, Beckwith also offers a logical argument for the oneness of God. He attempts to build God's

---

1. We favor the metaphysical framework presented by Alfred North Whitehead, which shares in Beckwith's conclusion about the unity of reference between Muslims, Jews, and Christians but also allows for a plurality of ultimates (including the Cosmos and Being Itself) distinct from the Abrahamic God (Supreme Being).

singularity into the very definition of God. At one place, Beckwith describes God as *"the absolute, uncaused, perfect, rational, unchanging, self-subsistent, eternal creator and sustainer of all that which receives its being from another."* While each of these terms could be unpacked and debated, we are more interested in the form of the argument, which goes from this definition to the conclusion that "there can only in principle be one God."

In an abridged version, Beckwith describes God as "he who is metaphysically ultimate and has underived existence." Let's consider each of these elements individually. First, "underived existence." That God's existence is thought to be necessary (underived) is not unique to Beckwith's articulation. Varieties of "cosmological arguments" for the existence of God are as commonplace in Christian thought (e.g., Aquinas) as they are in Islamic thought (e.g., al-Ghazali), all of which are grounded in the view that God's existence is necessary. But is there anything about the nature of an underived existence that requires only one entity can be underived? If one asserts that there are two or more underived elements of the totality, all of which are eternal (and hence underived), is there any inherent conflict? Would they all have to be viewed as gods? We think not.

What then of the second feature, "metaphysically ultimate"? There may be some understandings of metaphysics in which metaphysical ultimacy necessarily requires unity. But one of the greatest metaphysicians was Aristotle, whose metaphysics features four causes or lines of explanation that each arrive at an ultimate. But the ultimate material cause is not the same as the ultimate efficient or formal cause.

By "ultimate," one might mean all-inclusive. But this sort of ultimacy results in a metaphysical monism. If that One is God, then only God exists. Therefore, the same logic that excludes the possibility of multiple metaphysical ultimates seems to exclude the possibility of anything other than the metaphysical ultimate—including derived creaturely reality. So if Beckwith wishes to leave room for non-ultimate reality (such as human existence), he must intend something different by "metaphysically ultimate."

In this vein, Beckwith adds that "God cannot be *a thing* in the universe, but the being on which all things in the universe depend" (p. 68). Put another way, "God cannot be one of a kind. He must be Being Itself, which means that he is the absolute source of all the kinds of things that do exist." While some, like Tillich and Heidegger, have suggested thinking of God as "Being Itself, the vast majority of Muslims, Jews, and Christians seem to have in mind something more like God as "Supreme Being."[2] We have already discussed this distinction at some length in our chapter, but it's worth reiterating that the distinction between Supreme Being and Being Itself can also be understood as the difference between God as a personal deity, on the one hand, and Godhead as the formless ultimate reality, on the other.

More to the point, that there is a distinction at all between a Supreme Being (personal) and Ground of Being (impersonal) already implies the possibility of multiple ultimates. There is no inherent conflict between the necessary (underived) existence of both a personal ultimate (Supreme Being) and an impersonal ultimate (Being Itself). In process theology, the terms God and Creativity are invoked respectively to distinguish between these ultimates. As such, we don't think that Beckwith's assertion that God as metaphysically ultimate with underived existence, entails that there is only one God and that Christians, Muslims, and Jews necessarily worship the same God.

Learning About God: Beyond Progressive Revelation

The notion of "progressive revelation" is extremely important, and we are grateful to Beckwith for introducing it into the discussion. Progressive revelation speaks to the dynamic nature of knowing, which can be used to account for differences in views about a shared referent. Consider Copernicus. Prior to Copernicus, people believed that the sun rotated around the earth. But Copernicus proposed that the earth rotated around the sun, and this recognition launched the Copernican revolution—a fundamental shift in the way that humans understood the earth's relation to the sun. Yet this fundamental difference between the geocentrism of Ptolemy and the heliocentrism of Copernicus didn't entail that there were two different earths or two different suns being discussed. Rather, different views regarding the same subject matter was

---

2. Consider the language used by Jesus to describe God as "Abba" (Father), or other Abrahamic divine attributes like love, jealously, etc. These only make sense in reference to a personal Supreme Being, as opposed to an impersonal force like Being Itself.

the result of progressive knowledge—we learned new things about the earth's relation to the sun.

With respect to God, Beckwith argues, "According to the Christian understanding of progressive revelation, it was only later, under the new covenant, that God revealed he is Father, Son, and Holy Spirit, and even then the full implications of what that means for the universal church were not settled until well into the fourth century at the Council of Constantinople in 381" (p. 79). The point is that learning new things about God doesn't entail different Gods. On this matter, we emphatically agree with Beckwith.

Whether at the level of the individual or a community (tradition), learning is a process. What we would like to add, however, is that recognizing the dynamic nature of knowing isn't reason to assume that the object of our knowledge is static. All things flow. Like conflicting descriptions of the color of leaves between spring and autumn or the physical traits of a person who grows from a baby to an adult, discrepancies can be both the result of progressive knowledge and dynamic reality. We think the dynamic nature of existence is equally relevant to the dynamism of God, though we won't defend that view here.

While we have attempted to critique Beckwith's position, we do find benefits in supporting his conclusion. If the Abrahamic traditions recognized one another as worshiping the same God, perhaps they could live more peacefully at a table for three.

RESPONSE TO FRANCIS J. BECKWITH

GERALD R. MCDERMOTT

I agree with Frank Beckwith that Moses's God was the same God for Jesus and Paul—not only a philosophical abstraction ("underived unconditioned existence") but also and especially the infinite and personal God of Israel. Beckwith's final caveat that Judaism, Islam, and Christianity are three different faiths, however, is a clue that their different senses (as he puts it) do not all point to the same referent.

We need to go back to what Beckwith claims all three religions agree on: God as *the absolute, uncaused, perfect, rational, unchanging, self-subsistent, eternal creator and sustainer of all that which receives its being from another.* My contention is that Muslims do not agree with Christians on what three of these terms mean, so they cannot be said to "more or less believe the same things about God." On three terms there is far *less* than *more*.

Take the first term on which there is substantial disagreement: "perfect." Thomas Aquinas, whom Beckwith uses as his representative of Christian thought, said that to be perfect means to be fully actual without any potentiality. God is not lacking in anything, particularly goodness or love. His goodness is the highest goodness, and his love is the most perfect love. In fact, because God is also simple, there are no components in God. He *is* the highest good and the most perfectly imaginable love.[1] Thomas quotes the apostle John: "God *is* love." His essence is perfect goodness and fully actualized love.

While God is also his other attributes such as justice, love is his essence

---

1. Thomas Aquinas, *Summa Theologiae*, trans. Fathers of the English Dominican Province (Westminster MD: Christian Classics, 1981), Ia 1a.1.4; *Summa Contra Gentiles*, trans. Anton Pegis (Garden City: Image, 1955), 1:91.5; cf. *Summa Theologiae* 1a.1.3.

in ways that other affections of God are not. The "principle" of every divine affection is love.[2] So in some sense it seems to be the root of God's other affections. Thomas also says that "none of the other things that are said of God in terms of operation are said of Him according to more or less."[3] But of love this can be said: "God loves one thing more than another, according as He wills it a greater good."[4] One guesses that Thomas might be thinking that God loves all his human creatures, but perhaps he loves those who finally reject him less than those who persist in love for him.

For Thomas, therefore, love is part of God's perfection in ways that other attributes are not. But the perfection of Allah is fundamentally different. As I have detailed in my essay, Muslim scholars think the concept of God's love is incompatible with his transcendence. It suggests a humanizing of Allah's majesty that is impossible for the Islamic mind. Even if Allah's love is to be contemplated—and it is barely so for the Sufi minority—it is only for those Muslims who obey him. In that case it would be conditional love, if love at all. But even this might be going too far. Scholar of Islamic law Norman Anderson reports that "'love' or 'loving' finds no place among the seven 'Eternal Attributes' of God (al-Ṣifat al-Azaliyya) to which Muslim theology often refers."[5]

Avicenna, whom Professor Beckwith uses as his example of a Muslim thinker, could not conceive of Allah's having any intention for his creatures in the world. Like Aquinas, he taught the radical simplicity of God in which there are no attributes beyond his essence, which has no intention relating to the world. According to Avicenna, "Every intention is for the sake of the intended and is less in existence than the intended. This is because if a thing is for the sake of another, that other is more complete in existence than it."[6] So if something is more complete than another, that something cannot intend the other or anything for that other. There might be accidental effects from divine providence, but they cannot be intended.

---

2. *Summa Contra Gentiles* 1:91.7.

3. *Summa Contra Gentiles* 1.91.9.

4. *Summa Contra Gentiles* 1.91.11.

5. J. N. D. Anderson, *God's Law and God's Love: An Essay in Comparative Religion* (London: Collins, 1980), 98.

6. Avicenna, *al-Najah*, ed. M. Fakhri (Beirut, 1985), 305; cited in Shams Inati, "Ibn Sina," in *History of Islamic Philosophy*, ed. Seyyed Hossein Nasr and Oliver Leaman, vol. 1 (London: Routledge, 1996), 242.

What does that mean for Avicenna's conception of Allah and love? It must be excluded. For even if there are beneficial effects of Allah's providence toward the world, they were not intended. And without intention there cannot be love. How could I—or God for that matter—be said to love others without having any intentions for others? If someone helps me by accident, I might be grateful. But I certainly would not be able to think of that help as loving. For it was not intended to be a help.

And without love as part of Allah's perfection, Avicenna's depiction of God's perfection is quite different from Aquinas's depiction of God's perfection. They are two very different perfections.

If Avicenna and Aquinas are truly representative thinkers representing Islam and Christianity, then Muslims and Christians do not share a vision of God as perfect. For at the core of the Christian God's perfection is love, while the Muslim God's perfection repudiates the concept.

What about a second term in Professor Beckwith's list of "the same things" that he claims Muslims and Christians agree on (I will get to Judaism shortly)—that God is "rational"? What does this mean? For Thomas it means that God has a mind that is reflected in the rationality of the world he created. This is why our minds can understand so much of how the world works, because it is ordered in mathematical and rational ways that our minds can access and understand. As Thomas taught, the analogy between our created minds and the rational patterns in the world, on the one hand, and God's reason, on the other, contains infinitely more unlikeness than likeness.[7] Yet it is significant that the apostle John said that Jesus is the *logos*, which means rational word or reason. And Paul says that Christian worship is *logikēn latreian*, or "rational worship" (Rom. 12:1). Of course, worship is more than simply rational, for it is directed to a God who is infinitely more than our rational concepts. But it is never less than that—like worshiping a god who defies rational conceptuality.

When Avicenna and other Muslim thinkers describe God, Allah's transcendence is central, such that any attempt to suggest an analogy to human reason is resisted. It is something of a truism that for Muslims God's will is all we know, through his revealed law. Humans can use reason to discuss divine law, but to suggest a relation of God's will to human

---

7. *Summa Theologiae* Ia.13.

rationality is to misunderstand Allah in a fundamental way. God transcends all human categories so that there is no relationship whatsoever between God's nature and what we call rationality. Therefore to compare God's nature as "rational" for Muslims to the Christian God as "rational" is to compare apples and oranges—or more accurately, humans and their nonhuman Source. For Muslims "rational" when used of God's nature has nothing to do with human rationality; in fact it is categorically different. But for Christians there is some analogy between God's rational nature and human rationality. Bottom line: Muslims and Christians do not believe that God is "rational" in anything like the same way.

A third term that Professor Beckwith uses to claim that the Muslim and Christian concepts of God are the same is "unchanging." Many Muslims themselves would contest this claim. They are quick to point to the central Christian claim that God incarnated himself as a man in the person of Jesus, who lived in history and therefore endured change throughout his earthly life. The incarnation suggests that God changed in a fundamental way, at least in one of the three divine Persons. Christians might protest that the second Person of the Trinity remained unchanged in his deity and only changed in his humanity, and that God in his deity remained unchanged. This was Aquinas's view.[8] Yet here the difference with the Muslim view is clear: for Aquinas and all orthodox Christians one of the three Persons changed, and so in some sense God himself changed through time. Therefore Christians and Muslims do not think of God's nature as unchanging in the same way. There are significant differences.

If Muslim views of God's nature as *perfect, rational, and unchanging* are significantly different from Christian views of the same, Professor Beckwith's analogies to Clark Kent/Superman and Cassius Clay/Muhammad Ali fail. For they depend on the referent being the same. But when *perfect, rational, and unchanging* are applied to Allah, they mean very different things than when they are applied to the Trinitarian God. These differences suggest different referents, not the same God but two different Gods.

I agree with Professor Beckwith, however, when he says that although Moses's sense of God differed from that of Aquinas, they

---

8. *Summa Theologiae* IIIa.16.9.

had the same reference. Yet even Moses's sense was not qualitatively different from Aquinas's. For while Aquinas referred to the Trinitarian God, Moses wrote in the Torah that God's oneness was differentiated: there was God and the Spirit of God in Genesis 1, and God and the Word of God throughout Torah. So Moses knew that God's oneness was not mathematical but involved inner differentiation just as Aquinas did. Professor Beckwith is also right to say that Paul was referring to the Jewish God. He and his Jewish opponents had different understandings of the same God, the God of Israel. The difference concerned only one thing at the end of the day, whether Jesus was the messiah. As I argue in my essay, most Jews and Christians think that resurrection, incarnation, and Trinity separate Jews and Christians. But all of these are either Jewish concepts (resurrection) or developments of Jewish concepts (incarnation and Trinity). Only Jesus's identity separates Jews and Christians.

Of course, that is a big difference. It has implications for eternal destiny, but it is not a matter of worshiping different Gods. Both communities worship the God of Israel and find his revelation in Jewish scriptures that are 77 percent (Protestant) to 80 percent (Catholic) of the Christian Bible.

JERRY L. WALLS

It is hard to be critical of a paper that begins with Superman. Frank's paper is not only provocative but fun to read. Alas, I do not think his account, despite the appearance of Superman, defends truth or justice—but I am less sure about the American way. In any case, I agree with pretty much everything Frank says for about the first third of his essay. The story he tells about Adam, Baaqir, Candida, and their loss and recovery of faith in God is an illuminating way to approach these complicated and controversial matters. After recounting how they came to believe in God again through careful philosophical investigation, Frank asks a question to which it seems clear that we must return a resounding no: "Can anyone deny that Adam, the former Jew; Baaqir, the former Muslim; and Candida, the former Christian, all believe in the same God?" (p. 72).

As Frank goes on to concede, however, their common belief in God is only a matter of "mere theism," and it is "not even clear whether it is accurate to say they now have *faith* in God" (p. 72). While this common belief in God is rationally driven and philosophically sophisticated, religiously it is rather thin. It provides little, if any, idea of how this God feels about us, why he created us, or what he may require of us, if anything. Indeed, as I read this section of Frank's paper, I could not help but think of Hume's character, the skeptic Philo, and his advice about how we should treat the deliverances of natural theology: "If it affords no inference that affects human life, or can be the source of any action or forbearance . . . what can the most inquisitive, contemplative, and religious man do more than give a plain philosophical assent to the proposition, as often as it occurs, and believe that the arguments on which it is established exceed the objections which lie against it?"[1] Philo goes on to note that a well-disposed mind will naturally desire that heaven would be willing to provide us "some more particular revelation" and will accordingly "fly to revealed truth with the greatest avidity."[2]

Not surprisingly, this is exactly what our trio of religious seekers do, engaging in an earnest eighteen-month study of the three religions, reading not only their sacred texts, but their theologians and apologists. We can assume from their diligence they all acquire a well-informed understanding of each of the three religions, their distinctive truth claims, and the grounds and evidence for them. On the basis of their study, each converts to one of the Abrahamic faiths, but not the one they held before their journey through loss of faith and recovery of belief in God. And it is here that Frank's attempt to argue that they all still believe in and worship the same God runs into trouble.

The problem is not generated by any sort of attempt on Frank's part to downplay or trivialize the profound differences that separate the three religions. To the contrary, these are spelled out in considerable detail. But these differences do not pose a problem for the claim that all worship the same God since the differences are composed only of "additional things" they believe God has specially revealed that they did not know when they converted to mere theism. These pertain to matters like the divine nature, humanity, morality, and salvation. "Consequently, when Adam partakes in the Divine Liturgy, when Baaqir goes to shul, and when Candida says her five daily prayers (*salat*), they are all worshiping the same God" (p. 73). A bit later, he reiterates and expands on the claim that the sharp differences dividing the three religions do not pose a problem for his contention that they worship the same God. "The reason is remarkably simple. Each faith tradition holds the same basic understanding of what constitutes divine nature: God is *the absolute, uncaused, perfect, rational, unchanging, self-subsistent, eternal creator and sustainer of all that which receives its being from another.* So when Christians, Muslims, and Jews speak of God, they have the same reference" (p. 74).

But is it really this simple? I think not. The first problem with Frank's claims here is that he misconstrues the Christian account of what is the

---

1. David Hume, *Dialogues Concerning Natural Religion*, ed. Richard H. Popkin (Indianapolis: Hackett, 1980), 88.

2. Hume, *Dialogues*, 89.

most "basic understanding of what constitutes divine nature." Indeed, some of what he describes in terms of "additional things" specially revealed by God are in fact among the most basic truths of all, truths that are more fundamental than the truth that God is "eternal creator and sustainer of all that which receives its being from another." I am referring to the doctrine of the Trinity, the claim that God exists from all eternity in three persons, Father, Son, and Holy Spirit. Whereas God is only *contingently* a creator and sustainer, since he could have chosen not to create anything at all, he is *essentially and necessarily* a Trinity. As Colin Gunton put it, "The three persons of the Trinity exist only in reciprocal eternal relatedness. God is not God apart from the way in which Father, Son and Spirit in eternity give to and receive from each other what they essentially are."[3]

It is important to emphasize the nature of what it is the three persons give to and receive from each other in order to understand what they essentially are. We get some fascinating clues of this in the biblical material describing the interactions among persons of the Trinity. For instance, when the Father speaks from heaven at the baptism of Jesus and says "This is my Son, the Beloved, with whom I am well pleased" (Matt. 3:17), we see that the relationship is one of love and pleasure. We also get a remarkable glimpse into the eternal dynamics of the Trinity when Jesus prays to the Father that his disciples will "see my glory, which you have given me because you loved me before the foundation of the world" (John 17:24). Recognizing this eternal relationship of love and delight led C. S. Lewis to comment that "in Christianity God is not a static thing—not even a person—but a dynamic, pulsating activity, a life, almost a kind of drama. Almost, if you will not think me irreverent, a kind of dance."[4]

The extraordinary claim that God is love in his very essence, that he has been love from all eternity when there were no creatures to love, is vital to Christian theology. What is at best a minor note in Islam is absolutely fundamental for Christian faith. All that is distinctively Christian grows out of the essential truth that God is love. The incarnation and atonement exhibit God's eternal love in flesh and blood vividness. Indeed, Jesus informs us that "as the Father has loved me, so I have loved you" (John 15:9). This takes on layers of depth when

---

3. Colin E. Gunton, *The One, The Three and the Many: God, Creation and the Culture of Modernity* (Cambridge: Cambridge University Press, 1993), 164.

4. C. S. Lewis, *Mere Christianity* (San Francisco: HarperSanFrancisco, 2001), 175.

we recall Jesus's prayer in which he says the Father loved him before the foundation of the world. In other words, the love Jesus revealed is the love that has been shared among the persons of the Trinity from all eternity. Jesus's life, death, and resurrection is a narrative display of the aboriginal reality of eternal Trinitarian love.

It does not begin to do justice to the foundational claim that God is love in his essentially Trinitarian existence from all eternity to characterize this claim as only an "additional thing" we learn from special revelation that elaborates on the more fundamental definition of God arrived at by way of philosophical analysis. It is worth noting that Frank's account of what is basic in his definition of God appears to be derived from what takes priority in the *order of knowing* as understood in Thomistic philosophy. That is, we first arrive at the existence of God and some of his essential attributes by way of reason and philosophical argument and only after that proceed to consider what additional things we may learn by way of special revelation.

By contrast, as I discussed in my essay, what is truly basic and fundamental about God is what takes priority in the *order of being*, and crucial elements of this come to us by way of special revelation. Thus, in the order of being, nothing is more fundamental or basic than God's eternal existence in an essentially loving relationship between the three persons of the Trinity.

What this also points up is that the referent for any true description of God is the Trinity. Any account of the correct referent for our various definitions of God that does not include his Trinitarian nature is radically incomplete from a Christian standpoint. The point is the same whether we are talking about Frank's philosophical definition or his more biblical claim that he says would be agreed upon by Adam, Baaqir, and Candida—namely, "that God made a covenant with Abraham and that he called Moses to lead the children of Israel out of Egypt" (p. 74). If Christianity is true, the proper referent for both of these descriptions is the triune God: Father, Son, and Holy Spirit. This is the only God that exists. There is no "mere theistic" God, who lacks a Trinitarian nature.

In view of this, it is hard to see how Adam, Baaqir, and Candida, who are now fully informed about all three religions, can agree that they are worshiping the same God simply because they can agree on generic theism and shared beliefs about the Old Testament. Let us suppose one of the books they read when they were doing their research was *Mere Christianity*, and they encountered Lewis's famous "trilemma" argument that Jesus is either a liar, a lunatic, or the Lord of the universe. Suppose this was one of the arguments that moved Adam to embrace Christianity, whereas Baaqir and Candida, when encountering this argument found themselves more resistant to the doctrine that Jesus is God the Son.

Now suppose Adam was also deeply attracted to Lewis's delightful picture of the Trinity as a dance. He was also struck by Lewis's point that the Trinity is not merely a doctrine to be understood but a reality to be embraced.

> And now, what does it all matter? It matters more than anything else in the world. The whole dance, or drama, or pattern of this three-Personal life is to be played out in each one of us: or (putting it the other way round) each one of us has got to enter that pattern, take his place in the dance. There is no other way to the happiness for which we were made.[5]

If Adam now believes that Jesus is the second person of the Trinity, the only God who exists, and believes the only way to the happiness for which we were created is by entering the Trinitarian dance by embracing Jesus through faith, what will he now think about his friends who have rejected the claims of Jesus and maybe even find those claims blasphemous? Will Adam think his friends worship the same God he does because they assent to the claims of mere theism even as they consciously deny the Trinitarian nature of God?

I think not. It is one thing to say all three seekers believed in the same God when they shared a common commitment to mere theism *before* they seriously engaged with the distinctive truth claims of the various religions. But having come to understand those mutually exclusive claims, and each having embraced one version of those claims, they cannot retreat to generic theism as common ground in the way they did before. For Adam now recognizes that God as Trinity is even more fundamental in the order of being than God as creator and accordingly holds his Trinitarian convictions to be essential to his theism.

---

5. Lewis, *Mere Christianity*, 176.

By contrast, Baaqir and Candida now consciously deny Trinitarian claims and expressly exclude them from their theistic faith.

Let us illustrate the point with a story about Superman. Suppose Clark Kent is jealous of the fact that his girlfriend Lana talks about Superman all the time and seems to be infatuated with him. So one night on a date, he combs his hair like Superman, removes his glasses, and asks, "remind you of anyone?" Lana is puzzled and shakes her head. Clark unbuttons his dress shirt to reveal a big red "S" on his blue jersey, and says, "Come on, look at me. I am Superman." Lana is now even more confused and even annoyed. Clark then produces a steel bar and bends it in the shape of a horseshoe. Lana responds, "Oh Clark, are you so jealous of Superman that you are now dressing like him, trying to look like him, and even learned magic to impress me by pretending to bend that steel bar? Really, that is just too much." And she turns and walks out the door.

This is the situation of those who have been informed of the claims of Jesus and have understood why Christians teach that he is the Son of God, the second person of the Trinity, the true referent of the God of mere theism, but who reject those claims.

Before concluding, it is worth noting that sometimes Frank casts his argument in terms of worshiping the same God and sometimes, if not more often, in terms of believing in or referring to the same God. This is important because the former case is a more demanding one to make. As I argued in my essay, referring to the same God is only a necessary condition for worshiping the same God, but it is far from sufficient. In any case, Frank comments in his conclusion that it would be a mistake to take his chapter as a call to an interfaith ecumenism that takes the deepest beliefs of each tradition as "secondary or peripheral to its true essence" (p. 86). Indeed, in his final sentence, he remarks that "in recognizing that three distinct religious traditions refer to the same God one is not contending that they share the same faith" (p. 86). He does not mention common worship in his conclusion, and he only insists on the relatively weak claim that the three religions *refer* to the same God.

I am dubious that Adam, Baaqir, and Candida even refer to the same God after each of them have embraced in a fully informed way the religious claims of one particular religious tradition, claims that are logically incompatible with the other two traditions. But it seems clear at this point that they no longer believe in, let alone worship, the same God.

FRANCIS J. BECKWITH

The other contributors to this volume raise some very important criticisms about the case I make in my chapter. In this limited space I will respond to those concerns that I believe are the most serious and that require me to further clarify my position.

Jerry Walls is certainly correct that in the Christian understanding God is essentially and necessarily a Trinity and that both Judaism and Islam deny this. He is also correct that the Bible tells us many things about the triune nature of God, including the relations between the persons of the Trinity, that we would otherwise never know apart from scripture. However, these observations are perfectly consistent with the thesis I defend in my chapter, since my case depends almost entirely on whether one gets the uniqueness of the divine nature right even if one gets some things wrong about God, including any alleged special revelation from him. This is why many Christian writers, as different as St. Thomas Aquinas and William Lane Craig, make cases for the Christian faith by first establishing the existence of God and then moving on to other matters, including those that Jerry rightly notes are essential to authentic Christian belief. To see this, suppose that an aspiring philosophy student, Lemuel, comes to believe in the existence of God after reading Bill Craig's *Kalām* cosmological argument as published in his book *Reasonable Faith*.[1] However, after reading the portions of the book in which Bill defends Christ's claim of divinity and the historicity of his resurrection[2]—beliefs on which the truth of Christianity

---

1. William Lane Craig, *Reasonable Faith: Christian Truth and Apologetics*, 3rd ed. (Wheaton, IL: Crossway, 2008), 111–56.

2. Craig, *Reasonable Faith*, 207–404.

hinges—Lemuel is unconvinced of Bill's case for the veracity of these doctrines. Now suppose that three years later Lemuel does become convinced of these beliefs and enthusiastically embraces them. Does Lemuel now believe in a different God than the God he arrived at by way of the *Kalām* argument? Although I think the answer is no, it is, on my view, right to say that during the time between Lemuel's initial belief in God and his acceptance of these additional Christian beliefs that his understanding of God was incomplete and perhaps mistaken (especially if he was convinced that Christ's resurrection and claim to divinity were false beliefs). But at this point Lemuel does not even believe in the Trinity. He is merely convinced that God exists and that Jesus, who claimed to be divine, rose from the dead. And yet, it seems counterintuitive to say that he doesn't believe in (or worship) the right God.

Gerald McDermott correctly notes that in my chapter I claim that both Muslims and Christians (as well as Jews) believe that perfection is one of God's attributes. Gerry then goes on to point out that Christians and Muslims understand the meaning of God's perfection differently given what each faith tradition believes about God's love. That doesn't surprise me, since each tradition's view of God's love arises from what each believes has been specially revealed by God in its scriptures. But this is consistent with the view I defend in my chapter, which relies on the distinction (which I borrow from Aquinas) between the preambles of faith and the articles of faith. Gerry makes a similar move when discussing God's rationality. He cites both the apostle John's identification of Jesus with the Eternal Logos (John 1) and St. Paul's claim that "Christian worship is *logikēn latreian*, or 'rational worship' (Rom. 12:1)" (p. 95). Then Gerry contrasts this with what he takes to be the Muslim view: "It is something of a truism that for Muslims God's will is all we know, through his revealed law. Humans can use reason to discuss divine law, but to suggest a relation of God's will to human rationality is to misunderstand Allah in a fundamental way" (p. 95–96). But this apparent disagreement is not about God's rationality—that is, whether the universe was created by an eternal self-subsistent mind who gave existence and order to the universe.[3] Instead, it is about what each faith

---

3. "Allah is Creator of all things, and He is Guardian over all things." Qur'an 39:62, as quoted in *The Meaning of the Glorious Koran: An Explanatory Translation by Mohammed Marmaduke Pickthall* (New York: New American Library, 1988), 454, 223.

tradition takes to be revealed truth concerning either the internal life of God (whether the "Word is God") or the nature of divine law.

Wm. Andrew Schwartz and John B. Cobb Jr. claim that the distinction I make "between sense and reference is not unlike John Hick's neo-Kantian distinction between the *phenomenal* Real (the Divine as experienced/perceived) and the *noumenal* Real (the Divine in itself)" (p. 88). My noumenal-real-self disagrees! To be sure, the sense/reference distinction is similar, but unlike the phenomenal/noumenal distinction, it assumes that one can have some real knowledge about the entity to which one refers. This is why the morning star/evening star and Muhammad Ali/Cassius Clay examples work so well. One must have, as Schwartz and Cobb rightly put it, "a privileged epistemic position" (p. 89). For this reason, they say that I appear "to presuppose a fundamental unity of reference but without a comprehensive metaphysical framework to back it up" (p. 89). Although, because of space constraints, I do not offer any arguments for a comprehensive metaphysical framework, my use of Avicenna, Aquinas, and Maimonides—all neo-Platonic Aristotelians of sorts—indicates where my metaphysical commitments lie, and why I believe each thinker arrives at the same metaphysically ultimate being who has underived existence.

Given what the Christian, Jewish, and Islamic faiths have historically taught about God as the sovereign and providential creator of all that exists, and how tightly tethered that concept is to their sacred and authoritative writings, I don't see how embracing the idea of multiple ultimates, as Schwartz and Cobb suggest, is a realistic option for believers in those faiths. For it would require that they embrace the idea that there are aspects of reality outside the providence of God, a belief that finds no safe harbor in the Torah, the New Testament, or the Qur'an.

JEWS AND CHRISTIANS WORSHIP THE SAME GOD: SHARED REVELATION VIEW

GERALD R. MCDERMOTT

One *might* make a case from scripture that Christians and Muslims worship the same God. (I will turn to Christians and Jews later in this chapter.) When Paul came to Athens in Acts 17, he was "provoked" by the idols he saw all about him (v. 16). In this provocation, he was like all other pious Jews who were deeply disturbed by pagan idolatry. But at the same time, he suggested to the Athenian "philosophers" gathered at the Areopagus that there might be some connection between their worship and true worship: "What you worship in ignorance, this I proclaim to you" (v. 23).[1] He went on to say that God has set the times and places in which human beings live so that they "might grope for him and find him" (v. 27). He quoted pagan poets approvingly, as if they possessed some degree of religious truth: "For 'in him we live and move and exist,' as even some of your own poets have said. For 'we are his offspring'" (v. 28). These remarks might seem to imply that for Paul, people without knowledge of Jesus or the gospel can nevertheless have some connection with the true God.

Does the Bible Suggest That Pagans Worship the Christian God?

Luke's story of Cornelius is sometimes seen as another illustration in Acts of pagans who are ignorant of Jesus but who appear to be worshiping

---

1. All translations are my own unless otherwise indicated.

the same God. The angel told Cornelius that his prayers and alms had ascended "as a memorial before God" (Acts 10:4), suggesting that he was worshiping the true God despite not having yet heard about Jesus. After Peter heard Cornelius's story of the angel, and how the angel had told Cornelius to look for Peter, the apostle then declared that "God does not show partiality, but in every nation he who fears [God] and works righteousness is acceptable to him" (Acts 10:34–35). By omitting mention of Jesus here, it could be suggested that Peter was implying that gentiles without knowledge of Jesus might be worshiping the same God as those who know Jesus.

It is not only the New Testament that contains examples of people outside Israel who might seem to worship the God of Israel. In Genesis we are told of a Canaanite priest who appeared to worship the same God whom Abram (he was not yet Abraham at this point) worshiped. The text tells us that Melchizedek was a priest of El Elyon (roughly translated "God Most High") who declared that this El Elyon was "maker of heaven and earth" (Gen. 14:19). Then we read that Abram swore to "Yahweh El Elyon, maker of heaven and earth" (v. 22), suggesting that Melchizedek and Abram were referring to the same God. The use of the same description of God—El Elyon, maker of heaven and earth—by both Abram and Melchizedek lends support to the idea that people of different religions might be worshiping the same God under different names.

The Roman Catholic bishops at Vatican II never made this sort of explicit claim. But they did assert that the true God touches the conscience and perceptions of non-Christians even while they might worship other gods. The Vatican II fathers wrote in *Nostra Aetate*, "Though differing in many particulars from what she [the Roman Catholic Church] holds and sets forth, nevertheless [world religions] often reflect a ray of that Truth which enlightens all men."[2] This declaration alludes to the apostle John's statement that Jesus "was the true light—which enlightens every man—that was coming into the world" (John 1:9). In *Lumen Gentium* the Vatican II fathers asserted that non-Christians who "through no fault of their own do not know the gospel of Christ or His Church, yet sincerely seek God and, moved by grace,

---

2. "Declaration on the Relationship of the Church to Non-Christian Religions," sec. 2, in *The Documents of Vatican II*, ed. Walter M. Abbott (New York: Guild, 1966), 662.

strive by their deeds to do His will as it is known to them through the dictates of conscience . . . can attain to everlasting salvation."[3] Here the bishops maintained that the true God leads to himself some of those who do not know Jesus explicitly. Even though they do not worship the true God, the bishops proposed that these non-Christians are being led by God's Spirit and grace to eventual union with, and explicit knowledge of, the Son. This document adds that Muslims, "professing to hold the faith of Abraham, along with us adore the one and merciful God, who on the last day will judge mankind."[4] Here the Council fathers stop short of saying explicitly that Christians and Muslims worship the same God, but assert agreement between the two religions on God's oneness and mercy.[5]

While the Vatican II fathers were wary about saying pagans worship the Christian God, some Christian theologians of the religions have been less reticent. Raimundo Panikkar, for example, argued that Christians tie the Spirit too closely to Jesus and miss the reality of non-Christians who worship the same God but under a different name.[6] Jacques Dupuis asked why the Spirit would have to be limited to the incarnation when it was present before the incarnation. We can therefore learn new things about the true God from other religionists. In short, they worship the same God but with another name.[7]

Can we draw this same conclusion from scripture, that non-Christians and Christians worship the same God? Do the biblical passages that I have just discussed show enough of a connection between certain unevangelized people and the true God that we could extrapolate to Muslims and conclude that they worship the same God as Christians?

The Bible and Pagan Worship: Looking a Bit Closer

Not necessarily. Let's look a bit closer. In the Cornelius story, one might have expected Peter to conclude his speech with the declaration that in

---

3. "Dogmatic Constitution on the Church," sec. 16, in *Documents of Vatican II*, 35.

4. "Dogmatic Constitution on the Church," 35.

5. For a careful look at Vatican II on Judaism and Islam, see Gavin D'Costa, *Vatican II: Catholic Doctrines on Jews and Muslims* (New York: Oxford University Press, 2014).

6. Raimundo Panikkar, *The Trinity and the Religious Experience of Man* (New York: Orbis, 1973), 57–58.

7. Jacques Dupuis, SJ, *Christianity and the Religions: From Confrontation to Dialogue* (Maryknoll, NY: Orbis, 2001), esp. 181; Jacques Dupuis, *Toward a Christian Theology of Religious Pluralism* (Maryknoll, NY: Orbis, 1997), esp. 388.

every nation anyone who fears God and does what is right receives forgiveness through the name of Jesus. But that is not how Peter concluded. Instead, he declared that "all the prophets testify that all *who believe in him* [Jesus] receive forgiveness through his name" (Acts 10:43). Peter concluded the speech that started with a declaration of God's acceptance of all who fear God and do what is right with a specificity focused on belief in Jesus. This does not answer the question of whether the unevangelized worship the same God as Christians, but it prevents us from assuming too easily that they do.

Let us return to Paul in Athens. His sermon was actually full of derogatory references to Greek religion, focused particularly on human ignorance. He had noticed an altar "to an unknown god" and suggested to his hearers that they were thinking wrongly about God living in a temple and being served by human hands. He was not distant as they supposed, nor was he like gold or silver or stone. He could not be represented by an artistic image (Acts 17:23–29).

It is true that Paul's language about humans searching and perhaps groping for and finding him suggests that pagans can find God apart from the Christian gospel and church. But there are two problems with this interpretation. First, the sermon is otherwise pessimistic about the ability of any Greek religion to provide knowledge of God. After all, Paul fixated on the statue to an *unknown* god. Second, the Greek word for "grope" (*psēlapheian*) "denotes the groping and fumbling of a blind man."[8] Furthermore, since this verb is in the optative case, expressing wishing or hoping, and the word itself means "grope," it seems that Paul considered it unlikely that seekers could actually find the true God in Greek religions.

Paul concluded his sermon by the proclamation that in the past God had overlooked times of *ignorance* and now was commanding all human beings everywhere to repent. Judgment was at hand, and the proof was Jesus's resurrection (Acts 17:30–31). All in all, Paul seemed to be saying, the religion of this great Greek civilization was blinded by ignorance that leads only to idolatry.

Paul's verdict on Greek religion as a mass of error was consistent with his judgments elsewhere that twisted powers drive religions outside

---

8. Charles S. C. Williams, *A Commentary on the Acts of the Apostles* (New York: Harper and Row, 1958), 204.

of what we call Judaism and Christianity. As I have argued in another work, Paul believed that other world religions originated in pride and deception. Angelic powers originally created to serve God instead chose in their pride to rebel.[9] They convinced whole populations to worship them rather than the true God, and distorted God's truth along the way. They used what they knew of God's law to take captive those in their worship (Gal. 3:23). This is why Paul said that worship at their temples was consorting with "demons," and Christian believers need to steer clear of their rituals (1 Cor. 10:21–22).[10] There might be truths in other religions gained from God's revelation in nature and conscience, and perhaps scraps of insight about divine law gained from its unholy use. But this is different from direct contact with or worship of the true God.

Do Muslims and Christians Worship the Same God?

What about Muslims? When they worship Allah, are they worshiping the Christian God but under a different name?[11] In 2007 Muslim scholars from around the world released "A Common Word" that asserted yes in response to that question based on the following claim: Both religions teach the two great commandments—love for God with all of the self, and love for neighbor as oneself.[12] The Yale Center for Faith and Culture then released its own yes, agreeing with that claim.[13] More recently, Miroslav Volf released his book *Allah*, in which that claim was argued for, based on a comparison between the Bible and the Qur'an: "If what God is said to command in the Bible were similar to what God is said to command in the Qur'an, then this would suggest that the character of God is similar and that Muslims and Christians have a common God."[14]

---

9. Gerald R. McDermott, *God's Rivals: Why Has God Allowed Different Religions?* (Downers Grove, IL: InterVarsity, 2007), 67–80.

10. McDermott, *God's Rivals*, 67–68.

11. An illuminating approach to this question can be found in Timothy George, *Is the Father of Jesus the God of Muhammad? Understanding the Differences between Christianity and Islam* (Grand Rapids: Zondervan, 2002).

12. This section comparing the God of the Qur'an and the God of the Bible is adapted, with permission, from Gerald R. McDermott, "How the Trinity Should Govern Our Approach to World Religions," *Journal of the Evangelical Theological Society* 60, no. 1 (March 2017): 49–64; and from "The Triune God," in *A Trinitarian Theology of Religions*, by Gerald R. McDermott and Harold A. Netland (Oxford: Oxford University Press, 2014), 46–85.

13. "A Common Word: Christian Response," Yale Center for Faith and Culture, 2008 Conference, https://faith.yale.edu/common-word/common-word-christian-response.

14. Miroslav Volf, *Allah: A Christian Response* (San Francisco: HarperOne, 2011), 14.

So let's examine that question—whether the Bible and Qur'an contain those two commands. The first thing that must be said is that love for God is never commanded by the Qur'an and rarely even mentioned. Only three verses appear to use unambiguously what translators render as "love" in the human response to God (2:165; 3:31; 5:54), and two more may do so as well, depending on how the Arabic is translated (2:177; 76:8).[15] Yet none of these verses *command* love—they merely describe a relation to Allah—and they are at most five out of six thousand verses.

Daud Rahbar and other scholars agree that even if the Qur'an *mentions* love for God, it never *commands* it. Instead of love, fear of God is commanded by the Qur'an. A Muslim when he wrote his book *God of Justice*, Rahbar argued that the central theme of the Qur'an is God's justice, and its most common exhortation is to "guard yourselves fearfully against God's wrath."[16] Sir Norman Anderson, who for many years was a specialist in Islamic law at the University of London, concurred with this assessment: While the Bible presents God as a father or shepherd or lover to whom one returns love, "in Islam, by contrast, the constant reference is to God as sovereign Lord (*Rabb*), and man as his servant or slave ('*abd*)."[17]

If love for God is rarely mentioned and never commanded in the Qur'an, it is nevertheless important for the Sufi tradition, as the Yale Center has emphasized, pointing especially to the Sufi theologian al-Ghazali as the paradigmatic Muslim.

But there are problems with this use of Sufism. First, many Muslims over the centuries have denounced Sufism as a departure from orthodoxy, so it is strange to appeal to the Sufi tradition in support of mainstream Islamic teachings.[18] Furthermore, the Sufi understanding of love is different from what most Christians presume about their love for God and God's love for humanity. Joseph Lumbard reports that in al-Ghazali, love between the Muslim and God is no longer a duality

---

15. See Gordon Nickel, "The Language of Love in Qur'an and Gospel," in *Sacred Text: Explorations in Lexicography,* ed. Juan Pedro Monferrer-Sala and Angel Urban (Frankfurt am Main: Peter Lang, 2009), 232.

16. Nickel, "The Language of Love in Qur'an and Gospel," xiii, 5, 180, 181–83, 223, 225.

17. Norman Anderson, *God's Law and God's Love* (London: Collins, 1980), 98.

18. Nickel, "Language of Love," 241; Daniel Brown, *A New Introduction to Islam* (Malden, MA: Blackwell, 2004), 173.

but a unity in which the individuality of the human is annihilated.[19] According to another historian of Sufism, the concept "of God's love as pursuing the soul, a conception which had reached its highest development in the Christian doctrine of Redemption, was impossible to the Sufis" because, for Muslims, God's transcendence meant he would not have "feelings akin to their own."[20] One of the most famous early Sufis was Rabi'a al-'Adawiyya al-Qaysiyya (d. AD 801), who wrote of her love for God but said little or nothing of his love for her.[21] More recently, Murad Wilfried Hofmann has argued that "a love of God for His creation comparable to the love human beings are capable of . . . must be ruled out as incompatible with the very nature of God as sublime and totally self-sufficient." Dr. Hofmann, a convert to Islam, suggests that any talk of "God's love" inevitably "humanizes" and therefore distorts what is transcendent.[22]

According to both Sufi and non-Sufi Muslims, God does not have unconditional love for humans generally. Rahbar writes, "Unqualified Divine Love for mankind is an idea completely alien to the Qur'an."[23] God's love is conditional, expressed only toward those who do righteous deeds. The Islamicist Frederick Denny warns that God's mercy, which is offered to all, should not be confused with love, which is offered "only to select ones."[24]

In short, the God of the Qur'an never commands his human creatures to love him. Sufis have a long tradition of recommending love for God, but their status as "normative mainstream" in Islam is debatable, and their conceptions of love for God and his love for humanity are significantly different from Christian conceptions.

But what of the second claim about the Islamic God's principal commands—that Allah commands love for neighbor as oneself? Once

19. Joseph Lumbard, "From Ḥubb to 'Ishq': The Development of Love in Early sufism," Journal of Islamic Studies 18, no. 3 (2007), 351.

20. Margaret Smith, Rabi'a the Mystic and Her Fellow Saints in Islam (Cambridge: Cambridge University Press, 1924), 92.

21. Smith, Rabi'a the Mystic and Her Fellow Saints in Islam, 101; cf. Nickel, "Language of Love," 246.

22. Murad Wilfried Hofmann, "Differences between the Muslim and Christian Concepts of Divine Love," Bismika Allahuma, September 22, 2008, www.bismikaallahuma.org/archives/2008/differences-between-the-muslim-and-christian-concepts-of-divine-love/.

23. Daud Rahbar, God of Justice: A Study in the Ethical Doctrine of the Qur'an (Leiden: Brill, 1960), 172.

24. Rahbar, God of Justice, 199.

again there are problems. The first is that the Qur'an contains repeated admonitions to Muslim believers not to make friends with non-Muslims. For example, 3:118 reads, "O believers, do not take as close friends other than your own people." Similar warnings include 58:22 and 60:1. In the *Encyclopedia of the Qur'an*, Denis Gril observes that "love or friendship between human beings is not fully recognized by the Qur'an unless confirmed by faith." Instead, there is conditional love: "One can truly love only believers, since love for unbelievers separates one from God and attracts one toward this world. . . . Adopting unbelievers as friends or allies . . . is equivalent to lining up on the side of the enemies of God."[25] This is radically different from the command of Jesus to his disciples to love even their enemies (Matt. 5:43–48). Another difficulty is that, as we have already noted, there simply is no command to love one's neighbor in the Qur'an. So one can talk about love for neighbor in the Islamic *tradition*, but not as something commanded by the God of the Qur'an.

So what should we say about the claim that Muslims and Christians "worship the same God"?

At one level, of course, we have to say yes, because as monotheists we all agree there is only one God. Ontologically there can be only one eternal creator God. But the question the Yale Center asks is whether Qur'anic descriptions of God are "sufficiently similar" to biblical descriptions of God, and here we must demur.

Christians and Muslims agree that there is an eternal creator God, and there is substantial agreement on some of the attributes of God (such as omnipotence and omniscience). But in other respects, Muslims and Christians clearly disagree on what this one creator God is like, and the major disagreement concerns the Christian doctrine of the Trinity with its commitment to the deity of Jesus Christ.

Now, many maintain that what is rejected in the Qur'an is not the orthodox Christian teaching on the Trinity but rather certain aberrant, heretical views circulating at the time of Muhammad. Surah 5:116, for example, seems to assume that Christians believe that Mary, mother of Jesus, is one of the three members of the Trinity.

But rejection of the Trinity by Muslims cannot be explained simply as due to misunderstandings. For even when common misunderstandings are

25. Denis Gril, "Love and Affection," in Jane Dammen McAuliffe, gen. ed., *Encyclopedia of the Qur'an* (Leiden: Brill, 2003), 234, 235.

clarified, it is not unusual for Muslims to insist that the Christian belief in Father, Son, and Holy Spirit as God compromises the unity of God. At the heart of the dispute is the question of the deity of Jesus Christ.[26]

Here the Trinitarian rule (*opera Dei triune non divisa sunt*: the works of the triune God are not divided [among the persons]) is helpful. It reminds us that the Father's works are not to be divided from the Son's. The Son helps identify the character of the Father, for the Father's character is revealed by the Son: "Whoever has seen me has seen the Father" (John 14:9). If the Son told his disciples that God loved the world (John 3:16), that they should love God with all their hearts (Matt. 22:37), and that they should love everyone including their enemies (Matt. 5:44), we can infer that the Father has said and commanded the same. This Father is clearly different, then, from the Allah of the Qur'an.

Furthermore, the Christian teaching on the Son transforms even the most basic predicates ascribed to God and the Father of Jesus. For example, both Christians and Muslims say that God is one. But while Muslims insist that God is numerically one without differentiation, Jesus showed and taught that oneness is also triune.

Another predicate shared by both religions is that God is all-*powerful*. Yet the Son's demonstration that *true* power is found in the *weakness* of the cross is emphatically rejected by Muslims.[27] Therefore, if the Father is not divided from the Son, and in fact is revealed by the Son, even the most basic predicates of God as understood by Muslims and the biblical God are different. God is one in very different ways for Muslims and Christians, and the same applies to God's power. Hence I must agree with Lamin Sanneh, the great Yale scholar who grew up as a Muslim and now is an orthodox Christian, that affirming the sameness of the Islamic understanding of God and the biblical God "is adequate insofar as there is only one God, but inadequate with respect to God's character, on which hang matters of commitment and identity."[28]

---

26. See Kenneth Cragg, *Jesus and the Muslim: An Exploration* (Oxford: Oneworld, 1999); Geoffrey Parrinder, *Jesus in the Qur'an* (Oxford: Oneworld, 2013); and Neal Robinson, *Christ in Islam and Christianity* (Albany: State University of New York, 1991).

27. See 2 Cor. 12:9. This idea of the Son transforming the most basic predicates that the Islamic and Christian conceptions of God share was suggested to me by Timothy C. Tennent, *Theology in the Context of World Christianity* (Grand Rapids: Zondervan, 2007), 40–41.

28. Lamin Sanneh, "Do Christians and Muslims Worship the Same God?" *Christian Century* (May 4, 2004): 35.

Let me close this section with an analogy. Let us suppose that two strangers meet, share small talk, and then realize that they both know a Mr. Jones from the same city. The one asks the other to describe the Mr. Jones he knows. "He is a very loving person. He goes out of his way to befriend everyone he encounters. Not everyone responds with affection, and in fact some make it clear they don't want to be his friend. But Mr. Jones continues to share his friendship with them nonetheless. He treats them with kindness and grace, even if they treat him shabbily. Not only that, but he doesn't throw his weight around. He is big and strong, and could manhandle anyone who dares challenge him. But one time when a ruffian came along and slugged him because he wanted to take his wallet, Mr. Jones smiled and said, 'Why didn't you ask?' and handed him all the money in his wallet."

The other fellow shook his head and said, "Well, the Mr. Jones I know is great to his friends and those who agree with his beliefs, showering them with favors. But he has nothing to do with those who don't agree with him or show him respect. And if anyone ever tries to challenge him or, God forbid, attack him or his things, the challenger gets roughed up pretty badly."

The two strangers agreed these were two *different* men with the same name, for they had different characters. So, too, I would say, Allah and the God of the Bible are different gods because their characters are different.[29] They might share the same title—God—but they are fundamentally different beings. One has unconditional love for all human beings; the other has conditional love for Muslims alone. One is a Father and shepherd and lover calling for a return of love; the other is a Lord demanding service from his slaves. One commands love for neighbors and even enemies, while the other does not command neighbor love and frowns on love for enemies. One shows power by force, and the other by weakness. One is numerically one without differentiation, while the other is three in one. In short, those who worship one are not worshiping the other because they are two different gods.

Now, as I mentioned above, there is only one God, and he is the triune God of Christian orthodoxy. If Muslims intend to worship the

---

29. I use lowercase "god," because at this point in my argument I am speaking historically of two rivals for the claim of true God. When I speak normatively of which God is true, I use uppercase "God."

only Creator and Redeemer who exists, in that sense we have to say that they are intending to worship the only true God. But as we have just seen, the god of the Qur'an is a different kind of God. And the danger is that because the religions are not simply human projections but also spiritual projects animated by what Paul regarded as principalities and powers, they are seeking communion not with the true God but with a dark imitation.[30]

Does this possibility—that Islam and other religions are animated by dark powers—impugn the (relative) virtue and goodness we see in our Muslim friends? No. Paul saw that pagans without the Law can live virtuous lives (Rom. 2:14–15), but at the same time, he warned that their pagan cults might be inspired by dark forces (1 Cor. 10:20–22). Now, the comparison is not precise because Muslims are not pagans, since they are monotheists who recognize the God of Abraham. And there are very different kinds of Islam, so that Islamism that inspires terrorism and Sufism that generally decries religious violence are two drastically diverse religions.

Yet Christianity itself as a historical and worldwide movement has had plenty of its own demonic distortions. This was all the more reason why even in the first decades of the church, Paul, faced with comparable religious diversity and demonic forces at work within the church (2 Cor. 11:13–15), judged that religious rivals to the church of the Jewish messiah were diverse mixtures that might be inspired by cosmic powers.

What about the Jewish God?

If Christians do not worship the same god as Muslims, what about Christians and Jews? Many would deny that they worship the same god. After all, they think, Jesus came to start a new religion called Christianity and to dispense with Judaism. So did Paul. Both Jesus and Paul showed that Judaism was a religion of works while Christianity is a religion of grace. Both proclaimed that their followers are no longer under Jewish law, or any religious law, for that matter.

Furthermore, it is commonly held, Jesus taught that God transferred his covenant from Jewish Israel to the (mostly) gentile church of Jesus followers. Nothing could be more different from the Jewish

---

30. See Rom. 8:38; 1 Cor. 10:20–22; Eph. 6:12; Col. 2:15. See also chapter 4 in McDermott, *God's Rivals*.

idea of God—with only one divine person—than the Christian Trinity. Nor could the Christian idea of incarnation be more opposed to Jewish convictions that God would never inhabit flesh.

Resurrection is another concept that distinguishes Christian faith from Jewish faith. Today's Jews, it is said, reject the idea that Jesus rose from the dead, and have only a hazy idea of a general resurrection of souls at the end of time.

For these reasons, many Christians believe, it is ludicrous to imagine that Jews and Christians worship the same God.

Jesus and Judaism

There is only one catch to this powerful argument: none of its assertions are true. Let's take the first assertion, that Jesus came to start a new religion and put an end to the Judaism of his day. Jesus said something quite different in his Sermon on the Mount:

> Do not think that I have come to do away with the Law or the Prophets. I have not come to do away with them but to fulfill them. For I say to you in truth, until the heaven and the earth pass away, not one iota [the smallest letter in the Greek alphabet] or one horn [the smallest stroke of the pen in Hebrew] will pass away from the Law, until all things [in it] come to pass. Whoever annuls one of the least of these commandments and teaches men [to do] the same, will be called least in the kingdom of the heavens. But the one who practices [them] and teaches [them], he will be called great in the kingdom of the heavens. (Matt. 5:17–19)

Many Christians don't stop to realize that Jesus is talking about the Old Testament here, and Torah (the first five books) especially. He insists that its "least" commandment is to be kept and taught. Presumably this means the commandments that Christians today consider unimportant, such as Sabbath-keeping, circumcision, and kosher rules. These represent the distinctive marks of first-century Judaism, the Judaism that many Christians think Jesus was telling his disciples to abandon. But this passage from the Sermon on the Mount suggests quite the opposite. While there is no hint that the "least" commands are the most important, as some Pharisees might have believed, Jesus stated clearly that even the commands of Torah that we think of as particularly "Jewish" are not to be abandoned: *"Do not think that I have come to do away with the Law. . . . Whoever annuls one of the least of these commandments . . . will be called least in the kingdom of the heavens."*

Most readers of the previous paragraph will ask, "But didn't Jesus show that he was abandoning Jewish law by telling his disciples that they could pluck grain on the Sabbath? And didn't he proclaim that he was lord of the Sabbath" (Mark 2:23–28)? When he spoke with authority, without invoking the rabbis, wasn't that a signal that he was dispensing with religion based on Torah and setting up a new religion with his own words as a new law?

For centuries that was how Christians interpreted Jesus. But after the Holocaust, scholars started to ask what they had missed. How could the most Christianized country in history—Germany, the birthplace of the Reformation—have reached the point where it permitted a regime to destroy six million Jews? Starting with W. D. Davies, Krister Stendahl, and E. P. Sanders, and then later scholars such as Mark Nanos, Mark Kinzer, Scot McKnight, and Marcus Bockmuehl, Christians began to see that Jesus was far more Jewish than previous generations had imagined.[31] Specifically, they concluded that Jesus was Torah observant. He suggested new interpretations of Torah, pressing to its inner meaning, but he never advocated its abolition.

For example, they argued, Jesus endorsed sacrifices and offerings to the temple. He praised the offering of the poor widow at the temple (Mark 12:41–44), assumed that his disciples would bring their gifts for sacrifice to the altar of burnt offering at the temple ("If you are bringing your gift to the altar and there remember . . ." [Matt. 5:23]), and told the healed leper to be purified by offering a gift for sacrifice (Matt. 8:4; Mark 1:44; Luke 5:14). All of these sacrifices and offerings were

---

31. W. D. Davies, *The Gospel and the Land: Early Christianity and Jewish Territorial Doctrine* (Berkeley: University of California Press, 1974); Krister Stendahl, "The Apostle Paul and the Introspective Conscience of the West," *Harvard Theological Review* 56, no. 3 (July 1963): 199–215; Krister Stendahl, *Paul among Jews and Gentiles and Other Essays* (London: SCM, 1977); E. P. Sanders, *Jesus and Judaism* (Philadelphia: Fortress, 1985); Mark Nanos, *The Mystery of Romans: The Jewish Context of Paul's Letter* (Minneapolis: Fortress, 1996); Mark Kinzer, *Postmissionary Messianic Judaism: Redefining Christian Engagement with the Jewish People* (Grand Rapids: Brazos, 2005); Scot McKnight, *A New Vision for Israel: The Teachings of Jesus in National Context* (Grand Rapids: Eerdmans, 1999); Markus Bockmuehl, *Jewish Law in Gentile Churches: Halakhah and the Beginning of Christian Public Ethics* (Grand Rapids: Baker Academic, 2000).

stipulated in the book of Leviticus. After his death and resurrection, his disciples continued to go to the temple and participate in its liturgies and sacrifices (Acts 2:46; 21:26).

While Jesus taught that the future temple would be his body, he also showed respect for the existing temple. He referred to it as "my house," suggesting that he was jealous over the way it was being run by its priests (Matt. 21:12–13). He said God "dwells in" it (Matt. 23:21), and in Luke 20 retold the parable of the vineyard from Isaiah 5 in a way that challenged its priests (the tenants) rather than the vineyard itself (the temple).

Luke told us that Jesus's parents visited the temple every year for Passover, and showed the parents of Jesus's cousin praying at the temple during the time for incense offering, when faithful Jews normally did so (Luke 1:10).

But it wasn't only the temple that Jesus treated with a reverence similar to that of his Jewish contemporaries. Jesus also seemed to observe Jewish purity laws. He warned against walking over unmarked graves (Luke 11:44) and giving dogs what is holy (Matt. 7:6). He bade unclean spirits to enter pigs that plunged into the sea (Mark 5:1–13). We have already seen that he approved of the need for priestly purification after cleansing from leprosy. He also saw camels and gnats as unclean (Matt. 23:24). He was not always at ease with gentiles and Samaritans (Matt. 10:5; 18:17; Mark 7:26–27), even if he transcended traditional boundaries with those communities.[32] Therefore, he did not abolish the distinction between clean and unclean.

While Jesus admonished his followers not to do what the Pharisees did, he urged his disciples to "practice and protect" *(poiēsate kai tēreite)* their teachings (Matt. 23:3). This last command is a significant signal to Jesus's identification with the Jewish religion of his day, and it is missed by most Christian readers of the New Testament. The Pharisees' teachings included not only purity rules but also things like tithing and tassels. Jesus taught tithing (Matt. 23:23) and wore tassels on his prayer

---

32. This paragraph reiterates what I wrote in "Covenant, Mission, and Relating to the Other," in *Covenant and Hope: Christian and Jewish Reflections*, ed. Robert Jenson and Eugene Korn (Grand Rapids: Eerdmans, 2012), 23–24. This differentiated treatment of gentiles and Samaritans might have reflected the hierarchy of loves that Thomas Aquinas described (email from Gavin D'Costa, March 16, 2018), but it also reflected traditional Jewish distinctions.

shawl. When the Gospels mention the "fringe" of his garment that was touched by both the sick in Gennesaret and the woman who had hemorrhaged for twelve years, they use the same Greek root—κρασπέδ—that is used for the fringes the Pharisees wore and the tassels God commanded his people to wear in the Septuagint (Matt. 9:20; 14:36; 23:5; Num. 15:37–39).

So what about the Sabbath? The rabbinic tradition held that the purpose of the Sabbath was life, and so it was permissible to pluck grain on the Sabbath if you were famished.[33] Matthew's version of this story says exactly that—the disciples were hungry (12:1). So Jesus was in accord with Jewish tradition—not opposed to it—when he permitted his disciples to pluck grain on a Sabbath when they seem to have needed strength. Besides, Jesus appealed to the Jewish Bible and its depiction of David—the greatest of Jewish kings—to defend himself against critics: "Have you not read what David did when he was hungry . . . how he entered the house of God and ate the bread of the Presence, which it was unlawful for him to eat?" (Matt. 12:3–4). Here Jesus was invoking a rabbinic rule, that it is justifiable to break one of the lesser commandments in the law in order to fulfill a greater commandment.[34] This is why Jesus referred to the "weightier things of the law" (Matt. 23:23).

In sum, Jesus was not rejecting the Judaism of his day but illustrating its inner meaning. Therefore the Gospels do not support the notion that Christians worshiping Jesus as the Son of God are worshiping a God different from the God of biblical Judaism.

Paul and Judaism

But what about Paul?[35] Scholars have come to similar conclusions about Paul, though admittedly it is trickier for the apostle to the gentiles. There is tension, for example, between Paul's treatment of law in Galatians, where he is "almost stridently negative," and in Romans, where law is "good in and of itself but does not provide a sufficient solution to

---

33. Mishnah *Yoma* 8:6. Although this is late first century AD, Babylonian Talmud *Yoma* 35b (Baraita) attributes the principle to rabbis in the first century BC. See Bockmuehl, *Jewish Law in Gentile Churches*, 7.

34. Bockmuehl, *Jewish Law in Gentile Churches*, 6–8.

35. This next section is an adaptation of an excerpt from *Israel Matters: Why Christians Must Think Differently about the People and the Land* by Gerald McDermott, copyright © 2017. Used by permission of Brazos, a division of Baker Publishing Group.

the problems occasioned by the fall." Yet when the two letters are read together, Romans seems to "subsume the more pointedly negative construal of Galatians into a larger synthetic whole."[36]

Let me flesh this out a bit. Paul said that "every man who lets himself be circumcised is obligated to obey the entire law" (Gal. 5:3). Granted, he also said that he was "not under the law" (1 Cor. 9:20), but Bockmuehl and New Testament scholar Mark Kinzer suggest that by this Paul meant that he was not like Jews who lived in strict separation from gentiles. He was for bringing together Jews and gentiles now that the messianic era had begun. So Paul was "within" the Law (*ennomos*) but not "under the Law" (*hupo nomon*). Nor is he "outside the law" (*anomos*). All of these phrases are used by Paul in 1 Corinthians 9: "To those *under the law* I became as one *under the law*... so that I might win those *under the law*. To those outside the law I became as one outside the law (*though I am not outside the law* but *within the law of Messiah*), so that I might win those outside the law" (vv. 20–21).

The point is that while Paul did not take the narrowly ethnic approach to the Law that the most conservative Pharisees took, he could adapt to it if it helped win some of them to the Messiah. So he could be flexible in his approach to the Law but was never free from it. Nor did he want to be. There is no evidence that Paul ever broke basic Jewish rules for living by the Law, say, by eating nonkosher food or profaning the Sabbath or Jewish holy days.[37]

You might ask, then, what Paul meant by Galatians 3:10–14, where he said Christ "redeemed us from the curse of the law by becoming a curse for us" (v. 13). The best thing to remember first is that this is the same Paul who said, "The law is holy, and the commandment is holy and righteous and good" (Rom. 7:12), and that faith in Christ does not "overthrow the law," but in fact "we uphold the law" (Rom. 3:31). So it makes no sense to think, as many Christians have thought, that for Paul the law itself was the curse.

Michael Wyschogrod was a Jewish theologian who understood Paul's rabbinic context. He wrote that in the rabbinical framework, God

---

36. Gary Anderson, review of *The Church's Guide for Reading Paul*, by Brevard Childs, *First Things* 194 (June/July 2009): 46.

37. Kinzer, *Postmissionary Messianic Judaism*, 88. See David J. Rudolph, *A Jew to the Jews: Jewish Contours of Pauline Flexibility in 1 Corinthians 9:19–23* (Tübingen: Mohr-Siebeck, 2010).

is both law and mercy, but there is no way of knowing which aspect of God's character will predominate—the curse that is attached to disobedience to Torah or the mercy that tempers God's justice. "Jewish existence is thus a very insecure one." But for Paul, Jesus on the cross was the "lightning rod which drew all punishment to itself, thereby protecting all others." So the curse of the law is the *punishment* that comes from disobeying the law, which itself is holy and good.[38]

The Princeton historian John G. Gager contends that Galatians has been misunderstood because its audience has been misunderstood. In reality, he says, Paul was addressing only gentiles in this letter, and his purpose was to explain the relation of law to gentiles—which for Paul means none at all. "The Gentiles [in Galatia were] . . . being pressured by other apostles, within the Jesus-movement, to take on circumcision and a selective observance of the law." So Paul explained that "the law was never the intended path for Gentiles." Gager reasons that Galatians is addressed only to gentiles because "the descriptions of the circumstances of the Galatians before Christ can only apply to gentiles: 'we were slaves to the elemental spirits of the universe' (v. 3); 'you did not know God' (v. 8); and 'you were in bondage to beings that by nature are no gods' (v. 8)." Even the phrase "those who were under the law" refers to gentiles, for it "is not a characteristic phrase in Jewish texts for describing the relationship of the law and Jews." So the Paul of Galatians can be reconciled with the Paul of Romans. Galatians tells gentiles the law is not for them, while Romans insists the law for Jews is "holy and just and good" (7:12). The two are compatible because the legal and ceremonial rules of the Pentateuch (Torah) are for Jews not gentiles.[39]

There are many other signs that Paul respected the Law: he circumcised Timothy, made and kept a Nazirite vow, and participated in another Nazirite vow (Acts 16:1–3; 18:18; 21:21–24). In the last vow, Paul proved to "James and all the elders" of the Jerusalem church, who seemed pleased that "tens of thousands among the Jews [who] have believed" were "zealous for the law," that he himself was "liv[ing] in observance of the law" (Acts 21:18, 20, 24). Luke went out of his way in

38. Michael Wyschogrod, *Abraham's Promise: Judaism and Jewish-Christian Relations*, ed. R. Kendall Soulen (Grand Rapids: Eerdmans, 2004), 196–97. See also Hillary LeCornu and Joseph Schulam, *A Commentary on the Jewish Roots of Galatians* (Jerusalem: Academon, 2005).

39. John G. Gager, *Reinventing Paul* (New York: Oxford University Press, 2000), 86, 89, 91.

this story to show that Paul was *not* "teach[ing] all the Jews among the Gentiles to forsake Moses, telling them not to circumcise their children or walk according to our customs" (21:21). By "our customs" Paul surely meant eating kosher, Sabbath-keeping, and circumcision—and probably other Jewish-specific customs. In Romans Paul claimed that God's purpose in sending Jesus was that his disciples would fulfill "the righteous requirement of the Law" (Rom. 8:4).

In one respect, Paul was even more Jewish than Jesus: he took a more positive approach to Pharisees than we see in the Gospels. He proudly presented himself as a Pharisee (Acts 23:6), and Luke reports that Pharisees came to his defense (Acts 23:9). Throughout Acts 21–26, Paul "affirms his identity as a Torah-observant Jew, indeed, a Pharisee, and one not guilty of breaching the Torah or desecrating the Temple."[40] The great Catholic Bible scholar Raymond Brown speculated that if Paul had had a son, he would have circumcised him. Michael Wyschogrod wondered, "Could it be that Paul was, after all, an Orthodox Jew?"[41]

According to Mark Nanos, Paul "affirmed Torah unambiguously." His differences with his fellow Jews were not over Torah observance, but over who Jesus was: "The differences in Paul's time [between the Judaism of Paul and that of other Jews] did not turn around the traditional derogatory views of Torah, or reactions to those views. . . . They turned instead around the meaning of Christ for the people of Israel . . . and the rest of the nations."[42] Perhaps the real question for Jews and Christians is not whether Jesus or Paul accepted the continuing validity of the law—for there is mounting evidence that they did—but whether Jesus was, as Jewish theologian Irving Greenberg has put it, "a would-be redeemer for the nations."[43]

---

40. Mark Nanos, "The Myth of the 'Law-Free' Paul Standing between Christians and Jews," (paper, December 10, 2008), 6, www.marknanos.com/Myth-Lawfree-12-3-08.pdf. See also Nanos, "Paul and the Jewish Tradition: The Ideology of the Shema," in *Celebrating Paul: Festschrift in Honor of Jerome Murphy-O'Conner, O.P. and Joseph A. Fitzmyer, S.J.*, ed. Peter Spitaler, *Catholic Biblical Quarterly Monograph* (Washington, DC: Catholic Biblical Association of America, 2012); Nanos, "Rethinking the 'Paul *and* Judaism' Paradigm: Why Not 'Paul's Judaism'?" (paper, May 28, 2008), www.marknanos.com/Paul%27sJudaism-5-28-08.pdf.

41. Wyschogrod, *Abraham's Promise*, 232, 234.

42. Nanos, "Myth," 2, 6. See also Daniel R. Langton, "The Myth of the 'Traditional View of Paul' and the Role of the Apostle in Modern Jewish-Christian Polemics," *Journal for the Study of the New Testament* 28, no. 1 (2005): 69–104.

43. Irving Greenberg, *For the Sake of Heaven and Earth: The New Encounter between Judaism and Christianity* (Philadelphia: Jewish Publication Society, 2004), 229.

Was Christianity a New Religion?

So we return to the question: Did Jesus and Paul start a new religion, which would suggest that Christians and Jews worship different gods?

As I suggested above, Christians have had various reasons for saying yes to this question. One of the most important, and perhaps the one most widely used, has been the matter of Torah, the Jewish Law. Jesus set aside Torah, it has been said, and Paul said Torah is no longer binding, for Messiah Jesus has become the new Torah. Only his words, and the words of his inspired followers who wrote the New Testament, are binding on Christians anymore.

But what if it turns out that Jesus had no intention of setting aside Torah but saw himself as teaching and embodying the inner meaning of the Law? So that Torah was still binding for his Jewish followers and important in a different sense for his gentile followers but now seen with fresh clarity through his words and actions?

And what if it turns out that Paul was Torah observant, contrary to what most Christians have believed? That he, too, saw the Law as binding on Jews in all of its commandments, and a source of teaching—if not detailed observance—for gentile followers of Jesus? For example, that while kosher rules would not apply to gentiles, they would teach gratitude for food and the need to obey our Lord even when we don't understand all of his commandments?

If these things are true, then the principal rationale for the "Jesus and Paul aiming to start a new religion" thesis dissolves. Of course Judaism and Christianity *have* evolved into quite different religions. Today they are distinct. But Jesus and Paul did not have it in their minds to start a new religion. Jesus came to show his fellow Jews the fulfillment of their Law (himself!), and Paul brought this message to the gentiles so that they could be adopted into the Messiah's Abrahamic family.

There still remain, however, several important objections I articulated at the beginning of this section. For example, grace versus works. Didn't Jesus come to show a works-obsessed Jewish people that their relationship to God was not caused by their works? And wasn't Jesus trying to teach them that they could have a *personal* relationship to the God of Israel instead of standing at a distance at the foot of Mount Sinai, cowering in fear?

Christians have been saying this sort of thing to Jews and their rabbis for centuries. And rabbis have been responding in several ways for those same centuries. "Our relationship to God based on works? Don't you know," they have asked in return, "that we take a little baby boy at eight days and circumcise him, proclaiming to ourselves and the world that something cosmic has just happened: that this little boy has been brought into God's covenant family called Israel, and his destiny has been forever changed? Do we think this little baby has done anything to deserve this cosmic privilege? Of course not! He has been given a free gift from God—the very notion that you Christians call grace.

"And what do you think we believe is the reason for God's choice of Israel? It had something to do with the merit of our patriarchs Abraham, Isaac, and Jacob, as Torah suggests in Deuteronomy 10:15. But all of us—their descendants—are included by a divine gift, another act of grace that did not depend on our works.

"So we believe that we first enter the covenant by a gift—by grace. We also believe that if we are to *remain* in the covenant, we must keep observing God's law, which we regard not as a burden but as a wonderful gift given to us by our loving Father who wants us to have an abundant life: 'You shall walk in all the way that YHWH your God has commanded you, in order that you might live and things might go well for you, and that you might live long in the land which you possess' (Deut. 5:33). This is why the psalmist exclaimed, 'Oh [Lord]. How I love your Law!' (Ps 119:97).

"Here is where many Christians think we depart from their view of a God of grace. They think we have introduced a foreign idea—that to remain in God's covenant we must keep His commandments. But didn't your founder, Jesus, say something very similar—'If you want to *stay* in my love, keep my commandments' (John 15:10)?

"You also claim that we Jews know nothing of personal relationship with the God of Israel. If you think that, you must not know that our prayer book, which we use every day, draws from the Psalms throughout. The Psalms are living illustrations of the personal relationship that David and other psalmists had with God. We pray the Psalms as *our* prayers, to the God who loves Israel and speaks to Israel's people as His beloved sons and daughters."

Let's recapitulate the argument so far. I have tried to show that Jesus and Paul did not think they were starting a new religion to replace the

Judaism they grew up with. They did indeed teach that the Messiah had finally come in Jesus, and that for that reason the Judaism of the first century had reached an epochal moment when the greatest promises had begun to be *fulfilled*. Judaism was finding its inner meaning and great climax because the perfect Israelite had appeared as the embodiment of the Law and of Israel herself. But this does not mean that Judaism was being replaced by another religion of a fundamentally different character. It means instead that the God of Israel was bringing the people of Israel to their promised apogee when their messiah was revealed as the Son of God, the meaning of all they had ever known. Rather than opposing Jewish law, Jesus and Paul observed it, even as they testified that Jesus was its living embodiment.

Some readers will raise a few more obstacles at this point: incarnation, resurrection, and Trinity. Don't these fundamentally Christian concepts prove the incompatibility of the Jewish and Christian conceptions of God? In other words, the Christian God is incarnate, and the Jewish God is not; the Christian God rose from the dead, and the Jewish God seems unconcerned with resurrection; the Christian God is triune, while the Jewish God is unitary.

Incarnation

Let me suggest that things are not as simple as these statements imply. First, the idea of incarnation is not foreign to Judaism. The Old Testament speaks of God dwelling in his people, and the Talmud—which is the highest authority for the Jewish tradition—speaks of the same.[44] A noted Jewish philosopher/theologian has written at length about God dwelling in the people of Israel. Michael Wyschogrod has argued for "the indwelling of God in Israel," and has added that while Christians disagree with Jews on the location of the highest degree of incarnation, their difference is more quantitative that qualitative. He says that Christians take the concept of incarnation, which is Jewish, and "see the intensification of that indwelling in one Jew." The point is that while Jews reject the idea that Jesus is the incarnation of God, the *idea* of incarnation is a Jewish idea.[45]

---

44. Of course, Tanakh also speaks of God dwelling in the temple, as does Jesus (Matt. 23:21).

45. Wyschogrod, *Abraham's Promise*, 178.

Benjamin Sommer, professor of Bible and ancient Semitic languages at Jewish Theological Seminary, has written recently that "divine embodiment, paradoxically, emerges . . . as far more important to Judaism than to Christianity."[46] By embodiment Sommer means a "mysterious fluidity and multiplicity" by which the God of the Hebrew Bible takes on different bodily forms. For example, he comes down from heaven to earth to take a look at the tower human beings are building (Gen. 11:5), takes a stroll in the garden of Eden (Gen. 3:8), and walks to Abraham's tent and converses with him (Gen. 18). The prophet Amos says he "saw God standing at the altar" (Amos 9:1), and Moses spoke with God face-to-face, "as a man speaks with his friend" (Exod. 33:11). According to Sommer, Christianity was not doing anything radically new when it proclaimed that God took bodily form in the incarnation. "Biblical Israel knew very similar doctrines, and these doctrines did not disappear from Judaism after the biblical period" but continued through the eras of the Talmuds.[47]

Resurrection

Neither is resurrection a uniquely Christian doctrine. In fact, it is Christian *because* it is Jewish. The early church was able to accept Jesus's resurrection because its founders were readers of the Hebrew Bible and disciples in rabbinic schools where resurrection was a staple of Jewish eschatology. Jon D. Levenson, professor of Jewish studies at Harvard Divinity School, has argued that resurrection is integral to the Hebrew scriptures and "was a weight-bearing beam in the edifice of rabbinic Judaism."[48]

Trinity

What about the Trinity? Isn't that an insuperable difficulty for anyone trying to claim that the God of Jews and the God of Christians is the same? How can a God of three-in-one be the same as the God of those who protest that God is one and not three?

---

46. Benjamin D. Sommer, *The Bodies of God and the World of Ancient Israel* (Cambridge: Cambridge University Press, 2009), 10.

47. Sommer, *The Bodies of God and the World of Ancient Israel*, 135, 8.

48. Jon D. Levenson, *Resurrection and the Restoration of Israel: The Ultimate Victory of the God of Life* (New Haven, CT: Yale University Press, 2006).

The answer is that there was a substantial Jewish tradition that God's oneness is a differentiated oneness, a complex oneness rather than a mathematical oneness.[49] The most important reason for this tradition is the Hebrew Bible itself. In Genesis 1 we read of "God" and "the Spirit of God" (vv. 1, 2). There is no suggestion in the text that these are two gods, but somehow the Spirit of God is distinct and yet also God. Throughout the Hebrew Bible, we read about "God" and "the Word of God." For example, in 1 Samuel we read that "the word of the Lord was rare in those days" but that it came on a regular basis to Samuel (1 Sam. 3:1; 15:10). In all those instances the implication is that God is one, and yet somehow the Word is a distinct manifestation of God. Then in Proverbs 8 we are introduced to the "Wisdom" of God in such a way that Wisdom is both distinct from God and God itself. In all these cases, God's oneness is mysteriously complexified, as if there is an inner differentiation that does not compromise God's unity. God is still one, but within that oneness there are distinctions. This biblical phenomenon led generations of Jewish rabbis to speculate on the complexity involved in God's being.

For example, according to Jewish historian Daniel Boyarin, there was a "widely held [belief] by Jews in the pre-Christian era" of "a second divine entity, God's Word (Logos) or God's Wisdom, who mediates between the fully transcendent Godhead and the material world."[50] Therefore it was not a quantum leap that the early Jewish church had to make when it pondered how God could be one, and yet the Son of God could also be God, and then a third entity, the Holy Spirit, could be God too. The Jewish minds that wrote the New Testament could write in these ways because their Jewish tradition already held to

---

49. After reporting Justin Martyr's identification of Christ with the author of Tanakh, Daniel Boyarin writes, "Let me emphasize that not only Jewish thought is at work here, but Jewish hermeneutical practices as well: the association of the creative Word of *Bere'sit* with the Wisdom companion/agent of God from Proverbs. . . . It follows, then, that in Logos theology both John and Justin represent old, common Judaic patterns of religious thought and midrashic practice." Daniel Boyarin, *Border Lines: The Partition of Judaeo-Christianity* (Philadelphia: University of Pennsylvania Press, 2004), 106. For the tip of the iceberg of scholarship on differentiated oneness in Jewish thought, start with Erwin Goodenough, *The Theology of Justin Martyr: An Investigation into the Conceptions of Early Christian Literature and Its Hellenistic and Judaistic Influences* (Amsterdam: Philo, 1968); Jarl Fossum, *The Name of God and the Angel of the Lord: Samaritan and Jewish Conceptions of Intermediation and the Origin of Gnosticism* (Tübingen: Mohr-Siebeck, 1985); Alan F. Segal, *Two Powers in Heaven: Early Rabbinic Reports about Christianity and Gnosticism* (Leiden: Brill, 1077).

50. Boyarin, *Border Lines*, 30–31, 112–37.

inner differentiation within God's oneness. The Christian Trinity that eventually emerged from this raw material in the New Testament was therefore in continuity with, not in fundamental opposition to, Jewish tradition. The God of Israel had *long* been known to be one being with internal differentiation. Hence the early church could claim that it was worshiping the God of Israel, but with new clarity about the identities within that differentiation. Arguably, the authors of the Gospels and Epistles believed themselves to be writing about the God of Israel, not some new God distinct from the God of Israel. They thought they were worshiping the same God as their non-messianic Jewish brothers and sisters were worshiping, but believed that they recognized new developments in the history of that God's redemption of his people. That changed their understanding of this God of Israel, but it did not convince them that they were worshiping a different God.

Paul's Maturest Thinking

What is the proof of these last claims of mine—that the writers of the New Testament believed they were worshiping the same God of Israel as their Jewish opponents were? The best proof is Paul's letter to the Roman church. Here we find Paul's maturest expression of his thought, written not too long before his death. It had been almost thirty years since his conversion to following *Yeshua* as *Mashiach*. Although tens of thousands of Jews in Jerusalem had "become believers," still a majority of Jews in that generation had not. Paul had "great pain and unceasing grief" over these brothers who resisted his message about Jesus (Rom. 9:2). Perhaps he felt some anger, for he called them "enemies in terms of the gospel" (Rom. 11:28). Yet at the same time they "are beloved because of the fathers" (v. 28). How could they still be beloved if they were resisting God's Son by refusing to accept Paul's proclamation that he was the Messiah whom God had promised? The reason, he added immediately, was that "the gifts and the calling of God are irrevocable" (v. 29). God gave them "the adoption, the glory, the covenants, the giving of the law, the worship, and the promises" (Rom. 9:4), and he was not going to take any of them back. God does not do that, Paul kept insisting throughout his letters. He is faithful to his promises. He promised to take the Jewish offspring of Abraham as his people, and he was not revoking that promise even if the majority of them refused his own Son, the Messiah. They were still his people; they were still in covenant with him.

There is much to be said about these pregnant and remarkable statements, but the most important one for us is plain: Paul clearly regarded the God of the non-messianic Jews to be the same as his God. It was the God of Israel who called the Jewish people into covenant with him, and this God continued to love the Jewish people who refused his Messiah. He was not a new or different God. This same God had sent upon the majority of Israel a "partial hardening" (Rom. 11:25) so that they would *not* see that Jesus was their Messiah, and this was "for your sake," that is, for the sake of the gentiles (probably the majority in the church at Rome). The rabbis had taught that when the Messiah came, all of Israel would accept him and this age would come to an end.[51] Paul seems to have believed this, and so suggests here that God purposely blinded the majority of Israel so that space and time could be opened to bring in millions, perhaps billions, of gentiles in later centuries.

Whether my take on the reasoning behind the "for your sake" (Rom. 11:28) is correct, it is nevertheless manifestly evident that Paul believed his non-messianic Jewish brothers were still in covenant with the God of Israel. They were worshiping the same God he was worshiping, but he saw God's designs and Son in ways that they did not. These were not two different Gods, but different portions of Israel in different states of perception and obedience. This division was nothing new in the history of Israel, which for long periods of biblical history saw distinction between a majority that claimed the God of Israel and a faithful remnant. Paul referred to this distinction in Romans 9:6: "Not all who are from Israel are of Israel." But despite that fearful distinction, Paul made clear that the God of Israel remains in covenant with that part of Israel that does not recognize Jesus. They are still "beloved" to him. In some mysterious way, he is still their God. They worship the God Paul worshiped.

---

51. For example, the early (probably second-century AD) rabbinic text *Seder Olam* predicts that "first will come the messiah, then this world will come to an end, and finally the world to come will be inaugurated." Although this is from the second century, it probably reflects first-century thinking as well. Chaim Milikowsky, "Trajectories of Return, Restoration and Redemption in Rabbinic Judaism: Elijah, the Messiah, The War of God and the World to Come," in *Restoration: Old Testament, Jewish, and Christian Perspective*, ed. James M. Scott (Leiden: Brill, 2001), 271.

In sum, Jews do not differ substantially (while differing materially) from Christian on all the matters often taken to be matters of substantial difference: law, grace, works, incarnation, resurrection, divine unity with internal distinctions. They do differ on Trinity and the identity of Jesus. They would agree with Paul that "Messiah crucified" is a "scandal" to Jews (1 Cor. 1:23). Yet Paul regarded even those Jews who differed on Jesus but worshiped the God of Israel as having zeal for the same God but "without knowledge" (Rom. 10: 2). They needed to hear and receive the gospel (Rom 1:16), but they were worshiping the same God.

While the God of Israel is the Father of Jesus Christ and shares the same being and character as Jesus, Allah does not. YHWH forgives and saves through sacrifice as prescribed by Torah, and then through the perfect Sacrifice that was foreshadowed in the sacrifices of Torah. He shows in both Testaments that his people should forgive and love their enemies. He is Father to his people, love in his essence. This is true of the God revealed in both Testaments. None of this character can be found in Allah. While Christians and Jews share all (for Jews) or the vast majority (for Christians) of their scriptures, Christians and Muslims share none. For all these reasons, we must say that Christians do not worship the same God designated by Allah, but that Christians worship the same God as those Jews who regard the Old Testament as the Word of God.

WM. ANDREW SCHWARTZ AND JOHN B. COBB JR.

For Gerald McDermott, the question about whether Jews, Muslims, and Christians worship the same God is settled by whether they have the same teaching about God. If there are any major differences, then the "God" of the differing traditions cannot be the same. We think this is not the right way to decide.

Conceptuality vs. Actuality

There is an important difference between worshiping an idea of God (conceptions and descriptions) and worshiping the being of God (ontological actuality). That the two are not one and the same is implied by McDermott yet largely unexplored. McDermott admits that at one level we should certainly say that Muslims and Christians worship the same God, "because as monotheists we all agree there is only one God. Ontologically there can be only one eternal creator God" (p. 114). But this implied distinction between conceptuality and actuality, or what others in this volume have described as the difference between sense and reference, seems to undermine McDermott's conclusion that different teachings about God entail that what they teach about are different Gods.

Who or what is God? An idea? A summation of descriptions found in sacred texts? If God is understood as actually existing (as theists contend), then God must be more than a mere idea or concept. The ontological status of a *real* God is no minor matter. As Shakespeare wrote, "What's in a name? That which we call a rose by any other name would smell as sweet." Effectively, what Shakespeare was saying is that our names, our words, our descriptions of reality do not alter reality as such. The rose smells sweet regardless of what we say about it. Likewise, McDermott's admission that ontologically Muslims and Christians worship the same God seems to render his additional arguments about divergent descriptions irrelevant. God is God. No matter what we say or believe about God, the ontological reality remains. The distinction between conceptuality and actuality means that a difference in teachings about God is insufficient to conclude that Muslims and Christians worship different Gods.

McDermott continues his defense with an analogy of two strangers having a conversation about "Mr. Jones." As he explains, the contrasting descriptions of Mr. Jones leads the conversing strangers to conclude that they are speaking about two different men with the same name. We have made clear that we agree that two communities may be referring with the same word to different realities. For example, if one describes God as a compassionate divine person, and the other insists that God has no form and no feelings, we would judge that their references may

well be different. On the other hand, even quite different descriptions may not entail different references.

Imagine a scenario where McDermott's two strangers finish talking about Mr. Jones and begin talking about the figure shown here. One describes the figure as the profile of two faces looking at each other. The other describes it as a white vase. Faces are very different than vases. Does this mean the strangers are talking about different images? Certainly not. There is a single image capable of being viewed in more than one way. *So, why is it that conflicting descriptions of Mr. Jones suggests two different people, while conflicting descriptions of the face/vase figure refer to a single image?* Reality. In the case of Mr. Jones, there are actually two different people with the same name. In the case of the ambiguous image, there is actually a single image described in different ways.

However, such complexities are not relevant to the question of the objects of devotion by Muslims and Christians. Here the commonality of teaching is far more striking than the differences. The scriptures of both speak of a profoundly compassionate personal creative God.

Unless we suppose that the doctrine of the Trinity is about a different God, surely it does not entail a different object of worship from Islam. Of course, there are differences, just as there would be different statements about Mr. Jones even if they referred to the same person. The strangers might tell stories about very different things that Mr. Jones had done at different times in his life, for example. One might have found him easy going while the other found him formal and stiff. But if both also knew about some very distinctive things that Mr. Jones had done, that would make it hard to persuade them that they were speaking of different people. That the Qur'an and the Bible overlap extensively in this way can hardly be disputed.

The Importance of Difference

While McDermott argues that Muslims and Christians worship different Gods (because they have different teachings about God), he also affirms what most Christians have always affirmed: Jews and Christians worship the same God. By including the Hebrew scriptures in the Christian Bible, the church implies that it is speaking of the same God that Christians have come to know in Jesus Christ. Since McDermott thinks that differences in belief about God mean differences in what is worshiped, the only way in which he can assert this identity is to minimize the differences between Christians and Jews.

He has done a remarkable job. We can all profit from his careful study of the Jewishness of Jesus and Paul and the New Testament as a whole. There remains the difference that Jews did not join Christians in the belief that Jesus was the Messiah, but he agrees with us that a difference of that kind does not make the Christian God a different God from the one worshiped by Jews.

We celebrate our agreement on this point and thank him for his careful historical work. However, we think that his insistence on similarity has led him to underestimate the difference between Christians and Jews, especially with respect to the later doctrine of the Trinity. The New Testament teaching that we are to be baptized in the name of the Father, the Son, and the Holy Spirit can be understood in a way that does not violate Jewish categories of thought. But it will be harder to persuade Jews of the metaphysical Trinity of one substance and three persons, embodied in the later Christian creed. This creed is formulated in Greek philosophical terms that are alien to most Jews in order to make sense of the deification of Jesus, which is generally offensive to Jews. To us this in no way means that Christians have ceased to worship the God of Abraham but that our official beliefs are often interpreted in ways that are in great tension with the less qualified monotheism of Abraham and of Jews and Muslims. As process theologians we have problems with the philosophical idea of "substance" and believe that the biblical understanding of Father, Son, and Holy Spirit can today be formulated in ways that fit biblical thinking better than does the fourth century creed. The tension with Judaism can be reduced.

The insistence that diversity of teaching about God means that the teaching is about different Gods leads McDermott to judge that the Qur'an deals with a different God from the Christian one. Since there is, in fact, only one God, McDermott does not really mean that Muslims worship another God. He uses Paul's critique of the Greek gods to show that the lack of particular Christian teachings in the Qur'an means that their worship is not of the Christian God.

This is puzzling since Paul's critique is of Greek idolatry, and Islam is particularly strong in its avoidance of idolatry. McDermott seems to identify Islam with a form of paganism in his criticism, although he knows it is not a pagan tradition. He acknowledges that the emphasis on love that he finds missing in the Qur'an has become part of the Islamic faith, but he dismisses this as unimportant. Whereas Jewish rejection of the official Christian doctrine of the Trinity does not imply that theirs is a different God, a similar rejection by Islam does, apparently, have that implication.

Would it not be better to see all three traditions as intending to worship the God of Abraham? Already in the Hebrew scriptures there is diversity of understanding of God and of God's will for Israel and for humans generally. Christianity introduced changes that opened the doors to the gentiles, increased the influence of gentile traditions in the church, and generated far more diversity. The Qur'an grew out of the Hebrew teaching about God but also shaped it in a new way. It deeply honored Jesus, as Jews in general have not.

Christians may well think that both Jews and Muslims have failed to benefit from what Jesus revealed about God. We may think that this fuller revelation reshapes worship in crucial ways. But we still claim to worship the God of Abraham despite having many beliefs about God that were remote from Abraham's understanding. There is no reason to think that Muslims are worshiping a God other than the God of Abraham, although their beliefs like ours were certainly not all present in Abraham. That is their intention. Let us seek to understand Islam as it understands itself. We can then both recognize our disagreements about God and develop our agreements with it in the same spirit that animates McDermott's excellent work on Judaism.

Our view that the three Abrahamic traditions all worship the same God is based on the historical fact that they all claim to do so. All trace revelation of this God to the Hebrew tradition. Their teachings actually are remarkably similar. This does not mean that we think all the great spiritual traditions of the world emphasize the same God. They are not all paths up the same mountain. In our original chapter we noted that we see some as oriented to the cosmos or to this planet. Some are oriented to the metaphysical ultimate (Creativity or Being Itself). And some are oriented to the God that the three traditions here discussed trace to Abraham.

Among the Abrahamic traditions, Christianity has been most influenced by the idea of the metaphysical ultimate. This influence came to sharp focus in the work of the single most influential Christian theologian, Thomas Aquinas. He thought that God must be Ultimate Reality and the ground of all being. This led him to articulate and clarify the notion of *esse ipsum*. We translate this as Being Itself. Nothing can exist apart from participation in Being Itself. But Being Itself is not a being among other beings. Still, Thomas identifies the Supreme Being, the monotheistic God of Abraham, with Being Itself.

Many of the characteristics commonly attributed to God fit Being Itself much better than the Supreme Being or Person or Spirit. For example, Being Itself is indeed impassible and immutable, not affected by anything that happens. However, it is hard to fit these characteristics with the stories about God in the scriptures of the Abrahamic traditions.

The scriptures of the three traditions speak of God much more as the Supreme Being or Person. Many members of all these faiths insist that God is truly a Person or Spirit. Instead of describing the divine Person or Spirit as impassible, they speak of the perfect compassion of God—God feeling with the creatures in their joy and in their suffering. These Jews,

Christians, and Muslims worship the perfectly loving Supreme Person or Spirit rather than the impassible metaphysical ultimate. Some of them call the Supreme Person "God" and the metaphysical ultimate, the "Godhead."

Other Christians consider this belief, that God has the qualities of a Person, a misleading concession to popular piety. They hold that any language that attributes forms or qualities to Being Itself is, at best, symbolic and not literal. These understand their spirituality to be cultivating the relation to Being Itself or realizing that they are already instances of Being Itself. Worship in a typical sense is a less natural response to God as so understood than meditation.

We believe that the divine Person who encountered Abraham is a different reality from the metaphysical ultimate with which mystics and metaphysicians have been primarily concerned. We are glad that all the Abrahamic traditions are open to both features of reality, although we ourselves are more focused in our spirituality and worship on the scriptural Person or Spirit than the impersonal ultimate. A Whiteheadian metaphysic allows us to understand that Being Itself and the God of Abraham are both real, and that both are requisite for any world to exist. A possible formulation that provides a fresh way of understanding their relation is to note that although Being Itself has no form or quality, in its function in the world it is always characterized by the God of Abraham.

The point of the above is to show that we do not assume, automatically, that all spiritual traditions are oriented to the same God. Actually, most humans serve idols, as Paul noted about the Athenians. Today some people, even in our churches and despite Jesus's explicit warning, live more in the service of money than of God.

Even among those who are not idolatrous, there is devotion to different features of reality. In the language we favor, some are oriented to the natural universe, some to the philosophical ultimate, and some to the Supreme Person or Spirit. We are here focusing on the Abrahamic traditions. Abrahamic traditions cannot omit the Supreme Person or Spirit altogether even though they often attribute to God some of the characteristics that belong to Ultimate Reality.

If any of the Abrahamic faiths worships a different God from that of Abraham, it is Christianity. In what is often claimed to be its orthodox form, Christianity attributes to God characteristics, such as impassibility, that are not compatible with the compassion of the God of Abraham. Nevertheless, we believe the vast majority of Christianity is still shaped in its teachings and its worship more by the Bible than by the metaphysics some of its leaders have adopted. We hope that we can show that a better metaphysics also comes down in favor of worshiping the God of Abraham while welcoming mystics who explore the experience of attaining oneness with Being Itself.

FRANCIS J. BECKWITH

Gerry McDermott's essay is a model of clarity and rigor. He correctly notes and documents the differing beliefs that Christians, Muslims, and Jews have about God. When it comes to the question of whether Muslims and Christians worship the same God, he focuses on comparing the "God of the Bible" with the "God of the Qur'an." He concludes that Christians and Muslims do not worship the same God, for "Allah and the God of the Bible are different gods because their characters are different" (p. 116). When comparing Judaism with Christianity, McDermott concludes that they worship the same God because "Jews do not differ substantially (while differing materially) from Christians on all the matters often taken to be matters of substantial difference: law, grace, works, incarnation, resurrection, divine unity with internal distinctions" (p. 132). Because McDermott and I do not disagree on the question of whether Jews and Christians worship the same God, my assessment of his chapter will focus exclusively on his claim that Muslims and Christians do not worship the same God.

Islam, Christianity, and the Character of God

McDermott's central point is that the depictions of God's character in Islam and Christianity are so radically different that it should be obvious to anyone that each faith is not referring to the same God. He writes:

> One [the Christian God] is a Father and shepherd and lover calling for a return of love; the other [the Muslim God] is a Lord demanding service from his slaves. One commands love for neighbors and even enemies, while the other does not command

neighbor love and frowns on love for enemies. One shows power by force, and the other by weakness. One is numerically one without differentiation, while the other is three in one. In short, those who worship one are not worshipping the other because they are two different gods. (p. 116)

One difficulty with this approach is that there are places in the Christian Bible in which God does seem to instruct his followers to engage in heinous acts, including genocide, that do not appear to the casual reader to exhibit fatherly affection, weakness, or love of enemies. In recent years, this charge has been the staple of a small cadre of writers known as the New Atheists.[1] For this reason, one should be cautious in drawing such a stark contrast between the "God of the Bible" and the "God of the Qur'an" without first making the appropriate caveats and distinctions.[2]

Having said that, I do not think the character of God, as depicted in the Qur'an or the Bible, is decisive in answering the question of whether Muslims and Christians worship the same God. Take, for example, the encounter between Eve and the serpent in the book of Genesis, which I mention in my chapter. The serpent says to Eve: "'You will not die; for God knows that when you eat of [the fruit of the tree in the middle of the garden] your eyes will be opened, and you will be like God, knowing good and evil'" (Gen. 3:4–5). The serpent is, of course, lying. He is not only telling Eve something that God did not say, but he is also telling her something that is not consistent with God's character. In fact, her initial reply to the serpent's question (Gen. 3:1) indicates that she harbored doubts about his take on God's character: "The woman said to the serpent, 'We may eat of the fruit of the trees in the garden; but God said, "You shall not eat of the fruit of the tree that is in the middle of the garden, nor shall you touch it, or you shall die"'" (Gen. 3:2–3). And yet,

1. As Richard Dawkins puts it: "The God of the Old Testament is arguably the most unpleasant character in all fiction: jealous and proud of it; a petty, unjust, unforgiving control-freak; a vindictive, bloodthirsty ethnic cleanser; a misogynistic, homophobic, racist, infanticidal, genocidal, filicidal, pestilential, megalomaniacal, sadomasochistic, capriciously malevolent bully. Those of us schooled from infancy in his ways can become desensitized to their horror." Richard Dawkins, *The God Delusion* (London: Bantam, 2006), 31. Virtually all accounts of the New Atheists include Dawkins, the late Christopher Hitchens, Sam Harris, and Daniel Dennett.

2. See, for example, the response by two Christian scholars: Paul Copan and Matthew Flannagan, *Did God Really Command Genocide? Coming to Terms with the Justice of God* (Grand Rapids: Baker, 2014).

the serpent is not referring to "another God." He is referring to the same creator of the universe to which Eve refers.

Consider another example, one that both McDermott and I discuss in our chapters: St. Paul's encounter with his pagan audience while he preached on the Areopagus in Athens. Although McDermott is certainly correct that St. Paul exhibits nothing but contempt for the idol worshiping cults he sees throughout the city, the apostle carefully distinguishes between the "gods" of the idol worshipers and the one true God. As McDermott notes, St. Paul "had noticed an altar 'to an unknown god' and suggested to his hearers that they were thinking wrongly about God living in a temple and being served by human hands" (p. 110). This God, according to the apostle, is the sovereign providential creator of the universe on which all contingent existing things depend, "though indeed he is not far from each one of us. For 'In him we live and move and have our being'" (Acts 17:27–28). This appeal to natural theology—that one can know about the one true God without the benefit of special revelation—is consistent with what the apostle writes elsewhere: "For what can be known about God is plain to them, because God has shown it to them. Ever since the creation of the world his eternal power and divine nature, invisible though they are, have been understood and seen through the things he has made" (Rom. 1:19–20).

After identifying God, St. Paul goes on to share the gospel. But notice how he does it. He first establishes the correct reference to God and then explains how that God has appointed Christ to judge the world, and we know this is true because God raised Jesus from the dead (Acts 17:31). Contrast this with what occurred earlier in Acts 17 when St. Paul (accompanied by Silas) was trying to convince a Jewish audience of Christ's messiahship. In that encounter, there was no need for him to establish the right reference to God since that dispute was over whether Jesus is the Messiah promised in the Old Testament by the one true God, whose existence and reference was not contested between the two parties.

Let us suppose that some members of St. Paul's Athenian audience who leave unconvinced that Jesus is God's messiah nevertheless come to believe that the God described by St. Paul is in fact the one true God. It would seem perfectly correct to say that the members of this group believe in the same God as Christians and Jews do and at the same time reject the revelatory claims of both groups, including the belief that Jesus is God's Messiah, whom God raised from the dead. Now imagine that a member of this group of Athenian theists (ATs) comes to believe that this God has specially revealed to him that ATs ought to enslave, torture, and kill the followers of Jesus on the grounds that they mistakenly believe that God is triune. Their Christian victims could rightly say to them, "God would never command such a thing! It is not consistent with his character!" But so could have Eve, in response to the serpent, if she had not been so gullible. In both cases, each party is not referring to a different God; rather, one of the parties is wrong about the character of the God to whom they are both referring.

To illustrate his case, McDermott tells us the story of two strangers who claim to know a Mr. Jones from the same city. While sharing with the other what each knows about Mr. Jones from what they had culled from his beliefs and behavior, they come to the conclusion that the character of each "Mr. Jones" is so different that they must not be referring to the same Mr. Jones. But I do not think this illustration succeeds when it comes to the same God question, since the identity of God is not in dispute between Muslims and Christians: he is the sovereign providential creator of the universe on which all contingent existing things depend. (Or as I put it in my chapter: *he who is metaphysically ultimate and has underived existence.*)

Ironically, McDermott does not seem to dispute this. He writes, "So what should we say about the claim that Muslims and Christians 'worship the same God'? At one level, of course, we have to say yes, because as monotheists we all agree there is only one God. Ontologically there can be only one eternal creator God" (p. 114). However, what *is in dispute* are those divine character traits that McDermott attributes to what each faith believes God has revealed by means of sacred scripture: the Bible or the Qur'an. But given the fact that each faith gets the reference to God right, all this means is that one or both faiths do not possess specially revealed truth about the same one true God. Thus, Christians and Muslims worship the same God after all, even if it is the case that the latter or the former holds mistaken beliefs about that same God.

Another Way to Think About It

Let us now imagine that a new religion arises, which calls itself "Neo-Christianity." Its creed asserts that the divine nature is numerically differentiated—that the Godhead consists of Father, Son, and Holy Spirit, which is depicted in the religion's new scriptures as "a Father and shepherd and lover calling for a return of love" who "commands love for neighbors and even enemies," and shows power by weakness (p. 116). So Neo-Christianity claims to hold to all the distinctive features about God that McDermott affirms are found in the Bible and that are supposedly absent from the Qur'an. Now suppose that we delve more deeply into this new faith and discover that Father, Son, and Holy Spirit are not taught by the Neo-Christians to be one substance in three persons, as implied in the Nicene Creed (AD 381), but rather three separate superior beings who are called a Godhead because their unity is merely a oneness of purpose. We further discover that the Neo-Christians do not believe that this Godhead is the sovereign providential creator of the universe on which all contingent existing things depend, or at least not in the way affirmed by ordinary Christians. Rather, the Neo-Christians believe that each god in the Godhead is himself a creature in an uncreated eternal universe, and that such beings are called "gods" because they are the highest form of individual being that the universe is capable of producing and because they have the awesome power to "create" worlds, like Earth, out of preexisting matter (sort of like Plato's Demiurge) and offer the promise of eternal life to its human inhabitants that are brought into being by the Godhead's craftsmanship. So it is only in this highly qualified sense that Neo-Christians can claim (with some justification) that their Godhead is the sovereign providential creator of the world.

Do Christians and Neo-Christians worship the same God? The answer is no. But not because the Christian and Neo-Christian merely have different conceptions of God, for in that case they could very well be in the same position as Christians and Muslims (as I argue in my chapter) insofar as they could still be referring to the same God despite their contrary accounts of him. Rather, it is because Christianity and Neo-Christianity embrace fundamentally different understandings of what constitutes a divine nature, whereas with Christians and Muslims, though they disagree on what constitutes infallible revealed truth about God, they agree that there can exist in principle only one God: he who is metaphysically ultimate and has underived existence. Thus, even though McDermott is surely correct that Christianity and Islam attribute different characteristics to God, those characteristics are thought by each faith to be revealed truths about the only being that could in principle have a divine nature. For this reason, these differing characteristics, however important they are to the integrity of each faith, are not relevant to the question of whether Christians and Muslims worship the same God. Consequently, when McDermott writes that "Muslims are not pagans, since they are monotheists who recognize the God of Abraham" (p. 117), it makes me wonder whether the distance between our positions is really that great.

JERRY L. WALLS

I largely agree with Gerald's essay and find my differences with him to be relatively small compared to my disagreements with the other two essays. He and I agree that Christians and Muslims do not worship the same God, and his biblical-theological argument for this claim converges nicely with my philosophical-theological argument for the same conclusion. Moreover, I agree with much of the second half of his essay as well. I would not contest his observations about Jesus and Judaism or about Paul and Judaism. Nor would I dispute his claim that "Jesus and Paul did not think they were starting a new religion to replace the Judaism they grew up with" (p. 126). Gerald goes on in the same paragraph to explain: "It means instead that the God of Israel was bringing the people of Israel to their promised apogee when their messiah was revealed as the Son of God, the meaning of all they had ever known" (p. 127). So far, so good.

In the next paragraph, however, Gerald gingerly approaches the elephants in the room that have been threatening to stampede. He writes, "Some readers will raise a few more obstacles at this point: incarnation, resurrection, and Trinity" (p. 127). These doctrines obviously seem to be logically incompatible with Judaism and indeed an insurmountable barrier to any claim that Jews and Christians worship the same God. However, Gerald does not think these "few more obstacles" are as insurmountable as they might appear. Indeed, the relatively few pages he devotes to these doctrines suggests that they are rather minor barriers to be overcome.

Before considering his argument more carefully, let us recall these words from his critique of Islam with respect to its denial of the Trinity.

As he noted, sometimes critics attempt to downplay Muslim rejection of the Trinity by suggesting that they do not really understand the doctrine, that what they reject is only a caricature of actual Christian teaching. Gerald rightly rejects this claim:

> But rejection of the Trinity by Muslims cannot be explained simply as due to misunderstandings. For even when common misunderstandings are clarified, it is not unusual for Muslims to insist that the Christian belief in Father, Son, and Holy Spirit as God compromises the unity of God. At the heart of the dispute is the question of the deity of Jesus. (p. 114–15)

The Muslim rejection of the incarnation and Trinity is a major reason Gerald insists that Muslims do not worship the same God that Christians do, despite the fact that they agree on several important attributes of God. I want to argue that what applies here to Islam also applies to Judaism.

Let us now examine Gerald's attempt to surmount the difficulties posed by the three core Christian doctrines that he recognizes to be obstacles for his project. Although he starts with incarnation, I will begin with Jesus's resurrection. I do so because the resurrection was the singular event that led to the doctrines of incarnation and Trinity. It is very important to stress that these two doctrines were not the product of philosophical speculation; rather, the church was impelled to formulate them under the impact of the stunning events of the life, death, and resurrection of Jesus.

Gerald's discussion of resurrection is contained in one brief paragraph in which he contends that the "early church was able to accept Jesus's resurrection because its founders were readers of the Hebrew Bible and disciples in rabbinic schools where resurrection was a staple of Jewish eschatology" (p. 128). Now he is surely right that resurrection was a staple of Jewish eschatology and was affirmed by many Jews, including the Pharisees. However, the Jews were not expecting eschatology to break into history in the resurrection of a single man before the end of time, nor did they expect their Messiah to be crucified and resurrected. So Jesus's resurrection was a complete surprise to his disciples. Even though he predicted his death and resurrection several times before it happened, the disciples were by no means prepared for it. It was nothing less than the empty tomb and, more directly, the resurrected Christ staring them in the face during several appearances over forty days that persuaded them to accept his resurrection.

The issue between Jews and Christians was not merely the idea of resurrection or even the expectation of a resurrection at the end of the age. The issue was the claim that God had raised Jesus from the dead. This claim and its far reaching implications sharply divided Christians from Jews. Consider the incidents in Acts 3–4 when Peter and John healed a lame beggar and then addressed their fellow Israelites to explain how the healing had occurred:

> The God of Abraham, the God of Isaac, and the God of Jacob, the God of our ancestors has glorified his servant Jesus, whom you handed over and rejected in the presence of Pilate, though he had decided to release him. But you rejected the Holy and Righteous One and asked to have a murderer given to you, and you killed the Author of life, whom God raised from the dead. (Acts 3:13–15)

The implications of these words are extremely pointed: the man *you* killed, the Author of life, *God* raised from the dead. To be opposed to Jesus is to be opposed to the God of Abraham, Isaac, and Jacob. There can be no appeal to the God revealed in the Old Testament to warrant opposition to Jesus, for it is God who has put his stamp of approval on Jesus by raising him from the dead. Peter goes on to acknowledge that they acted in ignorance in killing Jesus, but he does not excuse them from the need to acknowledge their wrong. Rather, he boldly calls them to repentance, reminding them again that they are descendants of the prophets and of the covenant that God gave to their forefathers, beginning with Abraham.

In the next chapter, the issue is sharpened as the Jewish authorities approach them angrily because the apostles are "proclaiming that in Jesus there is the resurrection of the dead" (Acts 4:2). Again, the issue is not merely the idea or doctrine of resurrection but the more concrete claim that resurrection had actually happened in Jesus. Filled with the Holy Spirit, Peter goes on to drive home the implications of the resurrection:

> Let it be known to all of you, and to all the people of Israel, that this man is standing before you in good health by the name of Jesus Christ of Nazareth, whom you crucified, whom God raised from the dead. This Jesus is 'the stone that was rejected by you, the builders; it has become the cornerstone.' For there is salvation in no one else, for there is no other name under heaven given among mortals by which we must be saved. (Acts 4:10–12)

These are explosive claims with far reaching implications. Now that the God of Abraham, Isaac, and Jacob has raised Jesus from the dead, salvation cannot be found in any other way than by acknowledging and embracing Jesus. He represents the fulfillment of the promises given to the patriarchs, and there can be no viable faith in the God of the patriarchs that rejects what God has done in and through Jesus. The same message was proclaimed by Paul and Barnabas. Speaking to the Jews in Antioch, they announced "the good news that what God promised to our ancestors he has fulfilled for us, their children, by raising Jesus" (Acts 13:32–33).

When we turn to Gerald's discussion of incarnation, we see that he deploys a similar strategy to get past the obstacles to his case that Christians and Jews worship the same God. He goes into greater detail to show that in Jewish theology God is said to dwell in various things, from the Talmud to his people, and that there are several places in the Jewish scriptures where God is said to take bodily form. "The point is that while Jews reject the idea that Jesus is the incarnation of God, the *idea* of incarnation is a Jewish idea" (p. 127). Indeed, Gerald even quotes Jewish Bible scholar Benjamin Sommer, who has claimed that "divine embodiment, paradoxically, emerges . . . as far more important to Judaism than to Christianity" (p. 128).

As with his discussion of resurrection, I see a profound difference between accepting the idea of incarnation, and even affirming theophanies in which God briefly took on human form, and believing in the concrete reality of an actual incarnation in which the eternal Son of God took on human nature and lived a full human life among us. This difference takes on even more weight when we recall that the Son of God took on our nature to offer to God the Father the perfect obedience we owed to him, culminating in his sacrificial death for our sins, resurrection, and ascension. The significant divide between Christians and Jews represented by the Jewish rejection of the incarnation of Jesus is not in any way diminished because Judaism has an idea of incarnation. If anything, the fact that a religiously formed *idea* of incarnation was already in place should have made those who had the idea more disposed to accept an *actual* incarnation if God were to take on human nature and live among us to give us his ultimate revelation.

A similar critique applies to Gerald's discussion of the Trinity. He points to several Old Testament passages that have given rise to a "substantial Jewish tradition that God's oneness is a differentiated oneness, a complex oneness rather than a mathematical oneness" (p. 130). In view of these intimations of Trinity, the later explicit formulation of the doctrine can be seen as a natural development of earlier Jewish tradition. "Hence the early church could claim that it was worshiping the God of Israel but with new clarity about the identities within that differentiation" (p. 130).

Now I entirely agree with Gerald that the early church rightly insisted it was worshiping the God of Israel. I would go on to add that the Christian church rightly claims not just "new clarity" but God's definitive revelation of the eternal realities that were glimpsed in those earlier intimations of Trinity. Where I disagree is that I do not see how any of this warrants the claim that Jews who have rejected Christ are still worshiping the same God that Christians worship.

I reiterate that the life, death, and resurrection decisively alter the terms by which we can truly identify and worship God. What properly counted as the worship of God before Jesus does not necessarily count as proper worship after the coming of Christ. This seems to be what Jesus was communicating to his Jewish critics who appealed to their scriptures and the authority of Moses as grounds for rejecting his claims.

> You search the scriptures because you think that in them you have eternal life; and it is they that testify on my behalf. Yet you refuse to come to me that you might have life. . . . Do not think that I will accuse you before the Father; your accuser is Moses, on whom you have set your hope. If you believed Moses, you would believe me, for he wrote about me. (John 5:39–40, 45–46)

In short, Jews do not worship the same God as Christians for essentially the same reasons that Muslims do not. God's self-revelation defines the terms of worship. True worship is a response to what God has revealed. And both Jews and Muslims reject God's definitive act of revelation and consequently decline to accept what that revelation implies for what we are now required to believe about God and how we should respond to him with profound gratitude for what he has done for us in the life, death, and resurrection of Jesus of Nazareth.

GERALD R. MCDERMOTT

To Cobb and Schwartz

John Cobb and Andrew Schwartz are clever. They point to my acknowledgment that ontologically there is only one God, and suggest that I must therefore concede their thesis that all Abrahamic religions worship the same God.

But I never said that all religionists *reach* the only God who is. The scriptures make it clear that there are many who fail to reach the only God, just as they also make clear that many *think* they have reached him but are deceived: "When you spread out your hands, I will hide my eyes from you; even though you make many prayers, I will not listen" (Isa. 1:15 ESV); "Not everyone who says to me, 'Lord, Lord,' will reach the Kingdom of Heaven" (Matt. 7:21). Many who think they are worshiping the only God will be disappointed to find that they will not reach his kingdom. They worship, but unsuccessfully. They thought they were being heard and received by the true God, but they were not.

Professors Cobb and Schwartz actually seem to agree with me on this. They too acknowledge that there is only one Ultimate Reality. But they also say that not all spiritual traditions are oriented to the same God. Many, they say, are worshiping not the true God but idols. While they seem not to think this is true of Muslims, they nevertheless seem to agree that many are deceived in thinking that they are worshiping the only ultimate. So they seem to affirm with me that there is much indirection in religion—that many who think they are headed toward a certain Ultimate or God are mistaken. And that this is true despite the fact that there is only one Creator and Redeemer.

Cobb and Schwartz use a drawing to illustrate their thesis that one image is capable of being seen in two different ways. True enough, but notice the presupposition—that it is only one image. They presuppose what they are trying to prove: that there is only one God but seen in different ways and thus worshiped in different ways and reached by all three Abrahamic religions. But what if there are two separate images (of two persons) that look different indeed?

We would have to conclude they are different because they portray two persons. This is the case for Allah and the Father of Jesus Christ. (And Cobb and Schwartz acknowledge this when they say that two different people can have the same name but be mistaken for the same person.) Allah and the Christian God are represented in radically different ways by their two sets of scriptures, as I have argued in my previous essay and response. The Father of Jesus *is* love, but Allah is said by most Muslims (and the Qur'an) to have little or nothing to do with love. Cobb and Schwartz insist that Allah is "profoundly compassionate." But as I have tried to show, the Muslim God is compassionate only to Muslims. He does not show compassion to those who refuse to accept Muhammad as his prophet.

The New Testament's way of explaining worship to different beings under the same name "God" is to suggest that when some think they are worshiping God they are actually worshiping "demons" or "principalities and powers." I have discussed this earlier in the book. Cobb and Schwartz object that this cannot be true of Muslims because while Paul uses this language for Greek idol worship, Muslims address themselves to the God of Abraham. Thus they are not pagans like those Paul says worship demons.

But consider what the gospels say about Samaritans. They too were addressing the God of Abraham. In fact, they used the Jewish name for God—YHWH. Like the Jews (and Muslims), they opposed religious images. Like Jews, they kept the Law of Moses. Yet Jesus made clear that they were wrong to think that salvation came through their worship. He said to the Samaritan woman, "Salvation is from the Jews" (John 4:22). Samaritan worship addressed YHWH but did not "know" him. Jewish worship does "know" him (John 4:22).

Cobb and Schwartz make the further objection that I underestimate the importance of the Trinity for this debate. But I don't think that is true. I liken Jews who have not been shown the Trinity (by the Spirit) to Jews before the incarnation. They worshiped YHWH as he had been revealed to them, and God was pleased with those who worshiped him truly. Without the revelation of Jesus as Messiah, their "word[s] against the Son of Man will be forgiven" (Matt. 12:32). But if the Spirit reveals the true identity of the Son of Man to them, and they refuse it (and therefore the Trinity), they then "speak against the Holy Spirit," and this sin "will not be forgiven, either in this age or in the age to come" (Matt. 12:32). Surely this is not underestimating the importance of the Trinity.

To Beckwith

I have long admired Francis Beckwith's razor-sharp mind and clear philosophical analyses. In this case, however, I am not sure that his razor is cutting through the steely problem we are confronting.

His basic argument is that character is not decisive for determining divine identity—only his philosophical definition (*he who is metaphysically ultimate and has underived existence*) is.

Now I agree that his Neo-Christian gods, who are one not in being but purpose and who are creatures in an uncreated eternal universe, are different divine beings because of their difference in divine nature from the God of his italicized definition above, which he says is shared by Allah and the Christian God. He is describing the Godhead of Mormonism, and I have written elsewhere (as has he) that Latter-day Saints' conceptions of Jesus and God are fundamentally different from those of historic Christian orthodoxy.

But I think there is a basic problem with Professor Beckwith's philosophical definition of the God whom Muslims and Christians supposedly share: that definition is necessary but not sufficient to identify sameness of divine identity. He and some other philosophers might say that the italicized definition is enough to identify the two conceptions of God, but the vast majority of believers and theologians in both religions would disagree. Muslims say it is fundamental to Allah that he rejects the Trinity and called Muhammad to be his chief prophet, while Christians say that any God other than the Father, Son, and Holy Spirit is not the true God.

Therefore, I cannot agree that "the identity of God is not in dispute between Muslims and Christians" (p. 143). No Christians or Muslims would claim that it is enough to believe in a metaphysical ultimate who has underived existence. The average Christian would say that Beckwith's definition falls far short of God *because* it does not name the Trinity, and Muslims would reject its sufficiency *because* it fails to identify Allah and his revelation to his prophet. Hence it is *not* a "given" that, as he puts it, each faith gets the reference to God right. The being described in italics is neither Allah nor the triune God.

In other words, there is no general divinity onto which are added other details. The true God is a particular God, or he is not God at all. This is the faith of Muslims and Christians in their historic communities. The notion of a generic divinity is a construct of philosophers, not believers or theologians.

This is not a rejection of natural theology, as he suggests. I agree with Beckwith that Paul says non-Christians and non-Jews can know something of the true God by reason through nature (Rom. 1–2). But for Paul the true God is the God of Israel, who has sent the Jewish messiah, not a generic deity. Non-Christians know through nature something about *this* God, even if all they apprehend is that he is the all-powerful creator who has written his law on their hearts. When Paul speaks about the deities whom others worship, he refers to them as either dark powers that are different from the true God or fuzzy shadows wrongly identified as the true God.

Beckwith makes several arguments for his thesis that the character of a God is not decisive for that God's identity. His first is that the biblical God seems "to instruct his followers to engage in heinous acts, including genocide" (p. 141). Hence I should be "cautious" about drawing a "stark comparison" between the God of the Qur'an and the God of the Bible. My first response is to say that Muslims agree with Christians that the Bible is inspired (Muslims also say the biblical text has been corrupted wherever it conflicts with Muslim theology) and do not agree with this complaint. But they do agree generally with the character differences I identified in my initial essay—that God should not be called "love" and that Allah does not have unconditional love for all human beings. Second, these charges about the biblical God have been raised for two thousand years, from early pagan critics such as Celsus to the deists of the seventeenth and eighteenth centuries and now to the New Atheists. The character of the biblical God has stood the test of time and particularly in comparison to Allah: even if there are problem passages that defy easy resolution, comparing Allah and God as revealed through Jesus still provides overwhelming—even stark—difference.

Professor Beckwith then goes to the story of the fall and claims that when the serpent lied about YHWH, the serpent was depicting a different character but referring to the same Creator. I don't think so. Imagine someone who does not know your mother claiming that in a time of famine she would kill her own child in order to get food. You would probably say, "Nope. Wrong woman. You are thinking of someone else." In speaking to Eve, the serpent so distorted YHWH's character that he represented another god, a counterfeit YHWH.

This is part of the problem with Beckwith's Athenian theists. They know they are listening to a Jew (Paul) from Judaea, who believes God is triune (according to Beckwith's supposition). To suggest that these Athenians could separate part of Paul's claim (that his God is Creator) from the other part (that this God will judge them by the man Jesus, whom he raised from the dead) is wildly implausible. Paul was telling them that the one God is Creator and Judge, who raised the Judge from the dead. For one of them to think that this God wanted him and his friends to kill followers of the Judge was to reject Paul's God in favor of another.

The other problem is that these Athenians knew from the very beginning, according to Luke, that Paul's God was all about Jesus and resurrection. They asked him to speak to them because they heard he was talking about "foreign divinities," namely, "Jesus and the resurrection" (Acts 17:18). When some mocked and others wanted to hear him again, the object of their mocking and continued interest was the resurrected Judge, not a mere Creator (17:30–32). In other words, the character of Paul's God was integral to his identity: he was not only Creator (*metaphysically ultimate with underived existence*) but Judge and agent of resurrection.

For Luke, Paul, and the Athenians, being metaphysically ultimate might have been necessary but it was certainly not sufficient for divine identity. God was not just creator but the One who raised the Judge from the dead.

To Walls

Professor Walls and I agree that Muslims and Christians do not worship the same God, and we agree that what separates (nonmessianic) Jews and Christians is the identity of Jesus. But Professor Walls thinks I don't take seriously enough the latter difference, suggesting that I regard this as a "minor barrier." For while Jews agree in concept with the ideas of resurrection, incarnation, and differentiation within God, their conceptions of all these lack the concreteness and revelatory character of their fulfillment in Jesus. Therefore, "To be opposed to Jesus is to be opposed to the God of Abraham, Isaac, and Jacob" (p. 148).

Let me affirm that I do regard the identity of Jesus as far more than a minor barrier. It makes all the difference in the world. Jesus said that eternal salvation hangs on being joined to him as Messiah, the final revelation of God—indeed, the fulfillment of Torah (John 5:45–46). But I want to say two things in response to Professor Walls's friendly prodding. First, he himself has written that we don't know how clearly light has come to a particular person, and that the order of being is not the same thing as the order of knowing. If the light of revelation *about* Jesus has not come to a person, we cannot know that this person (in this case, a Jew) has rejected Jesus. And second, some Jews might be in the same order of knowing that all Jews were in before Jesus's appearance as messiah in the first century. So we cannot say with confidence that all who are opposed to Jesus are also opposed to the God of Abraham, Isaac, and Jacob. Some might be rejecting "another Jesus," just as Paul said false apostles were proclaiming to the Corinthians a Jesus different from the one he had proclaimed (2 Cor. 11:4). Jesus himself said that one could speak against the Son of Man and be forgiven if the Spirit had not yet revealed the true identity of Jesus (Matt. 12:32). That person would then be in the order of knowing of Jews who lived before that revelation.

Of course, once the identity of Jesus has been revealed to a Jew, that Jew is in a perilous position. At that point, to reject Jesus is to reject the God of his fathers, the God of Torah and Israel. But we must be humbly cautious, refusing to assume that Jews who have not been baptized were thereby damned. For centuries they were told by the church that they had to give up Torah observance if they were to follow Jesus (as I wrote in my previous response to professor Walls). They had also been told by God's Word in Torah that giving up observance would be to give up on the true God, the God of Israel, who had given them Torah. They believed they had to choose between God and some new teaching. Christians in their day thought Jews were rejecting Jesus and therefore the God of Abraham. But that might not have been the case. We must not claim to know what scripture does not make clear. Scripture clearly teaches that those who have been shown the true Jesus and reject him will miss the true God. It is also clear that to be saved one must confess that Jesus is Lord and believe that God raised him from the dead (Rom. 10:9). But scripture teaches that there is a difference between speaking against Jesus without revelation from the Spirit and speaking after such revelation (Matt. 12:32). And while we do not know how and when God might reveal Jesus's true identity to someone, we do know from near-death experiences that much can happen at (not after) the point of death.

There is also the question of culpability. Paul suggests that there are differences between gentiles and Jews. Gentiles are darkened in their understanding, alienated from the life of God because of their ignorance, and this ignorance is "due to their hardness of heart" (Eph. 4:18). But he wrote that Jews of his day who rejected the gospel did so because God had blinded their eyes "for the sake of" the gentiles (Rom. 11:28). God sent a "partial hardening" (partial because tens of thousands of Jews *did* accept the gospel; Acts 21:20) on the majority of Jews for the sake of "the fullness of the gentiles" (Rom. 11:25), that the gentiles might have time and space to enter the kingdom of the Jewish messiah. Even though thousands of Jews were rejecting the gospel, they were still "beloved" to him and their "calling" to be God's chosen people was still in place (Rom. 11:28–29). So their culpability was not the same as that of the gentiles. Paul suggested that the gentile hardening of heart was different from the Jewish hardening. The first (gentile hardening) seems to have been entirely self-caused, while the second (Jewish hardening) was primarily a work of God for the sake of others.

Now don't get me wrong. No one can enter the kingdom without confessing that Jesus is Lord and believing that God raised him from the dead (Rom. 10:9). This is true for Jews and gentiles alike. But we cannot know for sure what happens to Jews who refuse to become Christians in ways visible to us. We know God still loves them and that they are part of God's special and irrevocable covenant with them (Rom. 11:29). But their relation to God is part of "the mystery" of Israel (Rom. 11:25). To proclaim confidently that they do not worship the true God who is the God of Israel is to dissolve the mystery.

CHAPTER FOUR

NONE WORSHIP THE SAME GOD:
DIFFERENT CONCEPTIONS VIEW

JERRY L. WALLS

The question of whether Christians, Jews, and Muslims worship the same God is as intellectually formidable and fascinating as it is existentially galvanizing. What is at stake is about as far from a mere academic exercise as a question can be. What is on the line is the truth about God and what is required properly to know and honor him. The prospect looms large that millions of people are simply wrong about the most important questions of all and may be fatally misguided in their most passionate and foundational convictions. That would be bad enough if the consequences were only for this life, but the question is even more urgent because the matter of eternal salvation may be at stake. To be wrong about this question raises the prospect that millions of devoted worshipers may lose out on salvation and be finally consigned to eternal damnation.

Given these realities, the emotional appeal of an affirmative answer to our question is altogether understandable. Moreover, the very practical matter of all of us getting along seems to be served if we can all agree that Christians, Jews, and Muslims worship the same God. I shall, however, take the negative answer because I think it is true, whatever challenges it may pose on other grounds. While I will focus primarily on whether Christians and Muslims worship the same God, particularly in the first part of the essay where I discuss issues of reference, the argument I develop later will also apply to non-Messianic Jews.[1]

A big part of what makes this question so difficult is the fact that it intersects with a number of other questions that are distinct from it but closely related to it. Answering our question will require us to engage with a number of these other questions. Among these questions are the following. (1) Do Muslims and Christians refer to the same God? (2) Is it necessary for Muslims and Christians to refer to the same God in order to worship the same God? (3) Do Jews, Christians, and Muslims believe essentially the same thing about God? (4) If they do not, are these differences of belief about God necessarily reflected in essentially different forms and expressions of worship? (5) Can Jews and Muslims be saved even if they are not worshiping the same God as Christians?

God, Saint Nicholas, and Reference Shift

Let us begin with the first two questions, which we shall consider together. The first question is the more difficult one. The answer to the second seems fairly clear. If Muslims and Christians do not even successfully refer to the same God, it is hard to see how they could both engage in the more complex activity of worshiping the same God. So I shall take it as given that sameness of reference is a necessary condition for Muslims and Christians to worship the same God.

The whole matter of reference is complicated, however, and has been the subject of some of the most notable work in modern and contemporary philosophy. In a recent essay, Tomas Bogardus and Mallorie Urban insightfully explored these issues in connection with the question of whether Christians and Muslims worship the same God. Bogardus and Urban zero in on what they take to be the central question we need to get clear on to decide whether we believe Christians and Muslims worship the same God. That question is "what determines the reference of a name, and when and how do name-using practices shift their referents?"[2]

The notion of "reference shift" is central to their argument, so we must take some time to understand it. They employ this notion to point out problems in various theories of reference, including Saul Kripke's

---

1. Henceforth, when I refer to Jews, I mean non-Messianic Jews.
2. Tomas Bogardus and Mallorie Urban, "How to Tell Whether Christians and Muslims Worship the Same God," *Faith and Philosophy* 34, no. 2 (2017): 177.

famous causal theory.[3] Kripke's groundbreaking theory was put forth as an alternative to descriptivism, the theory that names refer by virtue of the fact that they are abbreviated or disguised definite descriptions of the person or place to which they refer. Thus, "Saint Nicholas" is shorthand for saying "the Christian saint who lived in the third and fourth centuries, who was the bishop of Myra, who was legendary for giving anonymous gifts, whose name appears in the poem 'The Night before Christmas,' and so on."

Kripke's alternative causal theory holds that historical and causal factors determine the reference of a name.[4] On his account, names originate in something like a baptismal ceremony in which a name is bestowed on a person. The name is handed on from person to person in a historical chain, and the name successfully refers so long as later users of the name are part of the causal chain that goes back to the original christening, and intend to use the name as it is commonly used. Speakers may alter the name in certain ways and even have different associations with the name than the original users of the name had, but so long as later users intend to use the name in the same way as persons did at the beginning of the chain, the name successfully refers. So on Kripke's account, my use of the name Saint Nicholas in the previous paragraph successfully refers because it connects through a historical and causal chain that traces back ultimately to the occasion when he was first christened as Nicholas.

Bogardus and Urban believe that Gareth Evans provided us with a more satisfactory theory of reference, one that combines the best of both descriptivism and Kripke's causal account, and one that can best come to terms with reference shift.[5] They explain as follows how Evans combines the two theories.

Evans departs from Kripke in this: a name-using practice in a community links a name word with a body of information about

---

3. Saul Kripke, *Naming and Necessity* (Cambridge, MA: Harvard University Press, 1980).

4. Bogardus and Urban helpfully summarize Kripke's critique of descriptivism in "How to Tell," 181–82.

5. It is worth noting here that Kripke was aware of the Santa Claus case and apparently recognized it as a problem for his view. Bogardus and Urban quote him as follows: "There may be a causal chain from our use of the term 'Santa Claus' to a certain historical saint, but still the children, when they use this, by this time probably do not refer to that saint." Kripke, *Naming and Necessity*, 93, quoted in Bogardus and Urban, 183.

its referent, a catalog of characteristics, what Evans sometimes calls a *dossier*. Now, for Evans, a name does *not* refer to whatever answers to most (or a weighted most) of entries in this dossier— that would just be a species of descriptivism. And neither, *pace* Kripke, does a name refer to whatever was originally dubbed by that name, irrespective of the information in the name's dossier, or the source of that information. Rather, for Evans, a name refers to the object that is the *dominant source* of the information in the name's dossier. In this way, Evans's theory marries the insights of Kripke's causal picture of reference with the insights of descriptivism.[6]

The critical idea here for Evans's view, and for our concerns, is the idea of the dominant source of information in the dossier.

What's Dominant in the Dossier?

Bogardus and Urban take pains to demonstrate that identifying dominance is not a simple matter. It is not merely a matter of the amount of information, but rather its centrality, and even on those terms, there may be a number of competing criteria to determine what is central. There is no need for our concerns to be detained by all the variations on what might count as truly central. Fortunately, as they suggest, we can employ a relatively simple test to determine whether some item of information is "given *sine-qua-non* weight by asking, 'What if nothing in the world answered to that bit of the dossier? Could the name still refer?'"[7]

And now we come back to Saint Nicholas, who recurs throughout their paper as an illustration of reference shift. As they note, "Saint Nicholas" is often used as another name for "Santa Claus." The question is whether Santa Claus, as used by millions of contemporary children (and parents), refers to the same person as Saint Nicholas. What if nothing in the world meets the description for "Santa Claus" in our dossier, but something answers to our information for "Saint Nicholas"? If we think that "Santa Claus" successfully refers to that person, then we judge

6. Bogardus and Urban, "How to Tell," 185. For Evans's theory, see Gareth Evans, "The Causal Theory of Names," *Proceedings of the Aristotelian Society, Supplementary Volumes* 47 (1973): 187–208; and Gareth Evans, *The Varieties of Reference* (Oxford: Oxford University Press, 1982).

7. Bogardus and Urban, "How to Tell," 191.

there is nothing in the dossier that is too severely a mismatch with the information in the dossier for "Saint Nicholas" that would undermine reference. On the other hand, if we judge that "Santa Claus" would not successfully refer to the same entity as "Saint Nicholas," then we judge that there is something in the dossier that is indispensable for "Santa Claus" that is radically at odds with information pertaining to "Saint Nicholas." Bogardus and Urban give us their assessment of this question as follows.

> We believe the answer to this question is "No," because some crucial information in the present-day use of "Santa Claus"—information about being a jolly Nordic elf who delivers presents globally on Christmas—radically mismatches some information in the dossier for "Saint Nicholas"—e.g., that he was human, not an elf, that he's got no global delivery service, that he's *dead*, etc. That jolly Nordic elf information is so central to the contemporary use of "Santa Claus" that, even if Saint Nicholas is the source of much of the other information in the dossier of "Santa Claus," Saint Nicholas cannot be the dossier's *dominant source*, i.e., the referent of the name. Rather, the name has shifted its reference, in this case, to the source of that central, crucial (mythical) information, i.e., to fiction.[8]

With this example in mind, we can apply a similar test to explore whether, from a Christian perspective, the name Allah as employed by Muslims has similarly undergone reference shift. "As a matter of historical fact, there is no doubt that the use of 'Allah' by Muslims traces back to—and branched off from—the divine-name-using practices of Jews and Christian, just as our practice of using 'Santa Claus' traces back and branches off from the use of names for Saint Nicholas."[9] But this sort of Kripkean historical causal account of the name Allah is not sufficient to establish that "Allah" has the same referent as "God," for perhaps the same sort of reference shift has occurred as that which we have seen in the shift that occurred with "Santa Claus."

---

8. Bogardus and Urban, "How to Tell," 192.
9. Bogardus and Urban, "How to Tell," 192.

From the Christian perspective, the God who created the world, who called Abraham, who led the children of Israel out of Egypt and gave Moses the Ten Commandments is the Trinitarian God who has existed from all eternity in three persons: the Father, Son, and Holy Spirit. Jesus is God's highest, definitive revelation. Consequently, no alleged revelation that denies that Jesus is the eternal Son of God, such as the Qur'an, could be a revelation from God. The experiences of Muhammad on the Mountain of Light were illusory or otherwise misleading. Now then, supposing all this is true, the question is whether "Allah" as used by Muslims, still successfully refers to this God.

If you return an affirmative answer to this question and insist that Muslims are in fact referring to the same God as Christians, this is "likely because you're using the name 'Allah' in an attributive way, giving some predicates in the dossier for 'Allah' maximal weight, taking them to be individually necessary and *jointly sufficient* for the proper application of the name."[10] Consider, for instance this passage from the Vatican II document *Nostra Aetate*: "The Church regards with esteem also the Moslems. They adore the one God, living and subsisting in Himself; merciful and all-powerful, the Creator of heaven and earth, who has spoken to men; they take pains to submit wholeheartedly to even his inscrutable decrees, just as Abraham, with whom the faith of Islam takes pleasure in linking itself, submitted to God. Though they do not acknowledge Jesus as God, they revere Him as a prophet."[11] The key point here is that if maximal weight is given to certain predicates for "Allah," such as creator of heaven and earth, all powerful, who has spoken to men, and these are taken as jointly sufficient for referring to God, then Muslims do so successfully when they use the name Allah.

Now, suppose you return a negative answer to this question of whether "Allah" as used by Muslims successfully refers to God. You judge that if the Christian story is true, Muslims do not refer to God when they invoke Allah.

This shows that there is some information in the dossier for "Allah" that you take to be central, and which you take to be

---

10. Bogardus and Urban, "How to Tell," 196.
11. *The Documents of Vatican II*, Vatican Translation (Staten Island, NY: St Pauls, 2009), 388.

radically incongruous with the Christian conception of God. Likely you take this information to concern the Trinity, the Incarnation, the Crucifixion, or the Resurrection. Or perhaps your interpretation of some verses in the Qur'an lead you to believe that it's central to the conception associated with "Allah" that Allah is not omnibenevolent, and you think this radically mismatches the Christian conception of God who loves the whole world (Jn 3:16), who loves and dies for sinners (Rom 5:8), etc. According to you, then, information radically incongruous with the Christian conception of God has become dominant in the dossier for "Allah" as used by Muslims. And so, for you, if Christianity is true, there has been a reference shift in the Muslim use of "God" from God to fiction.[12]

On this analysis, then, just as the name Santa Claus originated with a historical character (Saint Nicholas) and underwent a radical reference shift to a fictional character, in a similar way "Allah" underwent a profound reference shift in Islam to the point that "Allah" no longer referred to God, but rather to fiction, which is to say it refers to nothing at all.

Now it is important to keep in mind what all this philosophical analysis is intended to show. As the title of Bogardus and Urban's article indicates, they are concerned only to show how we can tell whether Christians and Muslims worship the same God. On the assumption that sameness of worship requires sameness of reference, they have attempted to show us when two names both refer to the same person or place, and when they do not. Their case hinges, of course, on the crucial matter of when reference shift has occurred to such a degree that sameness of reference has been lost. What we think about this matter determines whether we think the necessary condition of sameness of reference has been satisfied for sameness of worship to be possible. Only in their brief conclusion do Bogardus and Urban bring the issue of sameness of worship into focus by laying out the possible options for deciding whether the necessary condition for such worship has been met.

---

12. Bogardus and Urban, "How to Tell," 196. In a note for this passage, the authors write, "Read through the suwr of the Qur'an, and you'll find twenty or so descriptions of those Allah does not love, for example those given to excess (5:90, 7:55), the corrupt (2:205, 5:6–7), the sinners (3:57, 42:40), and the unbelievers (2:276, 3:32)."

If you think there's been a reference shift in both cases ["God" and "Allah"], then Christians and Muslims do not refer to—and so, do not worship—the same God. If you think there's been a reference shift in one case but not the other, then whether Christians and Muslims refer to and worship the same God will depend on whether you think Islam or Christianity is true. If you think there's been a reference shift in neither case, then the path is open on your view, for Christians and Muslims to refer to, and perhaps *worship*, the same God.[13]

I am particularly interested in the second and third options here. As someone who thinks Christianity is true, I am inclined to think there has in fact been a reference shift in the case of Islam but not of Christianity. That is, the dossier for "Allah" includes claims that are so radically at odds with core Christian truth claims that a reference shift has occurred such that "Allah" does not refer to God. Since Christians and Muslims do not even refer to the same God, they do not worship the same God.

So when a Muslim converts to Christianity (or vice versa), he should conclude that whatever it was he previously worshiped does not in fact exist, not merely that God is different in important ways than he previously thought, not unlike a child who is told the truth about Santa Claus. The child doesn't say, "Well, Santa is still real but is quite different than I thought. He is actually a dead saint rather than a jolly elf with magical powers for delivering presents to good little boys and girls all over the world." Instead, the new revelation leads them to say, "There is no Santa, and all those presents we thought were from him actually came from Mommy and Daddy." This is not to say that all converts articulate their new faith in these terms, only that this is the most accurate way to do so.

Before turning to the third option, it is worth noting here that some may hold that it simply is not clear whether a shift has occurred that is so radical that Christians and Muslims do not refer to the same God. Perhaps some may think the matter is rather hazy and indistinct. Perhaps they think the differences between "Allah" and "God" are profound but nevertheless think it is at best borderline to say a full-out reference shift has occurred.

13. Bogardus and Urban, "How to Tell," 197–98.

But what about the third option? What if you think there has been a reference shift in neither case? Does it follow that Christians and Muslims worship the same God? It does not. It only follows that "the path is open" to embrace this conclusion. Since sameness of reference is only necessary, but not sufficient for sameness of worship, one might well hold that Christians and Muslims refer to the same God but do not worship the same God. So the question now is what is required for Christians and Muslims to worship the same God, in addition to referring to the same God.

Sameness of Reference Is Not Enough for Sameness of Worship

In what follows, I argue that the conditions that are sufficient for sameness of worship do not hold even if it is arguable that reference shift has not occurred. That is, even if one thinks it is reasonably clear that sameness of reference is preserved, it is clear that the conditions that are necessary for worship have not been preserved.

Perhaps we can continue to think of the matter in terms of dossiers and shift. Perhaps there is a sort of shift that preserves reference but still undermines sameness of worship. Let us call this "worship misdirection." Assuming that Christianity is true, I will argue that when the misdirection is severe enough, those worshipers do not worship the same God as Christians do. I have chosen the term *misdirection* to underscore the fact that worship is a directed activity. It has a target, so to speak, and is intentional in nature. Moreover, the one who provides the direction for proper worship is God himself. He does so by revealing himself to us and informing us of what we must do to honor and praise him. Let us state this in terms of a general claim that I believe applies to "people of the Book," whether Jews, Christians, or Muslims. Let us call this the "generic worship principle."

> Generic worship principle: All worshipers of the God of the Book humbly acknowledge what God has revealed to them and offer grateful praise for what he has done on their behalf once they are properly informed of those truths.

Worship, then, is a response on our part to God's initiative to make himself known to us. We truly worship God when we acknowledge his revelation and respond as he has directed us. Consider these words from the Ten Commandments.

> I am the Lord your God, who brought you out of the land of Egypt, out of the house of slavery; you shall have no other gods before me.
>
> You shall not make for yourself an idol, whether in the form of anything that is in heaven above, or that is on the earth beneath, or that is in the water under the earth. You shall not bow down to them or worship them; for I the Lord your God am a jealous God, punishing children for the iniquity of their parents, to the third and fourth generation of those who reject me, but showing steadfast love to the thousandth generation of those who love me and keep my commandments. (Ex. 20:2–6)[14]

Notice first that God deserves honor and obedience because of his great act of salvation in bringing the Israelites out of Egypt. Note also that God is jealous of any worship that is directed to other gods, and he will not tolerate any form of idolatry. Moreover, God also reveals his character as a God of steadfast love whose word can be trusted.

Now let us consider a case of worship misdirection that is most pertinent to the text just examined, namely, the notorious incident of the golden calf that Aaron constructed while Moses was on the mountain receiving the law from God. It is most telling to consider the words spoken by the people after the calf was formed, and then Aaron's proclamation: "'These are your gods, O Israel, who brought you up out of the land of Egypt!' When Aaron saw this, he built an altar before it; and Aaron made a proclamation and said, 'Tomorrow shall be a festival to the Lord'" (Ex. 32:4–5).

In light of our discussion above, notice that this golden calf was identified as the one to be given credit and honor for bringing the Israelites out of Egypt, and the people fervently insisted that this was the god who should rightfully be worshiped. Thus, the golden calf is described in terms of the distinctive display of divine power God enacted in rescuing the Israelites from bondage, the very act that God ascribed to himself at

---

14. Unless noted otherwise, scripture passages in Walls's essay and responses comes from the NRSV.

the beginning of the Decalogue. So the Israelites identified this god as the one who delivered them. Both Moses and other faithful Israelites, as well as these people who were now worshiping this golden calf, would agree that "God" is the one who redeemed them from Egypt, not unlike both Muslims and Christians agree, in the words of *Nostra Aetate* (cited above), that the one God is "merciful and all-powerful, the Creator of heaven and earth, who has spoken to men."

Notice, moreover, that even Aaron went along with the people when he said they would honor the golden calf with a festival. Most remarkably, he seemed to identify the calf as the Lord, that is, as Yahweh, which is the name by which God had revealed himself. To hold a festival honoring the golden calf was to honor Yahweh. A clear historical causal chain links God's originally revealing his name as Yahweh and Aaron's use of the name in this passage.

But just as clearly, Yahweh was not being honored, praised, or worshiped in this incident. Indeed, his wrath was incited, and he said to Moses that the Israelites had been "quick to turn aside from the way I have commanded them; they have cast for themselves an image of a calf, and have worshiped it, and said, 'These are your gods, O Israel, who brought you up out of the land of Egypt!'" (Ex. 32:8). God was so angry that he threatened to consume the Israelites and start over with Moses, and they were only saved from this fate by Moses interceding for them.

So for the sake of argument, let us agree that the Israelites referred to the Lord in some sense when they identified him as the one who "brought them up out of the land of Egypt," a definite description that uniquely belonged to the Lord, and they rightly knew by a historical causal chain that the name of the God who delivered them was Yahweh. But even granting this, it is clear that they were not worshiping Yahweh in this incident but in fact were profoundly failing to honor and obey him. Their worship had been radically misdirected in such a way that they were not worshiping the same God who actually delivered them from Egypt.

The commemoration and celebration of Yahweh's act of delivering the Israelites from Egypt is the basis for one of Judaism's most distinctive annual enactments of worship, namely, the Passover. This annual act of remembrance celebrates the awesome display of God's love as well as his power in delivering the Israelites from slavery. Yahweh is the one who is to be praised and worshiped for this signal act of salvation, but Yahweh must never be confused with a golden calf. To worship him and to honor him for this act of salvation requires refraining from even the making of idols, let alone confusing them with Yahweh or bowing down to them and worshiping them.

The New Testament Revelation Changes Everything

This discussion could be extended considerably, but let us turn to another fundamental claim that underlies my argument that Christians and Muslims do not worship the same God. This builds on the more generic point about what is required of the God of the Book. Let us call this claim "New Testament revelation."

> New Testament revelation: The God of the Old Testament has revealed to us in the New Testament revelation that he has an eternal Son who was incarnate in Jesus, and who provided salvation on our behalf through his death and resurrection. Indeed, this is God's supreme act of self-revelation and act of love on our behalf.

To spell this out a bit, we can distinguish between what we might call the order of being and the order of knowing. In the order of being, the case has always been that God has a Son, indeed, that he is a Trinity. The eternal, aboriginal reality is that God exists in three persons— Father, Son, and Holy Spirit. The Trinitarian God created the world, called Abraham, gave Moses the Law, spoke to the prophets, and so on. However, during the time of the Old Testament, God's Trinitarian nature had not been revealed and was not known. In the order of being, the second person of the Trinity took on human nature many years after creation, died on the cross to atone for our sins, was raised from the dead, and ascended into heaven.

In the order of knowing, however, things unfold in just the opposite direction. In the order of knowing, it was the resurrection of Jesus that was the explosive event that led to the development of the essential Christian doctrines. It was the resurrection that showed that Jesus's death on the cross was not a mere tragedy, but rather a sacrifice for the sins of the world. It was the resurrection that made clear that he was not a merely human person, but also a divine one. As Paul put it, Jesus was "declared to be Son of God with power according to the spirit of holiness by resurrection from the dead" (Rom. 1:4). And it was reflection on the divinity of Jesus and his distinctive relation to the Father, as well as the coming of the Holy Spirit at Pentecost, that eventually led the church to formally define the doctrine of Trinity.

The vital importance of these points can hardly be overstated for this debate, and here we see that these points apply to differences between Jews and Christians as well as Muslims and Christians. The fact is that Jews, Christians, and Muslims believe radically different things about God and what he has revealed to us. Starting with the resurrection of Jesus and ending with the Trinity, Jews and Muslims deny all the distinctively Christian revelation about God. The hard fact of the matter is that the fundamental claims of these three religions are simply logically incompatible, and they cannot all be true. At least two of these religions are profoundly mistaken in what they believe about God and what he requires of us in terms of obedience and worship.

One way to try to mitigate these apparently intractable logical contradictions is by highlighting the mysterious nature of the Trinity, and indeed of the divine essence generally, and to promote a more apophatic approach to theology that makes minimal claims about what we can know. According to Reza Shah-Kazemi, the differences between Islam and Christianity may thus be resolved by focusing more on mystical intent than on dogmatic content. He defends such an approach at length in arguing that Christians and Muslims not only believe in, but ultimately worship, the same God. So long as theologians in these different religions focus on the "whole myriad of premises, assumptions and foundations," there is little chance of coming to agree that they believe in the same God.

> If, however, attention is directed away from the theological definition of Allah, and to its supratheological or metaphysical referent—the ultimate Essence (al-Dhat) which is absolutely ineffable and unnameable; and if, likewise we look beyond the theological definition of the Trinitarian conception of God, and focus instead on its supratheological and or metaphysical referent—the "superessential One" to quote St Dionysius to

whom we shall return later—then we shall be in a position to affirm that, despite the different names by which the ultimate Reality is denoted in the two traditions, the Reality thus alluded to is indeed one and the same.[15]

Now, it is significant to note that Shah-Kazemi identifies the incarnation and Trinity as the apparently most insurmountable obstacles to his line of argument.[16] What I find telling is that while he gives considerable attention to these doctrines, especially the Trinity, he ignores or gives scant attention to the decisive act of revelation that gave rise to these doctrines, namely, the resurrection.[17] And it is this dramatic event that must be squarely faced in any discussion of whether Jews, Christians, and Muslims believe in and worship the same God.

Indeed, emphasizing that the death and resurrection of Jesus are first and foremost affirmed by Christians as historical events is vital. The death and resurrection of Jesus were at the heart of the early Christian preaching that transformed the Roman Empire. As Paul summarized it, "For I handed on to you as of first importance what I in turn had received: that Christ died for our sins in accordance with the scriptures, and that he was buried, and that he was raised on the third day in accordance with the scriptures, and that he appeared to Cephas, then to the twelve" (1 Cor. 15:3–5). Unlike the doctrines of the incarnation and Trinity, which are highly mysterious and conceptually complex doctrines, the death and resurrection of Christ are relatively straightforward claims. In these events, God demonstrated not only the depth of his love for us but also his almighty power in raising Jesus from the dead. Again, it is hard to exaggerate the significance and far-reaching implications of these events.

Reflecting on the fact that what Christians see as a supreme act of divine love, Muslims deny even happened, is stunning. As Christ was

---

15. Reza Shah-Kazemi, "Do Muslims and Christians Believe in the Same God?" in *Do We Worship the Same God? Jews, Christians and Muslims in Dialogue*, ed. Miroslav Volf (Grand Rapids: Eerdmans, 2012), 79.

16. Shah-Kazemi, "Do Muslims and Christians Believe in the Same God?," 77.

17. Later in his essay, Shah-Kazemi identifies the "three mysteries—Trinity, Incarnation, and the Redemption wrought through the Crucifixion" as summed up in "the challenging enunciation" of Vladimir Lossky: "The dogma of the Trinity is a cross for human ways of thought." Shah-Kazemi, "Do Muslims and Christians Believe in the Same God?," 142. But the resurrection is not included.

dying on the cross, Christians see a marvelous expression of grace as he prayed, "Father, forgive them; for they do not know what they are doing" (Luke 23:34), whereas Muslims deny that Christ actually died on the cross. And while Jews do not deny Jesus's death on the cross, they view this event altogether differently than Christians do. Indeed, the first-century Jews who wanted Jesus crucified thought he was guilty of blasphemy and deserved to die.

Different Beliefs Demand Different Worship

These differences are not merely historical and factual disputes but reflect profound differences of belief about the love of God and the worship and gratitude that are due him. It is noteworthy that the most ecumenically central act of Christian worship, namely, the sacrament of communion, is a celebration of the death of Christ for our salvation and a looking forward to his return. The command to enact and participate in this sacrament comes to us directly from the lips of Christ. Communion is an essential component of Christian worship. Moreover, astonished gratitude at the death of Christ for our salvation is a theme that pervades Christian devotion. One of many places we can see this is in Christian hymnody. Consider a couple examples, first from Charles Wesley's hymn "O Love Divine, What Hast Thou Done."

> *O Love divine, what hast thou done!*
> *The immortal God hath died for me!*
> *The Father's coeternal Son*
> *Bore all my sins upon the tree.*
> *Th' immortal God for me hath died:*
> *My Lord, my Love, is crucified!*

Or consider these famous lines from Isaac Watts's hymn, "When I Survey the Wondrous Cross."

> *Were the whole realm of nature mine,*
> *That were an offering far too small.*
> *Love so amazing, so divine,*
> *Demands my soul, my life, my all!*

The "demand" for "my soul, my life, my all" is a demand of love. Christian worship is essentially shaped by the recognition and celebration of the extraordinary good news that the Trinitarian God, who is love in his eternal nature, has offered that same love to his sinful, rebellious human creatures. The same love that has existed from all eternity among the Persons of the Trinity was on display in the life, death, and resurrection of Jesus. "As the Father has loved me, so I have loved you; abide in my love" (John 15:9).

To direct our attention away from the joyful Trinity whose members love and delight in each other and have demonstrated a desire to share that love with us in so amazing a fashion; and to direct our attention instead, as Shah-Kazemi urges us, to the more generic notion of the "ultimate essence" or the "superessential One," is to experience a misdirection of worship that leaves us wondering how we can still be worshiping the same God. Likewise, the God who comes to us in the flesh can be interacted with and known and loved and worshiped in distinctively personal ways that are severely diminished if the incarnation is denied.

In this connection, thinking about the opening verses of Hebrews in light of the fundamental differences between Judaism, Christianity, and Islam is illuminating.

> Long ago God spoke to our ancestors in many and various ways by the prophets, but in these last days he has spoken to us by a Son, whom he appointed heir of all things, through whom he also created the worlds. He is the reflection of God's glory and the exact imprint of God's very being, and he sustains all things by his powerful word. When he had made purification for sins, he sat down at the right hand of the Majesty on high, having become as much superior to angels as the name he has inherited is more excellent than theirs. (Heb. 1:1–4)

This is a remarkably rich passage, and I can hardly discuss it in any sort of detail, but it powerfully exhibits the radical difference between the narrative that informs Christian theology, and Jewish and Muslim theology, and who it is that we worship, and why he demands our loving adoration. These differences are in many ways epitomized by the profound contrast the author draws between God speaking to us by prophets and speaking to us by a Son who is "the reflection of God's glory and the exact imprint of God's very being" (Heb. 1:3). An infinite chasm exists between a merely human prophet, however great he may be and however powerful the words he speaks, and the very Son of God "who contains all things by his powerful word." The differences between seeing Jesus as a merely human prophet, or worse, a sinner who deserved crucifixion, and seeing him as the one who "made purification for sins" and now sits "at the right hand of the Majesty on high" are so vast that the three positions are simply incommensurate.

Let us recall these questions at the beginning of this essay: (3) Do Jews, Christians, and Muslims believe essentially the same thing about God? (4) If they do not, are these differences of belief about God necessarily reflected in essentially different forms and expressions of worship? I have been arguing that the answer to question 3 is no and the answer to 4 is yes. The radically different beliefs that Jews, Christians, and Muslims have about God do entail essentially different forms and expressions of worship. Stressing this point is imperative. It is precisely the fact that these different expressions of worship are premised on radically different beliefs about who God is and how he has revealed himself most clearly that lead us to conclude that Jews, Christians, and Muslims do not worship the same God.

Putting the Argument Formally

Now I want to offer a more formal argument for this conclusion that Jews, Christians, and Muslims do not worship the same God. This argument assumes the Generic Worship Principle and the New Testament revelation spelled out and defended above. Given these principles, we can now observe that the New Testament revelation imposes distinctive requirements for worship. Let's call this the "New Testament worship requirement."

New Testament worship requirement: All worshipers of the God who is fully revealed only in the New Testament humbly acknowledge that he has an eternal Son who was incarnate in Jesus, and that Jesus provided salvation in our behalf through his death and resurrection, and they offer grateful praise for this when properly informed of these truths.

I emphasize here that the argument proceeds from the assumption that orthodox Christianity is true, that the only God who exists is the God who is fully revealed only in the New Testament. On the ground of that assumption there is good reason to think Islam represents a radical worship misdirection such that Christians and Muslims do not worship the same God. To return to the distinction between the order of being and the order of knowing, while God has always had a Son, it is only incumbent on us to acknowledge this and to worship God accordingly once he reveals the fact that he has an eternal Son who was incarnate in Jesus, and so on.

The notion that our response to the incarnate Son is decisive for determining whether we truly know and worship God is a major theme of the Gospel and Epistles of John. Now that the Word has been made flesh and dwelt among us, and we have beheld his glory, and grace and truth have come through him, there can be no appeal to Abraham that bypasses Jesus and his revelation. Before Abraham, Jesus was, and Abraham rejoiced to see his day. So those who are truly following in the steps of Abraham and worshiping the God of Abraham will rejoice in knowing Jesus. Nor is there any appeal to the Old Testament to evade the claims of Christ, for those very scriptures testify of Christ. Those who truly believe Moses will believe Jesus. There can be no knowledge of the Father without knowledge of the Son, and anyone who knows the Son knows the Father as well. The staggering truth that Jesus and the Father are one has given us the definitive word on what it means to know, to love, to honor, and to worship God.[18]

The fact that these paradigm-shattering words were addressed to the Jews of Jesus's day underscores the reality that these points apply to both Jews and Muslims. While it is true that the God who is the Father of Jesus is the same God who called Abraham and spoke to Moses, and that those who worship both the Father and Son are worshiping the same God who spoke to Abraham and Moses, it is no less true that those who refuse to believe and worship Jesus are not worshiping the God who called Abraham and revealed himself to Moses. The coming of Jesus has radically altered the terms of what is required to worship and obey the God of Abraham. This is the same point Paul makes in Romans 9–11,

18. See John 1:14–18; 4:23–26; 5:39–46; 6:46; 8:19, 39, 42, 58; 10:30; 14:7, 24; 16:2–3, 14–15, 27; 17:11, 21.

where he draws a distinction between ethnic Israel and true Israel. The chief issue is that ethnic Israel has stumbled over the stumbling stone, which is Christ. It is highly significant that in the context of Romans 9:33, Paul is quoting passages from the Old Testament in reference to Yahweh himself and applying them to Christ. So, to reject Christ is to reject Yahweh!

Now then, here is the formal argument.

1. No properly informed worshiper who consciously rejects the incarnation and resurrection of Jesus is a worshiper of the God who is fully revealed only in the New Testament.
2. All properly informed Jews and Muslims consciously reject the incarnation and resurrection of Jesus.
3. No properly informed Jews and Muslims are worshipers of the God who is fully revealed only in the New Testament.
4. If no properly informed Jews and Muslims worship the God who is fully revealed only in the New Testament, no properly informed Jews and Muslims worship the same God as those who worship the God who is fully revealed only in the New Testament.
5. No properly informed Jews and Muslims worship the same God as those who worship the God who is fully revealed only in the New Testament.
6. All properly informed Christians worship the God who is fully revealed only in the New Testament.
7. No properly informed Jews and Muslims worship the same God whom properly informed Christians worship.

Now I will comment on some of the premises of the argument as well as defend them. The argument is formally valid, so the soundness of the argument will of course hinge on whether all the premises are true.

The key term of premise 1, and one that recurs throughout the argument, is "properly informed." It is often alleged that Muslims (as well as adherents of other religions) misunderstand what Christians are claiming when we say that God has a Son, that God is a Trinity, and so on.[19] Given the difficult, and frankly stunning, nature of these

19. Cf. Shah-Kazemi, "Do Muslims and Christians Believe in the Same God?" 87ff.; Bogardus and Urban, "How to Tell," 197.

doctrines, this is altogether understandable. I am assuming, however, that there are many properly informed Muslims and adherents of other religions who are rightly informed about the actual substance of essential Christian doctrinal claims. In my view, to assume otherwise would be condescending. Thus, any who consciously reject those doctrines are not rejecting a mere caricature, or simplistic or polemically poised presentation of them.

With respect to 2, it is worth underscoring that rejection of the incarnation, death, and resurrection of Jesus is essential to Islam, and that Islam is polemically poised against Christianity in a way that other great world religions are not. This is due to the fact that Islam was founded after Christianity and is premised on the belief that incarnation, atonement, and resurrection are false doctrines. So, to be a properly informed Muslim is to know this history and to believe that Jesus was only a prophet, and that the revelation of the Qur'an supersedes that of the New Testament. Premise 3 is a preliminary conclusion that follows straightforwardly from 1 and 2.

Premise 4 is a conditional whose antecedent is 3. The question is whether the consequent follows from the antecedent. I have argued above that conscious informed rejection of Jesus's resurrection, atonement, and incarnation represents a radical worship misdirection such that Jews and Muslims are not worshiping the same God as Christians. Those who were convinced by my argument will be inclined to accept premise 4. Premise 5 follows from 3 and 4, and I take 6 to be rather obviously true. The conclusion, 7, follows from 5 and 6.

Final Salvation Is Another Matter

Finally, we come to question 5 in the introduction to this essay: Can Jews and Muslims be saved even if they are not worshiping the same God as Christians? The urgency of this question is what no doubt drives much of this dispute and urges us to agree that Muslims worship the same God as Christians. In addressing this issue, it is helpful to note that significant Christian thinkers ranging from some of the church fathers, to John Wesley, to C. S. Lewis have contended that persons who have not heard the gospel explicitly may nevertheless be in a saving relationship with God. Consider, for instance, this passage from John Wesley in which he discusses various forms of faith, ranging from materialism and deism to fully formed Christian faith. Speaking particularly of Muslims, he wrote, "I cannot but prefer this before the faith of the deists; because, though it embraces nearly the same objects, yet they are rather to be pitied than blamed for the narrowness of their faith. And their not believing the whole truth is not owing to their want of sincerity, but merely to their want of light. . . .It cannot be doubted that this plea will avail for millions of modern 'heathens.' Inasmuch as little is given to them, little will be required."[20]

In another sermon, Wesley wrote similarly about those who have not heard the gospel and their prospects for salvation. "We are not required to determine anything touching their final state. How it will please God, the Judge of all, to deal with *them*, we may leave to God himself. But this we know, that he is not the God of the Christians only, but the God of the heathens also; that he is 'rich in mercy to all who call upon him' [Rom 10:12], 'according to the light they have'; and that 'in every nation he that feareth God and worketh righteousness is accepted of him' [Acts 10:35]."[21]

This is the line of thinking that also appears in the famous scene near the end of C. S. Lewis's book *The Last Battle*, where Emeth, the worshiper of Tash, is accepted by Aslan. Unknowingly he was actually serving Aslan because his worship was motivated by a love for truth and righteousness. The point is that Christ died for all persons, whether they know it or not, and the Holy Spirit is working to draw them to Christ, whether they know it or not, and they may be responding truly to the "light" they have and consequently be on the way to final salvation.

However, our question is more complicated since our argument that Jews and Muslims do not worship the same God as Christians specifies the case to Jews and Muslims who are properly informed and consciously reject Jesus's resurrection, incarnation, and so on. The question then is whether such properly informed Jews and Muslims who are not worshiping the Christian God can be saved, assuming Christianity is true.

The answer to this question is straightforward for orthodox Christians, and the reason is clear. If God is a Trinity, and Jesus is the Son of God who died and was raised to save us, and salvation is a

---

20. John Wesley, *The Works of John Wesley*, ed. Albert C. Outler, 4 vols. (Nashville: Abingdon, 1986), 3:494.

21. Wesley, *The Works of John Wesley*, 3:296.

right relationship with God, then salvation requires accepting Christ and confessing him as Lord. Just as it is true that to persistently reject Christ is to reject the only God who exists, so it is true that to know him is to know the one true God. Jesus insists that because he and the Father are one, knowledge of God is inseparable from knowing him, and that to know him is to know his Father. "If God were your Father, you would love me," Jesus said (John 8:42). This Trinitarian logic runs especially through the Gospel and Epistles of John, as noted above. Notice: this implies it is possible to know God before knowing Christ explicitly, but it also means that anyone who truly knows and loves the Father will also love Jesus when they are truly introduced to him. Emeth was serving Aslan before he was aware of it, but his final salvation involved an explicit encounter with Aslan and knowledge of who he was. Again, what counts as a saving relationship with God and true worship of him is definitively revealed by the glorious light of the incarnation for those who have encountered Christ.

But this is where our knowledge stops, because we are in no place to judge how clearly the "light" of Christ has come to Jews, Muslims, and adherents of other religions who know little or nothing of the gospel. Even those we may think have heard of Christ quite clearly may not have done so because of various factors that prevent them from fairly or accurately hearing the gospel. Only God knows who has truly heard and seen, and how they have responded. And even if there are many properly informed Jews and Muslims who consciously reject Christ, it does not follow that they could not come to accept him in the future and come to share in the worship of the God who is only fully revealed in the New Testament.

In the meantime, let us muster as much clarity as we can while engaging these issues, even as we pray for charity on all sides, starting with ourselves. However, we should not confuse grace and love for all persons with Christian fellowship, nor should we assume or state that those who do not profess Christ as Lord are our brothers and sisters *in a common faith*. That fails to advance genuine respect and understanding, just as when we presume to know the hearts of others or their eternal destiny.[22]

---

22. Thanks to Tomas Bogardus and Ronnie Campbell for helpful comments on an earlier version of this chapter.

RESPONSE TO JERRY L. WALLS

WM. ANDREW SCHWARTZ & JOHN B. COBB JR.

Is it necessary that Muslims, Christians, and Jews refer to the same God in order to worship the same God? Jerry L. Walls answers this interesting question with an unequivocal yes. Like Francis Beckwith in chapter 2, Walls concentrates on matters of sense and reference in his answer. Whereas Beckwith concludes that Muslims, Jews, and Christians disagree at the level of sense but share a referent (the same God), Walls argues that different conceptions of God are the result of "reference shifts" (referring to different Gods).

He uses the example of Saint Nicholas, a name that was originally used in reference to a historical figure but that over time was used in reference to a fictional character—inspired by but departed from the historical origins. Walls argues that the shift in reference occurs when there is a significant discrepancy regarding the "dominant source of information" about the referent(s) in question (p. 163). In the case of Saint Nicholas, the dossier containing crucial information about Santa Claus today (a Nordic elf with flying reindeer) represents a radical divergence from the dossier of information about Saint Nicholas (third-century Christian bishop). Hence, a shift has occurred such that the name "Saint Nicholas" may be used in reference to two entirely different people (one historical, one fictional).

Much of what Walls argues seems reasonable. No doubt, the greater the agreement between two descriptions of an object, the greater the likelihood people are speaking about the same object. However, we consider the matter a bit more complicated. The underside of Walls's dossier argument is the recognition that naming (like all language) is always in some sense ambiguous. Even the phrase "dominant source of information" implies a generalization abstracted from the entirety of information as such. There is an inherent value judgment in this process, by which some information is deemed irrelevant or inaccurate simply because it deviates from the "dominant" narrative. A community's name-using practice involves subjective valuation. Deciding where to draw the line that circumscribes "dominant" information distinct from marginal information is a complex process. If the distinction between dominant and marginal information is somewhat arbitrary, then disagreements between dossiers becomes more ambiguous still. Like conflicting interpretations of an abstract painting, having differing dossiers does little to suggest the existence of multiple Gods.

The "Truth" of the Matter

Another problem we have with Walls's argument is the introduction of "truth" into the discussion of reference shifts. Quoting Bogardus and Urban, Walls writes, "If you think there's been a reference shift in one case but not the other, then whether Christians and Muslims refer to and worship the same God will depend on whether you think Islam or Christianity is true" (p. 167). Yet it's unclear how truth is relevant to reference shifts. Take the Santa Claus example. The fact that there has been a reference shift regarding St. Nick doesn't imply that there was, at some time, an actual human person to which the name referred. It's equally plausible that a reference shift can take place from one fantasy to another. There is nothing about the logic of reference shifts that requires the shift be from real to fake or true to false. The change in reference is just that, a change. So even if one concludes that there was a reference shift from God to Allah, this doesn't entail that either one is true. It could be that both are wrong, that neither the Christian God nor the Muslim God exists as a real referent. The point is, changes in reference may have relevance for answering the question about the sameness of God worshiped by Muslims, Jews, and Christians but no bearing on the truth of these traditions.

What's critical here is the distinction between our name-using practices and the actual referent of our names (*in sich*). One should be careful to distinguish between truth-claims and truth, between reality and our experience of reality. Walls's argument seems to blur these distinctions in a way that forces a binary ultimatum—concluding that Christianity is true and all other religions are false. We believe that reality is more complex and that this conclusion is the result of blurring matters of truth and reference.

Along these lines, we take issue with Walls's argument that religious conversion is like a child who was told the truth about Santa Claus, in which the former belief must be rejected as false. Faith is more accurately depicted as a process, which includes maturation. As such, the fact that one's conception of God as a child is different than one's conception of God as an adult doesn't mean that one's childhood faith needs to be rejected as false. Rather than saying, "The God I worshiped as a child doesn't exist," it is more appropriate to declare, "My view of God has deepened, expanded, and changed."

Reference Shifts or Shifting Referents?

Another major problem with Walls's reference shift argument is that it implies a static unchanging referent by which shifts in reference are shifts away from the original referent to something new. But why assume this? Isn't it possible that differences between dossiers are the result of a changing referent rather than a change in reference? Rather than shifting from one referent to another, perhaps there is a single referent that itself undergoes change. It seems just as possible that God's dossier needs updating, both because we learn more about God and because the "size" of God increases.[1]

This recognition is particularly keen with respect to Walls's discussion of the Trinity. Walls believes that Christians necessarily worship the Trinity in and through whom the death of the Son of God on the cross redeemed all who believe. This cannot be the same God, he thinks, as one who is not Trinitarian and has not experienced death on a cross. This position seems to us to create acute problems for Christians.

Jesus worshiped in Jewish synagogues. Presumably he worshiped the God of Israel as that God was revealed in what we Christians call the Old Testament. Those scriptures were for some time the scriptures of the early church. The Christians believed that Jesus was the Messiah toward whom those scriptures pointed. Most Jews did not agree.

---

1. See Bernard M. Loomer, "The Size of God," in *American Journal of Theology and Philosophy* 8, no. 1–2 (January and May 1987), 20–51.

But there is no hint in the early church that the God Christians worshiped was not the God who was revealed in those scriptures.

A few Christians later came to think that the God revealed in Jesus was not the God of Jewish scriptures. Walls may side with Marcion, but to claim that in doing so he represents orthodox Christianity does not seem possible. To say that we Christians do not worship the same God as the Jews, who share with us those writings, makes it seem that we are worshiping a different God from the one Jesus and Paul and the early Christians worshiped. Does Walls really want to affirm that?

It is true that over time the teachings of the church about Jesus and the Holy Spirit led to Trinitarian doctrine. If that ends Christian worship of the one God, then it does seem that Christianity no longer worships the God that Jews, as well as Jesus and Paul, worshiped. But most Christian thinkers have worked hard to show that affirming a Trinity is not to give up the monotheistic tradition so strongly affirmed in our Old Testament. We agree that Trinitarian thought can lead into tritheism and that this has led to Jews and Muslims strongly rejecting the Trinity. But if worshiping the Christian God requires giving up God's unity, then we, and many, many Christians, out of faithfulness to Jesus and to the scriptures we all honor, will be excluded.

In the early days the issue between Jews and Christians was about what the God revealed in our Old Testament had done. Christians affirmed that God sent the Messiah, who opened the door of the worshiping community to gentiles. Practically speaking, it meant that faithfulness to God did not require circumcision. Christians then and now disagreed about how drastically this disagreement separated them from Jews. Gradually the issues of incarnation and then, still later, the Trinity did become important. Perhaps some Christians did cease to worship the one God worshiped by Jews and Muslims. We hope not.

When Walls uses the Trinity as a sign of departure between Muslim, Jewish, and Christian notions of God, he states, "The hard fact of the matter is that the fundamental claims of these three religions are simply logically incompatible, and they cannot all be true. At least two of these religions are profoundly mistaken in what they believe about God and what he requires of us in terms of obedience and worship" (p. 172). We disagree. In fact, an alternative way forward is inherent in Walls's appeal to the Trinity. The nature of Trinitarian thinking suggests a way beyond the true-false binary presented in this dilemma. Much like the deep pluralism discussed in our essay, it is possible that Muslims and Jews focus their worship toward God the Father without focusing on God the Son or God the Holy Spirit. In so far as the Son and Spirit are distinct from the Father, this omission doesn't undermine Muslim and Jewish devotion to God (i.e., the Father). In so far as the Father, Son, and Spirit are indistinguishable, to worship God the Father is simply to worship God. In either case, Muslim, Jewish, and Christian worship of God isn't logically incompatible as Walls suggests.

Fingers and Moons

Toward the end of his essay, Walls offers a sevenfold formal argument. The crux of his argument rests on defining God narrowly (as fully revealed only in the New Testament) such that if Jews and Muslims reject this New Testament revelation, they must be worshiping different Gods (which Walls argues are false Gods).

Our first problem with this argument is the failure to distinguish between the God revealed in the New Testament and God *as* revealed in the New Testament. Like confusing a finger with the moon it points toward, Walls seems to be conflating God (the moon) and the New Testament revelation of God (the finger). Our statements about the world are distinct from the world. By distinguishing between God (in Godself) and the special revelation of God in the New Testament, we are inclined to reject Walls's first premise: "No properly informed worshiper who consciously rejects the incarnation and resurrection of Jesus is a worshiper of the God who is fully revealed only in the New Testament." God's existence isn't contingent on the New Testament. God existed before. God exists after. And God exists far beyond the New Testament revelation. As such, there is no reason to assume that the God revealed in the New Testament couldn't also be revealed in other places, times, and forms.

The second problem with Walls's formal argument is his use of the criteria "properly informed" throughout his premises. It seems that to be truly and deeply "properly informed" is to be informed in such a way that goes beyond descriptive knowledge about God toward relational knowledge of God. In this way, to be properly informed of the God revealed in the New Testament is to have a relationship with that God. Discrepancy regarding knowing "about" God (information) doesn't entail different Gods (being). In our assessment, personal relationships trump informational dossiers every time! Therefore, even if the dominant dossier of Muslims differs in critical ways from that of Christians, if both Muslims and Christians have relational knowledge of God, which we think is implied in the criteria of being "properly informed," then one should conclude that both Muslims and Christians worship the same God.

RESPONSE TO JERRY L. WALLS

FRANCIS J. BECKWITH

Jerry Walls, with his usual philosophical precision, offers an elegant defense of the view that Christians, Muslims, and Jews do not worship the same God.

Like Walls, I think that Gareth Evans's accounts of reference shift and dossier are probably right. No doubt, they are helpful in illuminating the question of this book. However, I do not think Evans's theory helps Walls's case. Take, for example, Walls's use of the Vatican II document *Nostra Aetate*, which states that Muslims "adore the one God, living and subsisting in Himself; merciful and all-powerful, the Creator of heaven and earth, who has spoken to men."[1] Walls argues that if you agree with *Nostra Aetate*, then you believe, as Evans would put it, that the "dominant source" of the dossier for "God" consists of "certain predicates for 'Allah,' such as creator of heaven and earth, all powerful, who has spoken to men" (p. 165). Thus, you believe that Muslims and Christians (along with Jews) worship the same God. On the other hand, if you think that the dominant source for God's dossier includes his Trinitarian nature, the incarnation, and other distinctly Christian doctrines, then you should come to the conclusion that Christians do not worship the same God as Muslims and Jews do. (However, you *could* surmise that Muslims and Jews worship the same God.)

Walls takes the second option as his own: "The dossier for 'Allah' includes claims that are so radically at odds with core Christian truth claims that a reference shift has occurred such that 'Allah' does not refer

---

1. *The Documents of Vatican II*, Vatican Translation (Staten Island, NY: St. Paul's, 2009), 388, and quoted on page 8 of Walls's chapter.

to God" (p. 167). For this reason, he argues that "when a Muslim converts to Christianity (or vice versa), he should conclude that whatever it
was he previously worshiped does not in fact exist, not merely that God
is different in important ways than he previously thought, not unlike a
child who is told the truth about Santa Claus" (p. 167). The mention
of Santa Claus is an allusion to an example that Tomas Bogardus and
Mallorie Urban employ to illustrate the concept of reference shift.[2] They
argue that a reference shift occurred at some point in the development of
the fictional Santa Claus from the historical Saint Nicholas, and thus we
should conclude that the real "Saint Nick" of history is not the fictional
"Saint Nick" who travels by way of flying reindeer. Walls reasons that
because the differences in the dossiers between the Christian God and
the Muslim God (and presumably the Jewish God) are just as profound
as the differences between the dossiers for the two Saint Nicks, Muslims
and Christians are not referring to the same God.

Relying on Borgardus and Urban, Walls makes the important point
that identifying what counts as a dossier's dominant source "is not a
simple matter." "It is," he writes, "not merely a matter of the amount of
information, but rather its centrality" (p. 163). Although this may true
in the wholesale, it is not always true in the retail, as in the case of the
same God question. As I noted in my chapter, the distinctly Christian
doctrines to which Walls appeals, in order to make a case for a reference
shift, presuppose the dominant source of the divine's dossier: *he who is
metaphysically ultimate and has underived existence.* One cannot say, for
example, that God is a Trinity—in the way in which the Council of
Nicaea meant it—without first knowing what a divine nature is. This is
why the dispute between Arius and St. Athanasius is best characterized
as a disagreement about the internal life of he who is metaphysically
ultimate and has underived existence. That is, the question for the
fathers of the council was whether subsistent being has within it eternal
processions and relations, including the Son being eternally begotten
from the Father. Consequently, if we were to ask the question whether
Arius and St. Athanasius worshiped the same God, we would have to
answer in the affirmative since they agreed on the dominant source of
God's dossier. On the other hand, if we were to ask whether Arius and

2. Tomas Bogardus and Mallorie Urban, "How to Tell Whether Christians and Muslims
Worship the Same God," *Faith and Philosophy* 34, no. 2 (2017): 192.

St. Athanasius held the same views about Jesus and the Holy Spirit, we would have to answer in the negative. As creedal Christians we would reasonably conclude that Arius held mistaken views *about* the only true God, but we could not say that he worshiped a different God, since he and St. Athanasius share the same reference: he who is metaphysically ultimate and has underived existence.

Walls does not see this because he seems to think of God and his properties in the way we think of ordinary objects like St. Nicholas, me, you, or the planet Venus. These objects—as many contemporary philosophers are apt to say—are individual complex substances that consist of a collection of properties and parts. This is why the reference shift conundrum about Saint Nick makes a lot of sense. Walls apparently sees the predicates Christians attribute to God—omniscient, omnipotent, omnibenevolent, triune, incarnate in Christ—as a list of properties that we can compare to the list of properties Muslims attribute to their God. On Walls's reasoning, since the doctrines of the "Trinity" and the "incarnation" clearly distinguish Christianity from its monotheistic competitors and are essential to the nature of the faith, "God" in the Muslim faith constitutes a reference shift. This is why he claims that supporters of the same-God thesis believe as they do, because they give maximal weight to "certain predicates for 'Allah,' such as creator of heaven and earth, all powerful, who has spoken to men" (p. 165). The implication here is that the same-God advocates are capriciously picking out as the dominant source those predicates of the Christian God and the Muslim God that confirm their thesis while ignoring those that may disconfirm it.

But this way of approaching the divine nature seems inconsistent with the metaphysical assumptions that made the Nicaean Creed a coherent formulation of the triune God.[3] To understand why, notice that in his list of the "predicates of 'Allah,'" which he derives from *Nostra Aetate*, Walls leaves out the most important: "living and subsisting in himself." For if God is "living and subsisting in himself"—which is just another way of saying that God is metaphysically ultimate and has underived existence—then God cannot in principle be creaturely or dependent on anything for his being. Moreover, as I argue in my

---

3. For a nice account of these assumptions, see David Bentley Hart, *The Experience of God: Being, Consciousness, Bliss* (New Haven, CT: Yale University Press, 2013).

chapter, there can only be one such self-subsistent being, and thus he must be the source of all contingent reality. Given this understanding of God, we conclude that he is the fullness of being, and for this reason, we attribute to him certain perfections of power, knowledge, being, and so forth, just as we find in scripture. But if Muslims and Jews believe in and worship this God, then they worship the same God as Christians do, even if one believes as Walls does that these non-Christian faiths are deeply mistaken in various ways.

To help clarify this point, let us return to two of the illustrations I employed in my chapter. When preaching on the Areopagus in Athens, St. Paul first distinguishes between the true and living God and the false idols worshiped by the masses:

> The God who made the world and everything in it, he who is Lord of heaven and earth, does not live in shrines made by human hands, nor is he served by human hands, as though he needed anything, since he himself gives to all mortals life and breath and all things. . . . For 'In him we live and move and have our being'; as even some of your own poets have said." (Acts 17:24–25, 28)

After establishing the right reference to God—he who is metaphysically ultimate and has underived existence—St. Paul presents the gospel by proclaiming Christ's resurrection and the last judgment (Acts 17:29–31). The text tells us that some in the crowd "joined him and became believers, including Dionysius the Areopagite and a woman named Damaris" (Acts 17:34). Suppose there were two others in the audience who, though not becoming Christian believers, left convinced that St. Paul was correct about God. We will call them Nikolas and Helen. Now imagine that several weeks later they encounter Dionysius and Damaris at a fruit market in Athens. The four strike up a conversation about St. Paul's preaching. Although pleased to hear that Nikolas and Helen have abandoned idol worship and now believe in the one true and living God, Dionysius and Damaris are sad that their new friends remain unconvinced of the rest of St. Paul's message. Would it be right for Dionysius and Damaris at this point to tell their friends that if they were to convert to Christianity, they "should conclude that whatever it was [they] previously worshiped does not in fact exist, not merely that God is different in important ways than [they] previously thought, not unlike a [pagan] who is told the truth about [Zeus]?" (p. 167). But that is precisely what Walls suggests, even though St. Paul unequivocally said that he was proclaiming to his Athenian audience the correct reference to the divine nature, the "God who made the world and everything in it" (Acts 17:24), the one in whom "we live and move and have our being" (Acts 17:28). This is why it should not surprise us that in his Epistle to the Romans St. Paul fully acknowledges that those unacquainted with special revelation can come to know enough about God to get the reference to him correct: "For what can be known about God is plain to them, because God has shown it to them. Ever since the creation of the world his eternal power and divine nature, invisible though they are, have been understood and seen through the things he has made" (Rom. 1:19–20).

Let us now recall the exchange between Moses and God on Mount Herob:

> But Moses said to God, "If I come to the Israelites and say to them, 'The God of your ancestors has sent me to you,' and they ask me, 'What is his name?' what shall I say to them?" God said to Moses, "I am who I am." He said further, "Thus you shall say to the Israelites, 'I am has sent me to you.'" (Ex. 3:13–14)

As I noted in my chapter, the consistent teaching of the church on this passage is that God is disclosing to Moses that he is the self-existent one, revealing that he is radically unlike any of the creaturely gods that are worshiped as idols. For this reason, Walls is mistaken when he claims that the Exodus account of the children of Israel's misdirected worship of the golden calf as God is analogous to Muslim and Jewish worship of God. Walls writes,

> Both Moses and other faithful Israelites, as well as these people who were now worshiping this golden calf, would agree that "God" is the one who redeemed them from Egypt, not unlike both Muslims and Christians agree, in the words of *Nostra Aetate* (cited above), that the one God is "merciful and all-powerful, the Creator of heaven and earth, who has spoken to men." (p. 170)

But this can't be right. For what made the worship of the golden calf misdirected worship was its nature as an idol, a finite object that is not the self-existent one of Exodus 3, the one God who is living and subsisting in himself of *Nostra Aetate*, and the one in whom "we live and move and have our being" of St. Paul's sermon. Whatever one may think of Jewish or Muslim worship, it is not the worship of idols.

Because of space constraints I cannot say much in response to Walls's formal argument (p. 178), except to say that it cannot get off the ground until he first tells us the definition of the term "properly informed Christian." Given the number of contemporary analytic Christian philosophers of religion who deeply disagree on the nature of God, the Trinity, the incarnation, the soul, and divine simplicity, it's tough to know who counts as properly informed.

RESPONSE TO JERRY L. WALLS

GERALD D. MCDERMOTT

There is much in Professor Walls's essay that I affirm. I am glad he reminds our readers that this question has grave implications. After all, the New Testament warns that salvation is a matter of being joined to the true God as a result of accepting and living in his revelation (Rom. 10:9–13). Jesus warns that on the day of judgment we will have to give account for every careless word we speak (Matt. 12:36) and for what we have done with his testimony about himself (Luke 12:8–9; John 12:48).

I also agree with Professor Walls that an affirmative answer to the question of this book has great emotional appeal. Who would not, in the abstract, want to affirm the deepest convictions of at least half the world? But we must be willing to follow the evidence where it leads, even if it conflicts with what at first is emotionally attractive.

Professor Walls is absolutely correct to warn us against judging the eternal destiny of a Muslim or Jew who we think has heard the gospel but seems not to have accepted it. We do not know how clearly the light has come to that person. I remember a young woman sharing her version of the gospel with me when I was seventeen. I am sure that when I told her yes, that I wanted God's wonderful plan for my life and that I was glad that Jesus had taken away my sins, she thought she had won another soul for the kingdom. As I look back, however, I now realize I had no idea what the gospel was. I was far more focused on the young woman and her interest in me than on what she said about Jesus. If I had said no, it would not have been to Jesus, whom I did not see or understand, but to her invitation to join her group. Walls advises two things in murky situations like these: we do not know what that Jewish or Muslim friend will encounter in the future, and we don't know how much light came in when that friend heard something that we think was the gospel.

I agree with Walls that sameness of reference is necessary to affirm the worship of the same God. In the case of Muslims, he is right to say that their information about God is radically incongruous with the Christian conception of God because of what has become dominant in the dossier for Allah. Namely, Allah is not benevolent toward all human beings. As I have argued in my essay and other responses, Allah does not love all of his human creatures; if he has love at all, it is conditional. Nor is he rational in anything close to the sense that the God of Jews and Christians is rational (see my response to Professor Beckwith). Nor is Allah perfect in the way that the God of Israel, whom Jews and Christians worship, is perfect, for at the heart of his perfection is love.

Walls is also correct to reject the mystical and philosophical essence of Being, which Professors Cobb and Schwartz suggest is the common referent for the worship of all Christians, Jews, and Muslims. As Walls properly observes, Jesus's commandment to his disciples to "do" the Lord's Supper in remembrance of him suggests that the object of their worship should include his death and resurrection, which have concrete and theistic implications that are light years from meditation on Being Itself.

But with all these agreements being registered, I do want to take issue with a few things. First, readers of his remark about "the first-century Jews who wanted Jesus crucified" might get the impression that this was true for all Jews in the first century. In fact, Jesus was popular with thousands of Jews in the first century. More and more historians have come to realize that the Jews who wanted him crucified were a small clique in the temple establishment who felt threatened by his popularity with Jewish crowds. This has been obscured by the mistranslation of *Ioudaioi* in John's gospel, where most of the time it should be rendered "Judeans" rather than "Jews." John portrays certain Judean leaders, not Jews in general, as wanting to kill Jesus. We learn from Luke in Acts that *myriadoi* (myriads) in Jerusalem were "among the Jews of those who have believed" (21:20). That means that less than two decades after Jesus's death, there were at least twenty thousand (at least two *myriads*, for one *myriad* is ten thousand) Jewish believers following Jesus in Jerusalem alone.

Walls goes on to assert that "to reject Christ is to reject Yahweh." Now, as we have seen, Walls has already qualified this generalization by warning us that we do not know if someone has rejected Christ just because we think they have heard someone "give" them the gospel. We do not know how much true light that person has been given.

But there are other considerations that are just as weighty. First, Paul indicates that even if Jews in his generation had rejected his message about Jesus, they were still "beloved" by Yahweh (Rom. 11:28). Their participation in Israel's being chosen by Yahweh was "irrevocable" (Rom. 11:29). Paul does not indicate at this point if their rejection of Jesus as messiah meant they were rejecting Yahweh, but he does suggest that Yahweh did not reject them. At the very least, Yahweh still loved them in a special way, different from his concern for gentiles. This was a special "calling" to Jews in Israel that gentiles did not receive (Rom. 11:29). Gentiles could be adopted as associate members in Israel if they were joined to Israel's messiah (Eph. 2:11–22). But there was a special relationship between Yahweh and his chosen people the Jews.

Both Paul and Jesus made this more complicated, which means it is even more difficult to know with assurance about a Jew who has rejected Jesus whether this means he has also rejected Yahweh. Paul said that God himself caused the majority of Jews in his day to reject Jesus (even if a large minority accepted and followed Jesus): "God gave them a spirit of stupor, eyes that would not see and ears that would not hear. . . . A partial hardening has come upon Israel, until the fullness of the Gentiles has come in" (Rom 11:8, 25 ESV).

Why would God do this? Paul tells the gentiles in Rome who make up the majority of the church there, "As regards the gospel, they [the Jews who reject Jesus] are enemies of God for your sake" (Rom. 11:28). Why *for your sake*? Apparently, Paul accepted the rabbis' prediction that when the messiah would come, "all Israel will be saved" (Rom. 11:26) and the world would end. So in order for time and space to open for billions of future gentiles before Israel's acceptance of the messiah would bring the end of the world, God purposely closed the eyes and ears of Jews. This hardening would last until the end of the "time of the gentiles." It was for the sake of the gentiles, that they might be saved.

Jesus added to the complexity. He said, "Whoever speaks a word against the Son of Man will be forgiven, but whoever speaks against the Holy Spirit will not be forgiven, either in this age or in the world to come" (Matt. 12:32). In other words, it is one thing to reject Jesus without the revelation of the Holy Spirit, but quite another if one has been shown by the Spirit who he is.

Then there is the further event of the Holocaust, which has only cemented the hardening for millions of Jews. Most Jews I know have lost family members at the hands of Germans and others who killed Jews in the horrors of the Nazi death camps. For many Jews, these were European Christians who followed "Christian" teaching that God had rejected the Jews because they had rejected Jesus. Most Christians do not think of Nazis or death camp workers as Christians, but Hitler had many "willing executioners" who went to church on Sundays and killed Jews on Mondays.[1] For these reasons it seems to millions of Jews that to accept the Jesus in whose name their relatives have been murdered is to reject not only their relatives but the God of Israel and his covenant with them. For them, to continue to love Yahweh is to reject Jesus.

Therefore, we must be wary of accepting Walls's statement in a uniform way: "To reject Christ is to reject Yahweh." What about the thousands of Jews in the centuries after Constantine who were told by the church that they must give up Torah observance if they were to accept Jesus and be accepted by the church?[2] Both Moses and Christ said that the Jews were to obey Torah (Deut. 11:1–32; 28:1–14; Matt. 5:18–19; 23:1–3), but the church told them they had to give up Torah to follow Jesus. For them, to obey the church meant to reject Yahweh. It was easy to conclude that the church's Christ must not represent the true Jesus who affirmed Torah.

Walls says, "No properly informed Jews and Muslims are worshipers of the God who is fully revealed only in the New Testament" (p. 178). This is true for all Jews and Muslims to whom the Holy Spirit has revealed the true identity of Jesus. To refuse it is to refuse the God of Israel, who is the true God. But it is helpful here to retrieve Walls's distinction between the order of being and the order of knowing. Walls observes that God's Trinitarian nature was not revealed or made known

---

1. Daniel Goldenhagen, *Hitler's Willing Executioners: Ordinary Germans and the Holocaust* (New York: Vintage Books, 1997).

2. Mark Kinzer, Postmissionary Messianic Judaism: Redefining Christian Engagement with the Jewish People (Grand Rapids: Brazos, 2005).

during the time of the Old Testament. What if many Jews today are still at that place in the order of knowing, so that it has not yet been revealed to them by the Holy Spirit that Jesus is their Messiah and therefore God is Trinitarian? This is made all the more plausible by Paul's declaration that God has closed the eyes of most Jews during the time of the gentiles. God himself has kept the Spirit's revelation from them.

This does not mean that we should not bear witness to them that Jesus is their Messiah. But it does mean that they are in a special situation, different from Muslims. The Jewish scriptures are our own. God has closed their eyes for the sake of the gentiles. He has not said this about Muslims. Jews are a special chosen people, unlike Muslims. God is still in special relationship to them, unlike Muslims. God loves Muslims like every other gentile people group. But God has chosen Jews like no other people group in the world. Their situation is different.

Walls brings up C. S. Lewis's Emeth in *The Last Battle*. His point is that "unknowingly he was actually serving Aslan because his worship was motivated by a love for truth and righteousness . . . [and others like him] may be responding truly to the 'light' they have and consequently be on the way to final salvation" (p. 180). I disagree with Lewis's inclusivism—and perhaps Walls's—that suggests that non-Christians can come to Christ without acknowledging Christ. But I am also agnostic about when and how God's Spirit reveals Christ to people who seek God's truth and righteousness, especially Jews who by the Spirit love the true God in the ways that they know. When Aslan, Lewis's image for Jesus, finally reveals himself to Emeth, he tells the warrior that he had always known him (Aslan) without knowing his name. We should concede that the same might be true of our Jewish brothers and sisters who worship the God of Israel, whom Jesus said was the true God (Mark 12:29; Matt 5:17–18; John 4:22). We can hope that if they are now worshiping Jesus's Father, they will—in God's way and time—accept Jesus as his Son once the Spirit reveals Jesus's identity to them.

JERRY L. WALLS

To Schwartz and Cobb

I appreciate Andrew and John's thoughtful response to my essay. However, it underscores the depth and degree of the disagreement that divides us. I will note as many of the points of disagreement as I can in the space available.

Among our most profound disagreements are those pertaining to truth and our ability to know it. Andrew and John observe that it is "unclear how truth is relevant to reference shifts," and they contend that it is "equally plausible that a reference shift can take place from one fantasy to another" (p. 183). They make these claims in response to the following line from Bogardus and Urban: "If you think there's been a reference shift in one case but not the other, then whether Christians and Muslims refer to and worship the same God will depend on whether you think Christianity or Islam is true."

In response, I am inclined to agree that reference shift can indeed take place from "one fantasy to another" (p. 183). So truth is not a necessary condition for a reference shift. But that is beside the point. The issue here is whether the belief in the truth of Christianity or Islam is sufficient to warrant the judgment that reference shift has in fact occurred in the religion one does not believe is true. It seems clear that it has. If one believes Christianity is true—that God has an eternal Son who became incarnate in Jesus of Nazareth—then any religion whose dossier includes a denial of these crucial claims no longer refers to the same God as the religion that insists that those beliefs are absolutely essential to a true account of who God is.

Andrew and John draw what they take to be a "crucial" distinction between the names we employ and the referent of those names. It is critical, they insist, that we distinguish "between truth-claims and truth, between reality and our experience of reality" (p. 183). They complain that I "blur these distinctions in a way that forces a binary ultimatum—concluding that Christianity is true and all other religions are false. We believe that reality is more complex and that this conclusion is the result of blurring matters of truth and reference" (p. 183–84).

I very much agree with these distinctions and have no idea why Andrew and John think I reject or even blur them. There is clearly a distinction between the names we use, the language we employ, the propositions we articulate, and the realities we designate or describe with our names, language, and propositions. Moreover, we should be under no illusion that our names and propositions exhaust the realities we refer to and describe, even when those names are accurate and those propositions true to the reality to which they correspond. This is especially true when those names and propositions apply to God, an infinite being who far outstrips our language about him.

Still, the propositions we use to describe God must be coherent and logically consistent. Contradictory propositions cannot both be true about God. It is either true or it is false that God eternally exists in three persons, that Jesus was the incarnation of the second person of the Trinity, that God raised him from the dead, and so on. But the "binary ultimatum" does not entail that religions other than Christianity are entirely false; indeed, those religions may teach important things about God that are true—that there is only one God, that he is all powerful, that he created the world. Yet if the distinctively Christian claims are true, then other religions are false insofar as they deny those claims. Recognizing the limits of language and the difference between truth claims and the reality they describe does not license embracing contradictory claims.

In view of this, there is a profound difference between the case where one's conception of God as a child develops into a more mature conception as an adult and the case where one converts to a new religion, from Islam to Christianity, for instance. In the former case, it may well be more accurate to say, "My view of God has deepened, expanded, and changed," rather than to say, "The God I worshiped as a child does not exist." But the change in one's conception of God in an adult conversion from Islam to Christianity is more radical than the change from a childhood conception of the Christian God to a more thoughtful and informed view as an adult. In the case of adult conversion, by coming to believe essential Christian doctrine, one *affirms* certain things about God that one previously thought it essential to *deny*. Indeed, it would be quite accurate to say the non-Trinitarian God one believed in before converting does not really exist.

I am also quite puzzled that Andrew and John suggest that I "may side with Marcion" or that I may disagree with their claim that "affirming a Trinity is not to give up the monotheistic tradition so strongly affirmed in our Old Testament" (p. 185). Trinitarian theology of course is insistently monotheistic, though New Testament revelation shows us that the oneness of God is more complex than the Old Testament might lead us to believe. But Christian orthodoxy is emphatic that the referent of the Trinitarian God revealed in the New Testament is identical with the referent of the God of Abraham, Isaac, and Jacob revealed in the Old Testament.

Finally, I would strongly dispute the suggestion of Andrew and John that Trinitarian theology provides us with the possibility that "Muslims and Jews focus their worship toward God the Father without focusing on God the Son or God the Holy Spirit" (p. 186). It is precisely this possibility that Trinitarian thinking precludes, as least for Jews and Muslims who are properly informed about Jesus and his claims. As the Gospel of John makes clear in passage after passage, now that Jesus has revealed the Father and taught us that he and the Father are one, there can be no true worship of the Father if the Son is rejected. To love and worship one person of the Trinity is to love and worship all three; to reject any one is to reject all three.

To Beckwith

I want to begin by thanking Frank for his challenging response to my article. I hope in this rejoinder I can further clarify our disagreements. I continue to think that some of our most fundamental disputes hinge on the distinction between the order of knowing and the order of being and the fact that he gives priority to the order of knowing construed along Thomistic lines. That is, he gives priority to generic theistic beliefs arrived at by way of philosophical argument and analysis that do not rely on the special revelation in scripture. These generic beliefs and the arguments that support them are accessible to all persons and are common property among the three great theistic religions. By contrast, I think the order of being, which we fully learn only from scripture, is necessary for defining what is essential to God, and for determining whether Jews, Christians, and Muslims worship the same God.

My differences with Frank surface, among other places, in his account of Nicaea. I am not an expert in historical or patristic theology, so I speak here with due reserve. But I would venture the suggestion that Frank has not characterized the matter quite right. He writes, "One cannot say, for example, that God is a Trinity—in the way in which the Council of Nicaea meant it—without first knowing what a divine nature is. This is why the dispute between Arius and St. Athanasius is best characterized as a disagreement about the internal life of he who is metaphysically ultimate and has underived existence" (p. 189).

Now to be sure, the very notion of Trinity assumes a common divine nature shared by the three persons of the Trinity, but explicit Trinitarian theology is rather modest in the Nicene Creed. Likewise, the Creed gives us little by way of detailed definition of the divine nature. Indeed, the statement about the Father is quite terse, identifying him only as the "Father Almighty, maker of heaven and earth, and of all things visible and invisible." By contrast, the bulk of the creed spells out the identity of the "one Lord Jesus Christ, the only begotten Son of God." The "great issue before the council," according to J. N. D. Kelly, "was not the unity of the Godhead as such; it was the Son's co-eternity with the Father, which the Arians denied, His full divinity in contrast to the creaturely status they ascribed to Him."[1]

The truth of Jesus' co-eternity and full divinity does, of course, have profound implications for the internal life of God, and it reveals to us things about the divine nature that are far more fascinating and delightful than the fact that God is he "who is metaphysically ultimate and has underived existence" (p. 189). It is no less essential to God the Father Almighty that he has a Son in whom he eternally delights than it is that he has all power. So if it is true in some sense that we cannot say God is a Trinity without "first knowing what a divine nature is" (p. 189), in another sense it is equally important to recognize that vitally important truths about the divine nature depend upon the prior knowledge that

---

1. J. N. D. Kelly, *Early Christian Doctrines*, rev. ed. (New York: Harper One, 1960), 236.

God is a Trinity. Only in knowing that God is a Trinity do we grasp that the divine nature is essentially relational, that love has been shared among the persons of the Trinity from all eternity.

But it is worth emphasizing that the "great issue before the council" of the full divinity of Christ was not driven by philosophical speculation. Again to cite Kelly, the most important objection that Athanasius had to Arianism was that "it undermined the Christian idea of redemption in Christ, since only if the mediator was Himself divine could man hope to reestablish fellowship with God."[2] The Christology that eventually led to full blown Trinitarian theology was driven by soteriology. The article on the "only begotten Son of God" in the creed spells out in some detail how he is the one "who for us men and for our salvation came down from heaven." This story of salvation not only teaches us crucial things about the nature of God but also defines the worship we owe to God.

So I would take exception to the way Frank characterizes things when he says I see "the predicates Christians attribute to God—omniscient, omnipotent, omnibenevolent, triune, incarnate in Christ—as a list of properties that we can compare to the list of properties Muslims attribute to their God" (p. 190). The issue here is not merely a comparative list of properties. To see why, consider the fact that one property in this list stands out as different from the rest and calls for comment, namely, "incarnate in Christ." We could add to this, "raised Christ from the dead." Notice that these attributes are not true of God necessarily, nor do they describe his essential nature as the others do. Rather, these are true of God because of how God has freely acted to show his love to us, to save us from sin and death, and to give us his ultimate self-revelation.

The implications for our worship of God are clear. True worship of God now requires us to worship Jesus and to offer to him our "sacrifice of praise and thanksgiving" for pouring out his love to us and saving us from sin and death. Even if Frank is right that Jews and Muslims *refer* to the same God as Christians by virtue of their agreement on the attributes that define generic theism, that is not nearly enough to secure the claim that they *worship* the same God.

The incarnation and resurrection of Jesus change everything. Indeed,

---

2. Kelly, *Early Christian Doctrines*, 233.

we see this in the case of Paul at the Areopagus that Frank cited. "While God has overlooked the times of human ignorance, *now* he commands all people everywhere to repent" (Acts 17:30, emphasis added). Why is repentance for all people everywhere now commanded? Because God has fixed a day on which he will judge the world in righteousness "by a man whom he has appointed, and of this he has given assurance to all by raising him from the dead" (17:31). For those who are properly informed of the incarnation and resurrection and who reject that revelation, we can no longer say that they are only "deeply mistaken in various ways," as Frank puts it, but still believe in and worship the same God as those who believe that revelation.

Finally, I would like to have heard more from Frank about my main argument and less about the relatively incidental matter of reference. He comments that the argument cannot get off the ground without a definition of the term "properly informed Christian." The phrase "properly informed" runs throughout the argument, and I used it to distinguish such persons from those who may reject Christianity because they misunderstand or have a caricature of Christian claims that God has a Son, that he is a Trinity, and so on. By contrast, the properly informed are those who are "rightly informed about the actual substance of essential Christian doctrinal claims" (p. 179). Any well-catechized Christian who is familiar with the New Testament would qualify. Frank's characters Adam, Baaqir, and Candida, who made an intensive study of the three great religions, would certainly qualify as properly informed. With this clarified, I would like to know which of my premises Frank rejects.

To McDermott

I appreciate Gerald's response to my essay and his affirmation of the large extent to which we agree. My disagreements with his response to my essay are not as fundamental as my disagreements with the other authors in this exchange, but I still take exception to some of his claims.

First, as a relatively minor point, I did not mean to imply that all Jews in the first century wanted Jesus crucified, as Gerald says one might think from what I wrote. My full sentence from which he quotes only a part is this: "Indeed, the first-century Jews who wanted Jesus crucified thought he was guilty of blasphemy and deserved to die" (p. 174). I suppose this sentence is ambiguous enough to be read as Gerald read it, but my claim applies only to those Jews who accused Jesus of blasphemy and demanded his crucifixion, not to all Jews.

Second, and more substantively, I disagree with some of what Gerald says about Jews who have rejected Christ. I agree with his observation "even if Jews in his generation had rejected his message about Jesus, they were still 'beloved' by Yahweh (Rom. 11:28)." Indeed, I would go further and insist that all persons who have rejected Jesus remain beloved by God and that God, like the father in the parable of the prodigal son, always desires the repentance of his rebellious children, welcoming their return. Gerald seems to think that God loves Israel more than he loves gentiles and suggests that gentile Christians are second class members of the body of Christ, "associate members in Israel" as he puts it (p. 196). Or as he wrote just a bit earlier, "at the very least, Yahweh still loved them [Jews] in a special way, different from his concern for gentiles" (p. 196).

To be sure, Israel has a special calling in God's scheme of redemption, but they were chosen for a special mission, to be the means through which "all families of the earth shall be blessed" (Gen. 12:3). But the ultimate condition for salvation is the same for Jews as it is for gentiles, namely, faith in Christ. If Gerald is claiming that God chose Israel for salvation in a way he did not choose gentiles, or that God is more concerned to save them than other people groups, I heartily disagree.

In the same vein, I would qualify how Gerald characterizes the Jewish rejection of Christ and in what sense God is responsible for it. Gerald writes: "Paul said that God himself caused the majority of Jews in his day to reject Jesus . . . (Rom. 11:8, 25)." And later: "So in order for time and space to open for billions of future gentiles before Israel's acceptance of the messiah would bring the end of the world, God purposely closed the eyes and ears of Jews" (p. 196). Putting it this way seems to suggest that God unilaterally caused the Jews to reject Christ and did so for larger providential purposes.

I would argue that the rejection of Christ by the Jews was not caused unilaterally by God, as Gerald suggests. To the contrary, they freely chose to reject Christ and the salvation he provided. I agree, however, that God has providentially used their unbelief to advance his purposes. Joe Dongell explicates this by pointing out the parallel between Pharaoh's rebellion and Jewish unbelief. Before God hardened

Pharaoh's heart, Pharaoh hardened it himself (Ex. 3:19; 5:2; 8:15, 32).
Dongell elaborates:

> God did not create Pharaoh's initial hostility any more than
> he caused Israel's initial unbelief. Rather God reinforced their
> tendencies to bring about a greater proclamation of his truth
> around the world. While some might have wondered whether
> the unbelief of God's chosen people would thwart God's plan
> to redeem the world through Israel, Paul assures us that God
> will triumph even more spectacularly by using Israel's unbelief
> to serve his larger purpose. While Paul does not flesh out the
> dynamics involved, the book of Acts repeatedly shows the Jews'
> hostile reaction to Christian preaching actually propelled the
> gospel to ever wider Gentile audiences.[3]

The distinction between Gerald's view here and mine is perhaps somewhat subtle, but there is a significant difference between the view that
God causes unbelief and rejection of Christ and the view that such rejection is freely chosen but still used by God to accomplish his purposes.[4]

I also concur with Gerald in his insistence that "it is one thing to
reject Jesus without the revelation of the Holy Spirit, but quite another
if one has been shown by the Spirit who he is" (p. 197). Indeed, the
illumination of the Holy Spirit is essential to any acceptance or rejection
of Christ that is truly a free choice for which one is responsible. It is a
vital part of the narrative of the book of Acts that after the Holy Spirit
came on the day of Pentecost, his presence and power accompanies the
preaching of the apostles throughout the book, whether that preaching
is accepted or rejected.[5]

As I draw these comments to a close, I reiterate that only God
fully knows who is properly informed and who freely accepts or rejects
Christ. And this brings me finally to the matter of inclusivism, which
Gerald addresses at the end of his response. He notes that he disagrees

---

3. Jerry L. Walls and Joseph R. Dongell, *Why I Am Not a Calvinist* (Downers Grove, IL:
Intervarsity Press, 2004), 89–90. Dongell cites in a footnote the following passages from Acts:
8:1–4, 14; 11:19–23;13:46–48; 17:1–15; 19:8–10; 23:1–11; 28:25–29.

4. I am of course assuming that God's causally determining an act is incompatible with
that act being freely chosen.

5. A notable instance of resisting the Spirit is Acts 7:51–60

with Lewis's inclusivism and perhaps mine as well if that means "non-Christians can come to Christ without acknowledging Christ" (p. 198). While I would not describe my position in that way, I would say that it is possible to be responding positively to the grace of God and to be in a saving relationship with God even if one has never heard the name of Christ. But I would go on to insist that such persons will accept Christ when they are properly informed about him.

And on this matter Gerald and I may actually agree. He writes that he is "agnostic about when and how God's Spirit reveals Christ to people who seek God's truth and righteousness." And then he concludes with this line: "We can hope that if they are now worshiping Jesus's Father, they will—in God's way and time—accept Jesus as his Son once the Spirit reveals Jesus's identity to them" (p. 198). This beautifully expresses a hope I share and on this note I happily conclude.[6]

---

6. For more on my view of inclusivism, see Jerry L. Walls, *Heaven: The Logic of Eternal Joy* (New York: Oxford University Press, 2002), 63–91; Walls, *Heaven, Hell and Purgatory* (Grand Rapids: Brazos, 2015), 187–211.

CHAPTER FIVE

FOCUS ON COMMON GROUND IN CHRISTIAN-MUSLIM RELATIONSHIPS: A MINISTRY REFLECTION

JOSEPH L. CUMMING

This "ministry reflection" draws on lessons I have learned from more than three decades of ministry among Muslims. My wife and I are privileged to count among our dearest friends many kinds of Muslims, ranging from nonliterate villagers and Bedouins in the Sahara to some of the most cosmopolitan intellectuals and senior religious leaders and scholars in the Middle East, South Asia, North Africa, and elsewhere. We have had private, heart-to-heart conversations with Muslim friends, and we have given television interviews in Arabic on Al-Jazeera and other channels. We have participated in formal dialogues with Muslim and Jewish leaders, and we have had informal chats about faith with ordinary friends. Our experiences include fifteen years of living in an Islamic Republic in North Africa with laws requiring 100 percent of citizens to be Muslims and laws stipulating the death penalty for apostasy. Our experiences also include extended times in other Muslim-majority nations and friendships with Muslim leaders in the United States and other Western nations.

Of course most of our conversations with Muslim friends—like conversations with any friend—are not specifically religious. As in all friendships, one discusses every topic imaginable. And much of our work is not specifically religious except in the sense that our humanitarian work to empower poor communities is motivated by faith in Jesus Christ.

Nonetheless, meaningful relationship with Muslim friends nearly always includes conversations about faith. Unlike secularist Westerners, few Muslims consider it rude to bring up religious questions in conversation; rather, most Muslims I know are eager to discuss matters of faith—asking what I believe and sharing their faith. They often express a sincere hope that I may come to embrace Islam.

Our work also includes ministry to Christian churches and Christian leaders—both in the West and in Muslim-majority contexts—who invite us to speak with them about Islam and Muslims.

A Priori Goals and Theological Convictions

Before further exploring lessons learned from these relationships, it may be helpful first to set forth a summary of *a priori* goals and theological convictions I bring to them. This is not to duplicate work done in other chapters of this book addressing more thoroughly biblical and systematic-theological issues. Rather, it is to help readers understand why I take the approach I do in conversations with Muslim and Christian (and Jewish) friends about questions of faith.

Goals

In my experience of formal dialogue with people of other faiths, the time factor limits the number of "top priorities" we can communicate to our partners. Some of the time available must be devoted to expressing respect for our partners as fellow humans, to reflect the love of Christ. Time must be devoted to listening to our non-Christian friends' top priority concerns, and the love of Christ requires that we take time to express understanding of their concerns and sympathy with whatever we can agree may be legitimate among their concerns. Similarly, love requires us to take time to learn about what is sacred to our dialogue partners and then to express understanding of their deepest convictions—whether or not we agree.

The remaining time limits the number of points we can communicate about our own priorities. We must refine long lists of issues we might like to raise, sharpening our focus to perhaps two other points. This forces me to assess—prayerfully, biblically, advisedly—just what are the two most important things to communicate to Muslim leaders. I prioritize these:

1. To enable friends to see the biblical Person of Jesus Christ—through both my attitudes and actions and my words—as supremely lovely
2. To promote religious liberty along the lines set forth in Article 18 of the Universal Declaration of Human Rights[1]

Some Christian friends would like me to prioritize discussing terrorism, political reform, women's rights, war and peace, or some other issue. These are all extremely important, but if I must focus on just two points, then I prioritize the Person of Christ and religious liberty.

In ministry among Christians, I similarly have two chief priorities. These are:

1. To help Christians *understand* Muslims and their concerns and convictions
2. To challenge Christians to *love* Muslims as Christ does

Theological Convictions

I am an evangelical follower of Jesus Christ. I believe that the good news of salvation by grace through faith in Christ and his atoning death and life-giving resurrection is the only hope for the world. I believe in the unique authority, inspiration, and inerrancy of the Bible. I uphold the historic Niceno-Constantinopolitan view of divine triunity and the Chalcedonian view of the Person of Christ. These convictions shape my engagement with people of other faiths and of no faith.

When Christians ask me (as they frequently do), "Do Muslims and Christians worship the same God?" my short answer is, "Yes and no. But mostly yes." Here is what I mean by this:

Yes

Christians seek to worship the one God who created the universe and who will judge us at the last day. Muslims also seek to worship the one God who created the universe and who will judge us at the last day. It is logically impossible for there to be two different "one Gods" who are

---

1. "Everyone has the right to freedom of thought, conscience, and religion; this right includes freedom to change his religion or belief, and freedom, either alone or in community with others and in public or private, to manifest his religion or belief in teaching, practice, worship, and observance." See http://www.un.org/en/universal-declaration-human-rights/.

both the only creator of the universe and only judge of the world. There *can be* only one such God.

We may have radically differing understandings—or misunderstandings—of what this one God is like and how we may know this one God. Or some of us may be worshiping in vain. But there cannot be two different "one Gods." The God we *seek* to worship is one. The intended *referent* of our worship is one.

Furthermore, the Qur'an explicitly states that Muslims should worship the same one God Christians worship: "Do not dispute with the People of Scripture [Christians and Jews] . . . 'Our God and your God is one'" (29:46; cf. 42:15).

Some Christians object that Muslims' conception of God's character sees God as distant, transcendent, and arbitrary, whereas Christians see God as immanent, approachable, and covenantally loving. This is a gross generalization about both Muslims and Christians. Many Muslims I know—notably Sufis—see God as immanent, approachable, and covenantally loving, and they find support for this in the Qur'an. Some Christians I know feel God is distant and arbitrary. Indeed, my own personal understanding of God in this area has changed over time, so that if differing perspectives in this area mean worshiping different gods, then I was worshiping a different god ten years ago, and I will doubtless be worshiping yet another god ten years hence, "if Jesus tarries." And so will you, dear reader.

But No

Nonetheless, Muslim and Christian understandings of God differ from each other in important and irreducible ways. These include the following:

1. 99.9 percent of Muslims (not all) reject divine triunity.
2. 99.9 percent of Muslims (not all) reject incarnation—that God chose to be manifest to humanity through the incarnation of Christ.
3. 99.9 percent of Muslims (not all) reject the idea that God's self-giving love found ultimate expression in Christ's atoning death.

These are not merely minor differences. From a Christian perspective, the doctrines of Trinity, incarnation, and cross are at the core of the faith. They are doctrines on which our eternal salvation depends. The Epistle of 1 John 2:22–23 says that to deny the Son is to deny the Father.

Additionally, there is one other reason why I cannot unequivocally answer yes to this question. Since 9/11 I have observed a puzzling phenomenon in Christian contexts. When most Christians hear someone say, "Muslims and Christians worship the same God," what Christians actually *think* they hear is, "Muslims do not need Jesus Christ." Even if the speaker explicitly says that all people—including Muslims—need Christ, nonetheless, post–9/11 Christians often filter out that information and instead *think* they hear, "Muslims do not need Jesus Christ." Since that is not what I intend to communicate, I avoid saying, "Muslims and Christians worship the same God."

But Mostly Yes

If we wish to maintain that those who do not accept Trinity, incarnation, and cross are *ipso facto* worshiping a different, false deity, then we must be consistent and claim also that 98 percent of devout Jewish people are worshiping a false god. Few Christians are prepared to make this assertion.

Some of the Christian leaders who have most prominently asserted that Muslims do *not* worship the same God as Christians have indeed been consistent in also saying they believe that Jews do not worship the same God. But I believe this stance is contrary to scripture.

Various passages in Acts (for example, 10:2; 13:16; 16:14; 18:7) describe non-Jewish monotheists who did not yet know Christ but are described as "worshipers of God" *before* they come to know Christ. Acts 10:4 seems clear that, at least sometimes, these people's worship was accepted by God as pleasing.

In Matthew 15:9 (and Mark 7:7), confronting those who explicitly reject him, Jesus quotes God's words in Isaiah: "These people . . . worship me in vain." Though Jesus polemicizes against these people's worship as unacceptable, he never asserts that they worship a *different* God.

In Acts 17, addressing Athenian pagans whose idols "appalled" him (vv. 16, 29), Paul nonetheless says, "The One whom you worship without knowing, this One I will proclaim to you" (v. 23).[2] If pagan Athenians and nonbelieving Pharisees worshiped God (though in ignorance or in

---

2. Unless otherwise indicated, scripture references are the author's translation.

vain), and if non-Jewish monotheists like Cornelius and Lydia worshiped God acceptably *before* knowing Christ, then it is difficult to deny the same generosity of spirit to our Muslim and Jewish friends.

Some suggest that a key difference between Muslims and Jews is that Jews recognize the authority of the Tanakh (Old Testament), whereas Muslims have a different holy book (the Qur'an). But this is oversimplification. Theoretically Muslims do recognize the authority of the Torah and Gospel as holy books, though in practice most Muslims focus almost exclusively on the Qur'an. Similarly, Rabbinic Judaism recognizes the authority of Tanakh, but in practice rabbinical study focuses largely on Talmud, as written codification of "oral Torah."

Conversations with Muslims

As explained above, my chief concern when Muslim friends ask me about faith is that they might see Christ in me and see the Person of Christ (not necessarily Christian religion) as attractive.

In theory Muslims venerate Jesus Christ profoundly. Muslims recognize that the Qur'an describes Christ as born of a virgin (19:20), as Messiah (3:45), as prophet (2:136), as among those closest to God (3:45), as Word of God (4:171), as teaching kindness and compassion (57:27), as miraculously feeding the hungry (5:112ff.), as healing the sick and raising the dead by the power of God (3:49), as being now alive in heaven (3:55), and as returning at the end of the age (43:61).

But in practice, in my experience, when most Muslims talk with a Christian friend about Jesus, they feel somewhat threatened and defensive. Why? Muslims are acutely conscious of fourteen centuries of war between Muslims and Christians, in which Christians—sometimes marching under the sign of the cross—have killed Muslims "in the name of Christ." Muslims feel conscious of wars continuing today in Muslim-majority countries, where Western powers, seen as "Christian," have played unhelpful roles at best. They feel conscious of the everyday discrimination and bigotry Muslims encounter in the West from "Christian" neighbors. Feeling threatened—even defensive—in such circumstances is natural. This is a generalization of course: not all Muslims feel this way. But this expresses the feelings of the majority of Muslims I know in diverse contexts around the world.

As Christians, we might object that these wars were started by

Muslims, or that Muslims too have committed atrocities, or that Muslims persecute Christians too. There is truth in that objection. But to begin with that objection is to ignore Jesus's command in Matthew 7:5 to remove logs from our Christian eyes before we seek to help Muslim friends with specks in theirs. Furthermore, to respond to Muslim friends' feelings with the playground retort "You started it!" will not have the effect of helping them see Jesus Christ in us.

Because of this background, most Muslims I know (not all) perceive a huge, unbridgeable chasm between themselves and the Bible's claims about Jesus Christ. Even if Christians have powerful apologetics that "prove" to them that the Bible's claims about Christ are true, many Muslims I know will nonetheless see that proof as happening inaccessibly "over there" on the "Christian" side of the chasm while they are permanently located—for better or worse—on the "Muslim" side of the chasm. I have literally had Muslim friends say to me, "I know you are right and I am wrong. I know what you Christians believe is the truth. But I was born a Muslim, and I will die a Muslim. Right or wrong, that is what I am, and that cannot change."

The chasm I describe here is not a Barthian chasm between God and humanity, which Christians believe Christ has bridged. I refer to a different, ungodly, artificial chasm between "Christendom" and "Islam" as two mutually hostile and literally armed camps. Christians bear perhaps 50 percent of the responsibility for creating this chasm, and Matthew 7:5 and 28:19–20 suggest Christians must accept primary responsibility for crossing it. Thus, in conversations with Muslim friends, I hope to show that the chasm between them and Jesus Christ is perhaps *not* as wide as it might seem.

Western readers especially must understand this chasm because it presents precisely the opposite challenge of what Western Christians face in discussing faith matters with neighbors who are unchurched nominal Christians or New Age-y "not religious but spiritual" people. Such friends sometimes do not recognize any significant distance between themselves and Christian faith. Sometimes we must gently note that merely labeling oneself "Christian" does not automatically produce meaningful relationship with Christ. Sometimes we must gently suggest that not all paths lead equally to the top of the mountain. Sometimes friends must first understand the problem of sin so that they may see the message of forgiveness as truly good news.

Occasionally I meet Muslims like this. One prominent Sufi leader told me, "All is one because God is one. Everything that exists actually subsists in God. So Christianity is true, and Islam is true, and all religions are true. God is one, and you are one with God, and I am one with God, and this Coke bottle is one with both of us in God. All is God, and God is all." I have had liberal, Westernized Muslim friends who said, "Christianity and Islam are essentially identical. We have a few tiny differences on small matters that can be ignored, but we agree on everything that really matters." In such cases, it may be necessary to express to Muslim friends that the Bible makes important truth claims about Jesus Christ, and these claims cannot be ignored.

But these are exceptions. When conversation turns to the Person of Jesus Christ, the large majority of my Muslim friends perceive a vast, unbridgeable chasm between themselves and that Person. I hope they may come to see that the chasm is not as wide as it may seem.

This does not mean ignoring or minimizing genuine differences and mutually incompatible truth claims on matters directly related to salvation. But it does mean highlighting where genuine common ground does exist. And it means showing that *some* of the width of that chasm (not all) is due to misunderstanding and misbehavior.

We see excellent models of this highlighting of common ground in the preaching of the apostles in the book of Acts. In every example of apostolic preaching in Acts, we see apostles first highlighting points of common ground with their audience before explaining the atoning death and resurrection of Christ (e.g., "fellow Israelites" [2:14; 3:12; et al.] when speaking to fellow Jews, or "God is no racist, but accepts people from every ethnicity" [10:34–35] when speaking to God-worshiping Gentiles).

Acts 17 is a particularly noteworthy example. In explaining his faith to pagan Athenian philosophers, Paul first praises their religiosity (vv. 22–23) and approvingly quotes pagan philosophers and pagan poets (v. 28), highlighting points of agreement, before proceeding to repentance and salvation through the resurrection of Christ.

I said above that we can show that some (not all) of the chasm is due to misunderstanding and misbehavior. The misbehavior is obvious. It is indisputable that Christians have behaved badly toward Muslims throughout history and continuing today. We may argue that Muslims have also behaved badly. We may argue over "who started it." But we cannot deny that Christians have sinned against Muslims. And Jesus clearly told us to take the logs from our own eyes first.

Tremendous power can be found in simple apology. When I say sincerely to a Muslim friend, "I am sorry for all of the wrong things Christians have done and continue to do to Muslims," this releases healing power in the relationship. Suddenly the chasm seems only half as wide as it did before. Suddenly my Muslim friend feels less defensive and threatened. Sometimes my Muslim friend even replies, "I, too, am sorry for all of the wrong things Muslims have done to Christians, and I am sorry you had to be the one to apologize first."

The misunderstandings that unnecessarily widen the chasm are less obvious. But they are extremely important.

When we affirm the Holy Trinity, most of our Muslim friends think they hear that we worship three separate gods. Some Muslims see these three deities as God, Jesus, and Mary (one interpretation of Sura 5:116), while others think we worship Father, Son, and Spirit as three separate divine beings. Few Muslims understand—and few Christians know how to explain—that we worship one God who exists in three distinct ways of being (*hypostases*), and that the ancient term *persona* may not imply all modern post-Cartesian, post-Freudian concepts of radically autonomous subjectivity, but rather (following the classical Boethian definition) "an individual subsistence of a rational nature." Few Muslims—and even fewer Christians—know Islam has its own doctrine, the doctrine of *ṣifat al-dhāt* (qualities of the divine Essence), which is similar though not identical.[3]

When we affirm that Jesus Christ is Son of God, most of our Muslim friends think they hear that God had carnal relations with Mary, begetting bastardized divine-human offspring. No wonder they find this repugnant: so do we.

Similar misunderstandings arise with Christian assertions about incarnation, about Christ's divine and human natures, and about the cross. Space in this chapter will not allow detailed examination of each

---

3. For further detail on this Islamic doctrine, see my article "*Ṣifat al-Dhāt* in Al-Ashʿarī's Doctrine of God, and Possible Christian Parallels," in *Toward Respectful Understanding and Witness among Muslims: Essays in Honor of J. Dudley Woodberry*, gen. ed. Evelyne A. Reisacher; assoc. eds. Joseph Cumming, Dean S. Gilliland, and Charles Van Engen (Pasadena, CA: WCL, 2012).

of these misunderstandings and how they may be addressed, but I have published a number of articles on them, and some of these can be accessed on my personal website.[4]

My goal in addressing these misunderstandings is not to ignore real, irreducible differences between Islamic and Christian understandings of God. Rather, it is to remove obstacles that make those differences seem larger than they actually are.

Another way to put this is that I do not seek to remove what 1 Corinthians calls the "stumbling block of the cross." Rather, I seek to remove other artificial, unnecessary stumbling blocks that cause Muslim friends to stumble long before they come near the stumbling block of the cross itself. Acts 15:19 says, "We should not make it difficult for those from other cultures who are turning to God."

Conversations with Muslim-Background Believers

My wife and I have many friendships with Christians who have converted to Islam and also with Muslims who have come to faith in Christ. The former describe themselves as having "embraced Islam" (Arabic: *i'tanaqa al-Islam*). The latter sometimes describe themselves as "Muslim-background believers in Christ"—abbreviated MBBs.

The asymmetry of terminology is noteworthy. The phrase "embraced Islam" makes religious adherence and identity central: one has left the "Christian" religion and embraced the "Muslim" religion. The phrase "Muslim-background believer in Christ" makes personal relationship with Christ central; religious identity is less important. This is even clearer with Messianic Jews who embrace Jesus as Messiah but do not see themselves as abandoning Judaism or "converting" to Christianity.

Through decades of ministry, I have personally known thousands of MBBs (and hundreds of converts to Islam and hundreds of Messianic Jews). Out of these thousands of MBBs, I can count on one hand those who believe they worshiped a different, false god before coming to know Christ. Nearly all of my MBB friends agree they did not truly *know* God before meeting Christ. Some say their worship of God was empty before they knew Christ, while others say it was meaningful but incomplete.

---

4. www.josephcumming.com/links. The Ṣifāt Al-Dhāt article cited above is available on this site under the title "Muslim Theologian Abu al-Ḥasan al-Ashʿarī's Doctrine of God, and Possible Christian Parallels."

But almost none say that in their Islamic piety they worshiped some false deity or idol.

Some were involved in occult practices outside mainstream Islamic thought—for example, summoning demonic spirits through incantations and numerology, or warding off evil through amulets, potions, and veneration of saints. These MBBs of course do recognize that occult practices involved idolatry. Mainstream Muslims also denounce such occult practices as idolatrous. But MBBs who participated in mainstream Islamic piety—seeking to worship the one God described in the Qur'an—do not believe they were worshiping a false god or idol. They believe, as Paul says in Acts 17:23, that they were worshiping God "in ignorance." This is also true of my Messianic Jewish friends. I have never heard any of them suggest they were worshiping a different god before they came to know Jesus as Messiah (unless, similarly, they were involved in non-mainstream occult practices).

I do know a handful of exceptions among my MBB friends. The most notable, and perhaps most admirable, example of this was the late Nabeel Qureshi, who recently departed to be with Christ. Nabeel and I first met when we participated together in an edifying public dialogue on this very subject on the radio in Britain.[5] We both learned from each other and came away from this dialogue with mutual respect and affection, even if we did not completely agree.

But among the thousands of MBBs I know, these exceptions can literally be counted on one hand. I note that each of these exceptional MBBs (I mean "exceptional" with a genuine tone of respect—even admiration) has lived in the West and experienced pressure from Christians to emphasize the chasm between Islam and Christianity. Each of these exceptional MBBs, when they first came to Christ, did *not* think they had changed from one deity to another. It was only over time, through further reflection and interaction with Christians, that they became convinced they had not only changed religions but also changed gods.

This must be set in context. Every MBB I know who has lived in the West (whether native-born or immigrant/visitor) has experienced pressure from the Christian community to emphasize the chasm between Islam and Christianity. One MBB friend told me how—at his very first meal

---

5. A recording of this dialogue can be streamed at youtu.be/QqUDguFgd0g.

with a Westerner—his Western host brought out a huge pile of pork, say-ing, "You must eat this to drive out the demon of Islam from your heart."

Many MBB friends have told me they feel pressured by churches to tell stories of how evil, extreme, and violent Islam is. Christians often see these MBBs as "trophies" who validate Christians' feelings that we have the superior religion. Incidentally, ex-Christian converts to Islam are often treated similarly—as trophies—by the Muslim community.

MBBs feel pressured to exaggerate any slight tendency toward extremism in their own personal history. This has tragically led a num-ber of prominent MBBs to escalate these exaggerations to the point of making fraudulent and bizarre public claims of having personally worked with multiple terrorist groups—despite the fact that this is vir-tually impossible as these groups hate each other. Some of these MBBs' claims have been publicly debunked, bringing disgrace on them and on the churches and institutions who promoted their claims.

Fortunately most MBBs resist these pressures, showing great integ-rity, despite evidence that they would reap financial rewards if they would only exaggerate a bit. This pressure is real and almost constant in Christian churches. This problem is present in non-Western contexts too. I have heard similar reports from MBB friends in local non-MBB churches in West Africa, the Middle East, South Asia, Southeast Asia, and elsewhere.

Henotheism

I worked among Muslims for sixteen years before the horrific events of 9/11. Before 9/11, most Christians were content to ignore Muslims most of the time, and to view them as an exotic curiosity when they did think of Muslims. When my wife and I spoke in Christian churches about our work among Muslims, Christians asked us many curious questions about Islam and Muslims, but no one ever asked us, "Do you believe that Muslims and Christians worship the same God?" Never. No one ever asked that.

Suddenly, on September 11, 2001, everything changed. Suddenly *everyone* wanted to ask about Islam. When we next came to the United States months later and spoke in churches, suddenly one chief ques-tion was on everyone's lips: "Do Muslims and Christians worship the same God?"

What changed? Why was this theological question suddenly *the* question burning in Christian hearts? Did Islamic doctrine change? No. Did Christian doctrine change? No. What changed was the political and social context in which Christians think theologically about Islam.

Throughout history, when Christians have perceived (rightly or wrongly) an existential threat to the survival of our society and our way of life, we have frequently been tempted by a subtle heresy known as henotheism. Henotheism is defined as "worship of a particular god, as by a family or tribe, without disbelieving in the existence of others"[6] or "worship of one deity (of several) as the special god of one's family, clan, or tribe."[7] It is an inherently tribal theology.

Rather than recognizing that God is the one God of the entire human race, henotheism worships the god of "our group." Henotheism effectively makes that god the agent of our group in our conflict with other groups. We pray that our god will defeat our enemies' gods and thereby grant victory to our armies over our enemies' armies.

Non-Christians are similarly tempted to tribalize or nationalize the one God of all nations. I have seen this in Muslims. In Paul's above-described Acts 17 encounter, Athenian philosophers criticized "advocating foreign gods" (v. 18). Though Paul highlighted common ground (vv. 22–23, 28), he also critiqued henotheism: "God who made the world and everything . . . made all nations from one" (vv. 24–26).

Perhaps the most shocking example of henotheism in history was the Nazis' adoption of the slogan *"Gott mit uns"* (God with us). These words are from sacred scripture (Matt. 1:23). In scripture the phrase communicates that in Christ (Immanuel), God is with all humankind. Matthew ensures we understand this by immediately following it with the story of gentile Magi coming to worship the newborn King. But in the hands of Nazi ideologues, this message of "God with us—the whole human race" was transmuted into "God with us—the German nation—to ensure our victory over our nation's enemies." The Christian God becomes *our* God. He serves the purposes of *our* nation to lead us to victory over those who threaten our existence.

---

6. "Henotheism," *Random House Unabridged Dictionary*, https://www.dictionary.com/browse/henotheism.

7. "Henotheism," *Collins English Dictionary*, https://www.collinsdictionary.com/us/dictionary/english/henotheism.

This may be a subtle heresy, but it is a heresy with the blood of millions on its hands.

The same Nazi ideologues who promoted this henotheistic distortion of Christianity simultaneously resurrected ancient Germanic pagan worship of Wotan, Freia, and other deities. How is it that German Christians fell for what now seems such a transparently pagan trick? They were just as intelligent as we, just as sincere as we, and—in many cases—just as devout as we. It may be partly because they genuinely felt an existential threat to their nation and civilization.

It is easy for non-Germans with eighty years' hindsight to see that Germany faced no real existential threat to survival in 1939. It may be more difficult for Christians caught up in post–9/11 passions to recognize that Western civilization does not really face an existential threat now either. And even if we recognize this individually, we cannot escape the social web in which we are enmeshed. That social web perceives itself—rightly or wrongly—as facing an existential threat from Islam.

In this context, the ancient temptation of henotheism again rears its head. We do not want God to belong equally to all humankind. We want God to be *our* God. We want God to be loyal to *our* group. We want God to reassure us that our group is right, that the group that threatens us is wrong, and that our God will ensure our ultimate triumph. We want the biblical "Gott mit uns" to mean not that God is with the whole human race, but that our God is with our civilization, our religion, our nation, defeating the false god of Islam, and ensuring our final victory over "barbarians."

In 2003 an American army general recounted to an evangelical church his encounter with a Muslim enemy who believed "Allah will protect me." The general told the church: "I knew that my God was bigger than his. I knew that my God was a real God and his was an idol."[8] This is creeping henotheism (on both sides). My point is not to shame this general—a sincere brother who repeatedly apologized afterward—but to ask what it is about post–9/11 churches that makes visiting speakers feel this is what we want to hear. Especially from military leaders who are devout Christians.

Romans 3:29–30 says: "Is God the God of the Jews only? Is he not

8. William M. Arkin, "The Pentagon Unleashes a Holy Warrior," *Los Angeles Times*, October 16, 2003, http://articles.latimes.com/2003/oct/16/opinion/oe-arkin16.

the God of the Gentiles also? Yes, of the Gentiles also, since God is one." If the apostle's God is the God of pagan Greeks, then how much more of Muslims? As 1 Corinthians 8:4–6 says, "There is no God but one. For although there may be so-called gods in heaven or on earth . . . yet for us there is one God . . . from whom are all things and for whom we exist." There is no room for henotheism in New Testament faith.

Some readers may wonder whether I am naive about the genuine threat Islamic extremism represents. For readers who do not know my story, let me briefly share that I have personally been targeted by Islamist militant lynch mobs on more than one occasion, and once they nearly succeeded in killing me. I have been arrested at gunpoint for my faith by Muslim police who warrantlessly searched my home to confiscate Bibles; I have been interrogated about my faith by Muslim police countless times, once in a torture room surrounded by implements of torture; I have had close friends who were tortured with electric shocks and beatings, and other friends who have been murdered by Islamist militants. In one case, the militant explicitly stated that I was his next target. So I know a bit about Islamist militant violence.

When the lynch mob nearly killed me, I heard them chanting, "*Allahu akbar! Allahu akbar!*" ("God is greater") over and over as they beat me until I lost consciousness and fell to the ground, preparing myself to die. I believe a demonic spirit of henotheism animated that chant— "*Our* God, the God of our Islamic religion, is greater than this infidel Christian and his false god." When Christians gathered in AD 1096 to launch the First Crusade, crowds whipped themselves into a frenzy, chanting "*Deus vult! Deus vult!*" ("God wills it!"). They too felt Islam represented an existential threat to Christian civilization. I believe they too were animated by a demonic spirit of henotheism. Indeed, I believe it was literally the same demonic spirit of henotheism who prompted those Crusaders to chant "*Deus vult!*" and who later prompted an Islamist lynch mob to chant "*Allahu akbar!*" as they sought to murder me.

I said this heresy is subtle. Most of us do not go all the way to consciously thinking or verbalizing such explicitly henotheistic or violently tribal ideas. But the social web in which we are enmeshed means that such ideas nonetheless subtly and unconsciously influence the way we think theologically about Islam and Muslims—and the kinds of questions we ask about Islam.

When I speak in a Christian church about Islam and Muslims, what question do you think Jesus would like people to ask me after the service? I would suggest that he who laid down his life in love for the reconciliation of all nations would want people to ask questions like these: How can I show love to my Muslim neighbors? How can I meet a Muslim friend? How can I show hospitality to Muslims in my community? How can I pray for Muslims? How can our church show love to Muslims in other countries around the world?

So, ultimately, my answer to the question "Do Muslims and Christians worship the same God" is this: "That is a legitimate question, and I will answer it, but first please think about what prompted you to ask that particular question before any other. Should you perhaps have asked a different question? What question do you think Jesus would ask?"

CHAPTER SIX

FOCUS ON RESPECTFULLY HELD DIFFERENCES IN CHRISTIAN-MUSLIM RELATIONSHIPS: A MINISTRY REFLECTION

DAVID W. SHENK

It was a windy August day in 1963. My wife, Grace, and I had just arrived in Mogadishu with our two young daughters. (Our two sons were born later in Somalia.) A slip of paper was my claim to legitimate entry: my New York University diploma. Our team was known as the Somalia Mennonite Mission (SMM).

A porter at the back of the jostling crowd called to me: "You be with Somalia Mennonite Mission? Mission be good people. Mission people like to pray." We never imagined we would be addressed so publicly when we arrived in Somalia. Only two years earlier the leader of our team in Somalia had laid down his life for our Savior.

On our first evening in Somalia, several students from our SMM English classes invited me to tea at a street-side kiosk surrounded by acacia shrubs. After good spirited banter, they asked, "Why have you come to Somalia?"

I responded, "We have come because God has appointed us."

"That is good," the students exclaimed, "but we already worship God. You should preach in India where they worship millions of idols."

That conversation was a precursor to many more of bearing witness to Jesus among Muslims. Such forums were usually spontaneous, for

God-talk wafted wherever we went. Not only did the Somalis have questions about our mission. So did the SMM team. It is amazing how Islam pushed us deeper into theology. One of the most frequent questions we heard was: "Do Christians and Muslims worship the same God?"

This essay responds to that question and centers on how Christians can affectively minister to Muslims while focusing on our respectfully held differences. As I will demonstrate, a commitment to peacemaking in the way of Christ opens surprising possibilities, but such efforts need not downplay the differences between Muslims and Christians. Often, our key distinctions have led to fruitful dialogue and ministry opportunities.

In exploring the key differences between Christians and Muslims, this essay is narrowly focused on the Muslim quest for *tawhid*—that is, to bring everything under the rule of God as revealed in the Qur'an. I say almost nothing about the *Shariah* or Muhammad, the seal of the prophets in Islamic theology. My focus is *tawhid*.

Why this narrow focus? That unitary commitment is the center of Islam. The Qur'an defines that center, and Muslims are committed to unite all things under the authority of the Qur'an. The gospel is likewise an invitation to unite all things under God. For Christians, the goal is to unite all things under the authority of Christ. But what difference does it make if Christ or the Qur'an is the center?

When Muslims who are committed to *tawhid* meet Christians, there are four questions they often ask: (1) Have the Christians altered the Bible? (2) What is the meaning of the name *Son of God*? (3) How is it possible for the Messiah to be crucified? (4) What do you mean by *Trinity*? *Tawhid* is at the heart of each question. Christians must therefore offer Muslims satisfactory answers to these questions. As I comment on *tawhid*, I will give special attention to these four persistent questions. This essay should help equip the reader to respond to the four great questions Muslims ask, while also highlighting some key differences. But before more deeply considering these questions, I will first examine the question of whether Muslims and Christians worship the same God, which sets the stage for the primary focus of this essay—*tawhid*.

Do Muslims and Christians Worship the Same God?

As mentioned earlier, one of the questions we were often asked was whether Muslims and Christians worship the same God. Our answer cannot exclude the importance that Jesus plays in our understanding of God. Exodus 6:2–3 provides the account of Moses at the burning bush. God said to Moses. "I am the Lord. I appeared to Abraham, to Isaac and to Jacob as God Almighty, but by my name the Lord I did not make myself fully known to them."[1] This is the account of God as Yahweh coming down to meet and save his people from slavery in Egypt. It is also the account of God as Elohim or Elohai (the God) Almighty creating the universe. All Muslims, Jews, and Christians believe that the God of Abraham is the true God.

However, God as Yahweh is distinctive. Yahweh has come down to meet and save us. In Islam God never comes down to us. Islam has no account of the Father seeking the Prodigal Son. In Islam God mercifully sends down instructions. In the gospel God comes down and suffers for us and because of us. In Jesus we meet God as Yahweh, as Savior! In Jesus we also meet God as Elohim (the almighty Creator). In Jesus we meet God in his fullness—as Elohim and Yahweh.

Understanding the House of Islam

The beliefs and practices of Muslims are referred to as the House of Islam. The *umma* is the Muslim community who reside within the house of Islam. Within the Christian movement, we refer to the congregation of believers as the church. The beliefs and practices of Christians are sometimes also referred to as ministries of the church. This is why the church has pastors whereas the *umma* has instructors (imams). Very early in our journey with Muslims, we began to invite the imams to join our circle and converse about the House of Islam or explore the Christian and Muslim commitment to bearing witness. Quite frequently we would meet in the mosque, other times in our home or in a restaurant.

The imam would often begin by reciting the *Fatiha*. (That is the beginning and the ending of the formal obligatory prayer.) Within that prayer the supplicant implores God to show the "straight path." An imam in Java told me that one day he came to understand that Jesus is the fulfilment of the *Fatiha*, for Jesus is the Way. The imam never returned to the mosque. In Jesus he had met the Way.

---

1. Unless otherwise noted, scripture quotations in this essay come from the NIV.

The Qur'an is sharply critical of hypocrites who masquerade as Muslims but are in reality not true Muslims. Therefore, we need to decide with clarity to whom we are committed. A divided loyalty cannot survive. If possible, it is important to clearly identify our faith commitment. In Somalia we were known as the Somalia Mennonite Mission. Our relief and development program was "in the name of Christ." Our identity was not a secret.

Prayers for healing bear witness to Muslims that Jesus is our intercessor and the Great Physician. If it is appropriate, I share the prayer that Jesus the Messiah taught his disciples. Although Muslims do not address God as loving Father, I cherish the opportunity of introducing our Muslim hosts to the family prayer. Frequently the family prayer opens the way to bear witness to Jesus in whom we meet God as our loving Heavenly Father.

After the ritual prayers are concluded, the imam likely describes the pillars that preserve the House of Islam. In one such incident, the imam told the Christians the five pillars of duty. He began with the confession of faith that there is no God but Allah and that Muhammad is the seal of all the prophets. Muslims believe that confession divides humanity into Muslims and non-Muslims. Then the imam recited the five pillars of duty:

1. The confession of faith
2. Giving alms to the poor
3. Praying five times daily facing Mecca
4. Taking the Hajj to Mecca if possible
5. Fasting during the month of Ramadan

Some imams will include a sixth pillar: jihad—the struggle to defend the House of Islam when it is under threat.

Those pillars of duty are supported by five pillars of belief.

1. Belief in God
2. Belief in angels
3. Belief in the prophets of God
4. Belief in the books of God
5. Belief in the final judgment

Muslims believe these teachings and practices were revealed to the prophet Muhammad through the angel Gabriel. The inner core of these pillars is *tawhid*: God is one and God's will is one.

On one occasion, an imam invested nearly two hours expanding on the essence of the pillars of belief and the pillars of duty. Then he said, "You might acquire paradise if you submit to these pillars." The imam continued, explaining the concept of a scales wherein good duties and practice go on the good side of the scales and the wrong that we do goes into the wrongful side.

Then we shared from the New Testament where eternal salvation is assured in Jesus the Messiah (John 14:6). The imam was astonished and encouraged us to continue in the Christian way. Thereafter, the imam would share in the village that these Christians are on the way to paradise. The Christian assurance of salvation is often compelling and attractive for Muslims.

The Four Great Questions

Now, back to the four questions Muslims who are committed to *tawhid* most often ask Christians:

1. Have Christians altered the Bible?
2. What is the meaning of the name *Son of God*?
3. How is it possible for the Messiah to be crucified?
4. What do you mean by *Trinity*?

Tawhid is at the heart of each question.

The Bible

The Muslim scriptures and traditions communicate that Jews and Christians have been mandated by God to make their scriptures available to Muslims and other believers as well. Especially mentioned are the Torah, the Psalms, and the Gospels.

However, around the world we meet Muslims who are dismissive of the Bible, for most Muslims believe the Bible has been corrupted. I will look at just two reasons for the Muslim objection to the Bible: (1) the Bible is mostly history, and (2) the Bible is translated into other languages.

A student of mine said it well. One day he asked for a Bible. The next evening he returned to my office, placed the Bible on my desk, and went out into the night saying, "This is not scripture. This is history." In contrast the Qur'an is not history. Muslims believe that the Qur'an is instruction on what we should do and believe. They believe the Qur'an was sent down from heaven just as it is inscribed on tablets in heaven.

Yet the Bible is more than instruction. God acts in history. That is why the Bible is history! Biblical history describes the acts of God in history, especially in Jesus the Messiah. The Bible reveals that God is love! The Bible describes God seeking lost sinners. The Bible also describes our response to God—our yes and our no.

In Islam God sends a book down from heaven. In the Bible God himself comes down to redeem us.

We remind our Muslim friends that both the Qur'an and the Bible proclaim that God will never let the scriptures be changed! Nevertheless, Muslims are perplexed by the translation of the Bible into many languages. For Muslims the Qur'an is in Arabic. That guarantees unchangeableness into languages other than Arabic.

We seek to explain to Muslims that we believe God's intention is that his Word be available to all language groups around the world. That is why the church translates scripture into many languages.

Jesus the Son of God

The second question is about Jesus. Shortly after our arrival in Somalia, the first young men to be baptized pulled me into the shade of an acacia shrub for conversation about Jesus. They explained that God is unknowable in Islam. Yet God wants us to be his friends. So the only way for us to know God is for God to become a person. Just like an ant who wants to converse with ants must become an ant. This means that we meet God in his fullness in the Messiah. Indeed, the students had given a good explanation of Jesus as Son of God.

The Christian confession that Jesus is the Son of God opens doors to describe the gospel. We share with Muslims that the angel Gabriel announced that Jesus would be called the Son of God. The name is not a human concoction but rather proclaimed by the angel who announced the coming of Jesus. The angel appeared and proclaimed that the Messiah is the Son of God. Several times God spoke from heaven announcing the coming of the Messiah and his mission.

Jesus is also the Word of God! The first verses of the Bible proclaim: God spoke! The earth was created. God speaks and the whole universe is called into being. We can never separate the Word from God, for God and his Word are one. In Jesus the Word lived among us. The scriptures say, "The Word became flesh and made his dwelling among us. We have seen his glory, the glory of the one and only Son, who came from the Father, full of grace and truth" (John 1:14). The Son of God is the incarnation of the Word of God. This is the mystery and the meaning of Jesus as Son of God.

In the Qur'an we read that Jesus the Messiah is the Word of God. But the Bible means something different. The Qur'an means that Jesus was created, just like Adam was created (Qur'an 4.171). Sometimes in our zeal to find bridges between the *umma* and the church, we twist meanings. Jesus the Word in the Gospel of John is not the same as Jesus the Word in the Qur'an. We sow confusion when we distort the meaning. It is much preferable to invite Muslims to look at the gospel text with an invitation to hear the meaning of Jesus as Son of God as revealed in the Bible.

During a visit to Bangladesh my host took me to visit the nearby Madrassa. The school was completely filled as all the students wanted to hear the guests. Then came the first question. "Do you believe Jesus is the Son of God?"

One reason this question is so important is because of a misunderstanding. It seems that Muhammed asked his friends who were monks what the meaning is of Jesus as Son of God. The monks suggested that the name Son of God means that God gave birth to a son. God had a wife, the Virgin Mary. This causes tragic confusion. Christians need to be clear in their witness that faithful Christians are not polytheists. There is a chapter in the Qur'an proclaiming the miraculous birth of Jesus to the Virgin. We invite Muslims to read the biblical account as proclaimed by the angel Gabriel.

The Crucifixion of Jesus

The primary reason Muslims deny the crucifixion of Jesus is their perception that the cross communicates a weak savior. God is all powerful. Therefore, the Messiah cannot suffer on a cross. Although the Qur'an seems to deny the crucifixion, there is room exegetically to consider the possibility of crucifixion. But theologically: Never! The death and crucifixion of Jesus points to two different centers.

In Mecca the Black Stone resides in the center of the House of Islam. Muslims believe that the stone came from heaven. Prayer and the annual pilgrimage are directed toward Mecca and the stone, a symbol that reminds Muslims to faithfully submit to God's will on earth.

The Christian journey has no black stone. Rather the Christian community receives the broken bread and wine reminding Christians of the broken body of Jesus in his crucifixion and resurrection. In the Gospels we meet the Savior who is our redeemer.

In Revelation 21 we read that God is building the City of God. This is the church, who are the presence and sign of the kingdom of God. It is comprised of twelve foundation stones and twelve gates. The gates are the tribes of Israel, and the stones are the apostles. This means that God has been building the city for a very long time! The gates of the city never close. The city is redeemed and formed by the Lamb of God, who has given his life for our salvation.

The house of Islam is comprised of pillars of duty and faith. In the center of the Muslim house is the Black Stone, whereas the center of the city of God is the Lamb slain and resurrected. Christ the crucified Lamb is in the center of the church, redeemed people from every tribe, language, nation, and people. In the Biblical vision, the church and the Lamb are surrounded by the scriptures (the apostles and prophets). In Islam scripture is also prominent. The apex of the Qur'anic belief is the Black Stone, a focus on what we must know and do. In the center of the House of Islam, Muslims kiss the stone. The apex of the biblical vision is the Lamb slain, Jesus crucified and risen. What difference does it make to welcome Jesus into our center? Our Muslim friends venerate their prophet. What difference does that make in their lives?

Although Islam denies that Jesus was crucified, the Qur'an proclaims that a son of Abraham was redeemed from death by God's interventions in a tremendous substitutionary sacrifice. The church has a wide open door to share our sense that this passage is a redemptive sign, for every year Muslims offer sacrifices remembering that God saved a son of Abraham.

There is a prevailing notion that if we explore the Qur'an and the Bible, we discover that both scriptures are essentially the same. That is simply not true. There are areas of convergence. But within each convergence we encounter divergence. Why? Islam and Christianity have different centers: the Qur'an and Jesus Christ. A Christ-centered movement embraces the cross. An Islam-centered movement does not know the cross. God in Islam sends his will down. God in Christianity comes down to save us.

Only the church knows that God is in Christ reconciling the world. Believers in Jesus are emissaries called to proclaim that good news even though the world might not comprehend.

When the Galileans tried to make Jesus their king by force, he left them immediately and retreated into the wilderness for a night of prayer. Thereafter, Jesus set his face toward Jerusalem, where he met the cross. In these movements Jesus and Muhammad chose opposite directions. In due course Muhammad defeated the Meccans with ten thousand soldiers. In contrast Jesus entered Jerusalem with throngs of singing children. He was taken to the cross and crucified. By crucifixion and resurrection, Jesus breaks the cycles of violence and invites us to receive his new creation of peace everlasting.

Three hundred years after Christ, Constantine defeated his enemies under the sign of the cross. Even since, many Christians have perceived the cross as a sign of killing the enemy. What a travesty of the love of God. The outstretched arms of the crucified Jesus are the invitation of God for reconciliation and forgiveness. Instead, the cross has become the symbol of killing the enemy. It is not surprising that for many the cross is about destruction; God's intention is restoration. (2 Cor. 5:11–21)

The objection to the cross runs very deep within the *umma*. The legacy of the crusades lives on in modern wars. In times like these our world desperately needs to hear of the man on a cross who cried out in forgiveness and reconciling love. The cross of Constantine and the Muslim jihads has given the church and the world a tragic and heavy burden. In contrast, Jesus offers salvation! He is our peace in these tumultuous times.

The Trinity

God as Trinity means that God is love. The mistaken assumption is that Trinity is a trilogy of gods. It is very important to clearly present the truth that Trinity is our inadequate way to express the mystery of God as creator, God as personal, God as Spirit. Trinity is the diversity within God. Trinity is the loving unity within God.

The concluding discussion on the Trinity pulls together the threads of our dialogue concerning questions Muslims ask Christians. The following story illuminates how divisive the Trinity can be: When I saw Lugman coming, I opened our apartment door to welcome him. Something quite dreadful must have gone wrong at the morning Friday prayers at the mosque across the street from our home. Lugman rebuffed my welcome and shouted that Trinity teaching must stop. I responded that Trinity means we should love each other as God loves. He was astonished.

Muslims speak of God as creator. Muslims also speak of the Spirit of God and the eternal Word of God. We invite Muslims to hear what the Bible reveals concerning God as Trinity. Trinity is not a word found in the Bible, but it is a term Christians have used to help to express how Christians experience God. We meet God as the resurrected Lord. All of these dimensions of God mean that God is love. He so loved us that he came to earth to live with us. God so loved that he suffered for us and because of us. God so loved us that he raised Christ from the dead that we might live with God eternally.

In Islam God sends his instruction down; in the gospel God comes down. That is why we say "Trinity." Trinity is our attempt to express the mystery that God in Christ came down to redeem us. Trinity is an expression of our experience of God. We cannot separate God from his essence for God is love. We cannot separate God from his Word because God and the Word are one. We cannot separate God from his Spirit because God and his Spirit are one. God the creator, God the Word, and God the Spirit are love and cannot be separated.

"That is wonderful!" Lugman responded.

On at least one occasion afterward, he addressed me as "dear brother David."

Engaging Muslims, Pursuing Peace
Our Journey with Muslims

Over the years, 140 teachers and development workers had joined the SMM in the common commitment to education and spiritual transformation. Ten years later we were required to leave by a change of government.

It was not the Muslim authorities that excluded us. Rather it was Soviet-style Marxism.

We continued our education legacy by developing a community center in the predominantly Muslim area of the city of Nairobi, Kenya. We developed a multifaceted center known as the Eastleigh Fellowship Center. (The center became well-known for its basketball team, the Menno Knights!) The center became a "sign of the kingdom" throughout Muslim communities in northeastern Africa.

Later Somali clans in Kenya and Somalia became ensnared in interclan wars. The Mennonites became quite involved in interclan peacemaking in the name of the Messiah. Before long, the Mennonites were referred to as the peace clan. These were fruitful years, first in Somalia and then in Kenya. Small fellowships of believers emerged.

In more recent years, Grace and I have served in a variety of ways within Muslim societies with a special focus on peacemaking with both a global and a local focus. As emissaries of the Messiah, we minister within Muslim and Christian communities by bearing witness to the Messiah and his peace.

Tragically, the cross maintains its crusader legacy for most Muslims and reminds them of war against the Muslims. Our team embraces a dramatically different perspective. Our calling is to bear witness that the outstretched arms of the Messiah on the cross are a revelation of Christ inviting repentance and reconciliation. The cross is the revelation of God's suffering love. The cross is the atoning sacrifice of Jesus

Protecting the House of Islam

One of the most difficult realities in Christian engagement with Muslims is the restriction on conversion. In our ministry efforts to Somalis, we encountered two beliefs that restricted the freedom to choose: (1) Islam is the truth, and (2) Christians are misguided. Because of these two beliefs, which formed their worldview, many Muslim Somalis believed the government should prohibit propagating Christianity. To them, the notion that a person has the right to convert or to be converted is nonsense, because only Islam is true. This, however, stands in contrast to my worldview—I confess Christ as Lord, and I am prepared to give an account of the hope within me in gentleness and respect (1 Peter 3:15).

Several years ago, Grace and I were pulled into a conflict where a young woman in a restrictive Asian country was threatened by a family member because she had become a believer in the Savior. Her father and I were about the same age, and it was soon evident that we shared mutual respect for one another. We met with pastors and Muslim leaders, about eight of us. The Muslim leadership decided we should meet in a public sitting area at a hotel. The Muslim clerics explained that Islam is the truth and that a dimension of their mission was to convert me to Islam.

The Muslim clerics also explained that the most serious responsibility of the Muslim community was to protect the community from any influence that pulls a person away from Islam. When a government or a family is diverting a person away from Islam, then that government is failing in its responsibility.

After about three hours of theological conversation, I recommended that we make a three-point statement. I based my suggestion on biblical scriptures.

1. The fear of God must not be forced on anyone, for we are created as free humans.
2. Jesus has promised that all who follow him will be eternally secure.
3. A person's relationship to God is personal between the person and God.

The Muslim and Christian leaders agreed! Two years later Grace and I visited the family. The elderly father assured me that the three commitments still stand.

The decisions we made have the potential of transforming the whole region. The participants were prominent in their community. If the religious leaders encouraged a more tolerant spirit, their council would most likely prevail. If SMM hoped for cultural space for church formation and community development, we needed to build trust. An official said it this way: we trust the SMM, and we request that you don't embarrass us. The meetings I have described were a precious engagement in trust-building within a very restrictive context.

Befriending Muslims, Finding Paradise

A friend and I were chatting at a tea stand in Eastleigh. A young man appeared. He had just arrived in Nairobi from Mogadishu riding on the open back of a truck for more than a week. At great risk he had traversed regions occupied by the al-Shabab, a jihadist movement in northeastern Kenya. We listened briefly to his story as a refugee escapee.

Then my colleague interjected, "We are people of prayer. Is there any area of your life wherein you need prayer?"

I expected him to say, "Pray that I will find a place to sleep and food or that I will find protection."

Rather, he said, "Tell me how to acquire paradise."

As our taxi arrived the young Somali refugee confided, "For a long time I have sought the answer to my question. At last my prayer to know the Way is fulfilled."

The teenage Somali refugee in Eastleigh is the face of thousands of Muslims around the world who welcome Christians to join in a cup of tea beneath their acacia shrub. The invitation to linger over tea might surprise you, as happened to me in Kampala a few months ago. This was a celebration of the book *A Muslim and a Christian in Dialogue*, written forty years ago by Badru Kateregga and me. A thousand people were present for the opening event. I asked, "Why have you invited us?"

Our hosts responded, "We have invited you because you have been friends for forty years. Your friendship gives us hope that Muslims and Christians can seek peace and pursue it."

In Sarajevo I asked a gentle grandmother, "You were a Muslim. Now you are Christian. Why have you become a Christian?"

With a tear on her cheek she said, "I am a Christian because a Christian became my best friend."

As can be seen from the above examples, engaging Muslims does not require that we shrink back from our Christian convictions and differences as we minister to them. In all things we should seek to make Jesus Lord and to be ready to give a defense for the hope within us. Yet we should always do this with gentleness and respect. Let us therefore seek peace and pursue it (1 Peter 3:11)!

INDEX